IN THE
SHADOW OF MEN

IN THE
SHADOW OF MEN

VALERIE O'BRIEN

POOLBEG

Published 2010
by Poolbeg Books Ltd
123 Grange Hill, Baldoyle,
Dublin 13, Ireland
Email: poolbeg@poolbeg.com

© Valerie O'Brien 2010
The moral right of the author has been asserted.

Copyright for typesetting, layout, design
© Poolbeg Books Ltd

1 3 5 7 9 10 8 6 4 2

A catalogue record for this book is available from the British Library.

ISBN 978-1-84223-426-6

Typeset by Patricia Hope in Sabon 11/15
Printed by Litografia Rosés S.A., Spain

www.poolbeg.com

About the Author

Valerie O'Brien was born Valerie Sheehan in Cork, where she lived with her mother, father and four sisters before embarking on a career in the Irish defence forces that spanned ten years. She also qualified as a beautician. She currently lives in County Kildare with her two children, where she values every moment she spends with them. She is finally fulfilling her lifelong dream of becoming a writer. This is her first book.

Acknowledgements

I would like to thank all the staff at Poolbeg, especially Kieran and Paula, for giving me this amazing opportunity to tell my story and fulfil a lifelong dream of mine. A big thank you to Niamh, David and Sarah for all of your help. I'm especially grateful to Brian for your great editing, guidance and advice. I would like to thank my family – Mum, for continually encouraging me to put my story on paper; Dad, for all of your support and the endless things you do; and all of my sisters and friends for listening to me over the last few months. Thanks also to PDFORRA. Thanks to Orla for all of your advice and encouragement. Thanks also to Jean Kenny. To Andy for your endless supply of coffee and advice. Finally, a special thanks to my children, Alex and Christopher, for your patience and love while Mommy wrote her book.

Note: Some names have been changed in this book to protect the identity of individuals.

For Alex and Christopher with love

Contents

1	In My Blood	1
2	Army Brat	8
3	Becoming a Soldier	17
4	Recruit Training	29
5	Breaking New Ground	45
6	Out of the Frying Pan . . .	50
7	. . . Into the Fire	58
8	The 4th Infantry Battalion	64
9	Clonmel	78
10	Portlaoise Prison	87
11	Decision Time	92
12	Trouble Ahead	99
13	Highs and Lows in Lebanon	108
14	Christmas in Lebanon	128
15	Under Fire	142
16	Bad to Worse	149

17 Home, Back, and Home Again   157

18 Should I Stay or Should I Go?   171

19 Becoming a Mother   181

20 Back in the Fray   188

21 Promotion   202

22 Betrayed   221

23 Journey to Eritrea   230

24 The Ber Hiba   245

25 Curry and Condoms   265

26 On Leave   276

27 Going Off the Rails   284

28 Coming Home   305

29 From Marriage to Special Forces   318

30 The Final Straw   332

31 Moving On   342

1

In My Blood

The year was 2002 and I found myself sitting in a bar called the Ber Hiba, a local hostelry frequented by Irish soldiers. I was stationed in Eritrea, a small war-torn country in north-east Africa. The bar also operated as the local brothel. I sat casually on an old wooden chair in the same dimly lit corner I had occupied for the previous few months. Strikingly beautiful Eritrean girls with caramel-coloured skin brushed past me every now and then. The bar was full of Irish soldiers and filled with the same hustle and bustle as every night. I silently wondered to myself how I had ended up in a place like this. Looking back now, I suppose I was groomed for a life in the military from an early age . . .

One of my earliest childhood memories is of pottering around at my grandfather John's feet. I would gently tug on his grey trousers as he cooked my Sunday breakfast.

The wireless played in the background, frying pan full of Irish sausages, bacon and eggs. The familiar aroma of his cooking hung in the air while my grandmother Molly busily hovered around making tea in her cream and brown teapot.

My grandmother's house was always full. Grandchildren would swish in and out after Sunday mass, trying to grab pieces of buttered toast and crispy bacon. My grandfather always cooked my toast on one side only. He did this because he was an army chef. That's the way he cooked toast for hundreds of soldiers.

My grandfather served in the Irish defence forces for forty-four years. He worked as a chef in the 4th Infantry Battalion, Collins Barracks, Cork. He served on six missions with the Irish army overseas. Most soldiers at the time served in the Congo only once, fewer still twice; just a handful of Irish soldiers served on three missions. My grandfather served on four missions to the Congo. He also served in Cyprus twice.

I would sit on his knee, mesmerised, as he vividly described his adventures in the mysterious land of the Congo, which romanticised Africa in my young mind. He described how, on their arrival, their train pulled up at a hot, dusty platform, where they were greeted by what they thought was a welcoming party. The Irish troops, baked by the golden African sun, the stifling hot air reducing their breath to wheezing, were delighted. Naïvely, they assumed that the scantily clad Congolese men were performing a dance to welcome the United Nations peace-keeping soldiers. In fact, they were performing a war dance, frantically leaping up and down, kicking the red and brown dirt up from beneath their feet to swirl high in the air. The piercing war cries of Congolese warriors was a warning to the new arrivals. They were being told that their presence was not welcome in the Congo. On that occasion they avoided any conflict but would not be so lucky later on.

My mother Breda didn't particularly like to discuss her father's missions to the Congo, as her family had been faced with the grim possibility that he might never have returned home. She would become visibly upset as she recounted how, on 8 November 1960, a massacre had taken place in the Congo, the Niemba ambush. It was the greatest loss of life for the Irish army in a single incident. The family heard nothing from my grandfather for the following two weeks and had no way of knowing whether he had been involved. They listened to every single news bulletin on the radio in the hope of getting some glimmer of news about the Irish soldiers. They grew more concerned as the days rolled by. After two weeks of despair, they finally learned that he had not been involved in the massacre. They hadn't received any letters or word of his welfare from the Irish army. Finally, it was announced that a battalion from Dublin had been involved in the massacre. My grandfather had been attached to the 4th Infantry Battalion from Cork.

During a later trip, they did not receive a letter from him for two months. Fearing the worst, the large family would huddle around my grandmother and wait patiently for any news on the Irish soldiers. The brown wireless crackled through the living room, but all appeared to be calm in the Congo. Then, suddenly, one sunny afternoon my grandfather simply arrived home. The air was crisp when he knocked on the front door of the single-storey house on Spring Lane, Blackpool, Cork city. The whole family gathered around and looked at him curiously. He had no eyebrows, eyelashes or hair. Apparently, the old cooker he had been using had blown up and he had lain in an army tent in the intense African heat for weeks, covered in gauze and linseed oil, until he was well enough to travel home. He had been badly burned but miraculously recovered without any scarring.

These storied captured my imagination and intrigued me. Not only had my grandfather been an excellent chef but he was also an outstanding soldier. He won numerous "All Army" medals for shooting and was mentioned in a book by Raymond Smith called *The Fighting Irish in the Congo*. He's also included in a group photograph that still hangs on the wall of the museum in Collins Barracks, Cork.

My grandfather retired from the army in 1983. It was only a year earlier that a platoon of women was first permitted to join the forces, but they were only allowed to serve in administrative roles. They were not permitted to carry out duties or serve in the infantry battalions. Sadly my grandfather passed away in 1984 and didn't see his granddaughter follow in his footsteps.

My own father Art also served in the Irish defence forces for forty-four years, recently retiring as a barrack quartermaster (BQMS). He served in Lebanon once and in Cyprus twice. I remember missing him when he was absent in my childhood. I would wait patiently on Sunday evenings for his phone call home. I would sit on the pink and blue carpet of our stairs, staring out the hall window, rays of golden sunlight beaming back at me, gently tapping my fingers against my face and my foot off the soft carpet beneath my feet in anticipation. I loved it when he called. He would fill me with stories of Lebanon, recounting the week's activities. I became familiar with the conflict between Israel and Lebanon when I was only six years old. I was fascinated listening to his stories.

Every single day, without fail, I would march up to my teacher and tell him how many days were left until my father came home. When he eventually arrived home, he brought with him beautiful dolls wearing pink and white lace-embroidered dresses. Each of his daughters – there were five of us, Lynda, Jackie, myself, Deirdre and Maria – also received her own special gift. Mine was a white watch with a heart-shaped face and delicate pink and red roses on the straps. It was the early 1980s in Ireland. The majority of families struggled financially, so I greatly appreciated the gifts that I received. He also presented me with a fabulous dressing gown made from golden brown silk with minute pearl-dropped buttons. The top of the gown was sewn together with gold thread, the likes of which I had never seen before.

I had an active childhood and definitely could be described as a tomboy. I was never far from my father's side; he brought me everywhere with him. I ran for

Leevale athletics club and played basketball and camogie. Almost every day without fail, I had either a hurley or a basketball in my hand.

I also loved dancing. I would run down the long narrow laneway near our home to the local dance hall, with its corrugated tin roof, which had a tendency to turn orange from the lashings of rain that fell on it, held up by four roughly plastered brick walls. Inside a cold chill sliced the air and two bare light bulbs gently bobbed back and forth overhead. I wasn't used to much luxury but this was primitive by any standards. We danced every week on the old creaking wooden floorboards. My mother had hopelessly tried to enrol me in Irish dancing but my friends and I inevitably drew the beady-eyed scrutiny of the stern teacher. We were told that under no circumstances was disco dancing permitted, so we left to join the Wednesday afternoon disco-dancing class instead.

Life passed quickly and without much drama until, at fourteen years of age, my whole world was turned upside down overnight. One evening my mother summoned all the girls to a family meeting in the kitchen of our home. She was pacing up and down the brown linoleum floor with a cigarette in her hand, wearing her blue velvet dressing gown. She turned to us and smiled broadly before announcing that the whole family would be moving to Cyprus for a year. My father had applied to serve overseas with the army there. It was a mission that the whole family was allowed to go on.

I was shocked. I didn't want to live in Cyprus. I would have to say goodbye to my friends and give up my beloved sports. My two older sisters were working and decided to remain behind, while my younger sisters and I were to travel.

I had never seen my mother so happy. She told us that Cyprus was a beautiful country with long sandy beaches and hardly any grey rainy days. We were going to be living in a former British army base in the capital, Nicosia.

My aunt threw a huge goodbye party for our family. Relatives swarmed in and out of the back living room, drinking sparkling white wine and eating triangular salad sandwiches, wishing us all the best. I stood in the centre of the room, wondering what was happening.

I had never been outside Ireland before, but that was about to change. For the next twelve months I would travel the length and breadth of Europe and some of the Middle East. My mind was about to be opened and broadened beyond my wildest dreams.

2

Army Brat

When we reached our new home in Nicosia, I was pleasantly surprised. A white picket fence enclosed our new garden, with grey flinty gravel lining the driveway to our cosy new bungalow. Creeping green ivy spread out across the soft golden bricks and onto the bright orange roof tiles. The front garden was a tan colour that looked like sand. Exotic pink flowers decorated the edges, nestled alongside luscious green plants and trees. Inside, wood-panelled shutters covered the windows and green carpet ran across the floor of the living room, a bland grey army-issue couch at its centre. There were three large bedrooms.

The houses were located in married quarters on the sprawling United Nations base. Over 2,000 peacekeeping soldiers were serving in Cyprus at the time, roughly 250 of those stationed on our base, which was known as UNFICYP HQ (United Nations Forces in Cyprus Headquarters).

It was official: I had now become an army brat – the term used to describe soldiers' children who grow up and live on military bases.

That summer we spent our days lazing next to the sparkling blue swimming pool in our camp. Almost every morning I would walk the two miles through the dusty barren fields to reach the swimming pool. I would dive in at the deep end, allowing the warm blue water to lap against my skin. My sisters would join me, as would other Irish UN kids. A local Greek man ran a kiosk where you could buy burgers and greasy chips. Laughter filled the air while I read, lounged and swam, without a care in the world during that beautiful Cypriot summer.

Every day my sisters Deirdre, Maria and I would discover exciting new features on the base. The old Nicosia airport sat derelict at its centre. We would walk the short distance to the airport daily to inspect and explore the area. The remains of a large passenger plane damaged by gunfire during the war sat on the runway, a stark reminder of the reason why the UN forces were present in Cyprus. The area was always eerily quiet, with chunks of the white-walled airport displaying the remnants of war. The walls had been peppered with machine-gun fire.

UN peacekeeping forces had first arrived in Cyprus on 13 March 1964 due to outbreaks of communal violence between Turkish and Greek Cypriots. On 20 July 1974, Turkey launched an extensive military operation in Cyprus. Fighting was especially fierce in the vicinity of Nicosia International Airport – the very same area where my sisters and I would walk each day. On 16 August 1974 Turkish forces declared a ceasefire and UNFICYP marked the ceasefire lines, taking on the responsibility of patrolling the buffer zone between them. The country was divided in two, Turkish Cypriots occupying the northern part of the island and Greek Cypriots living in the south. The border ran throughout the island and the area which separated the two sides became known as a buffer zone.

We lived within the buffer zone on the base in Nicosia. The majority of personnel living on the base were either British or Canadian. Smaller international groups were made up from other nationalities, including some Irish. A small group of Irish soldiers remained in Cyprus in an administrative and logistical role once the main contingent had left. A squadron of young British soldiers was based close to the airport. Each day I would watch them marching on parade in their desert-camouflaged uniforms. They would march back and forth to the commands of their regimental sergeant-major. He was a tall man, a thick black moustache overhanging his lips. A stiff dark brown wooden cane was gripped tightly underneath his arm and I suspected that every soldier was terrified of him.

Alongside the airport lay a large white hangar, formerly used to house airplanes. The British troops had erected a basketball court, volleyball court and gym inside the hangar, which I used regularly. I got to know some of the older male physical training instructors (PTIs) when I visited the gym to train. I would stare in awe as they roared out orders to the platoons of soldiers they were training daily. I watched as the platoons went on what they called the milk run, a pre-breakfast training session.

They would only just be completing their early morning training session, drenched in stale sweat.

It was during that summer that I truly became engrossed in all things military. I often baby-sat for families and would question the soldiering fathers at length. I wanted to know how exactly you joined the army. I knew that female soldiers played a small role in the Irish defence forces. Women had been accepted in the Irish army on only a handful of occasions since my grandfather's service. They always trained collectively together and later went on to serve in administrative roles only.

My two elder sisters, Jackie and Lynda, and a lot of our family came to visit us during our first summer on the base. There was a constant stream of visitors through the house. That long hot summer was an experience that I will never forget, but all too soon it came to an end and September was upon me before I knew it.

I was enrolled in a private school in Nicosia, called the Grammar School. "Other ranks" children attended the Grammar School while officers' children attended a separate school called the Falcon School. The lives of officers' children and other ranks' children were kept very much apart.

The pupils were drawn from across the globe. Even though the school was officially an English-speaking school, the teachers would conduct the lessons in English but all questions and answers were given in Greek. I found it difficult to adjust to this. I often fell behind, struggling to understand the lessons as I tried hopelessly to grasp this new language.

During my first few weeks at the Grammar School I met two wonderful girls, Aishya and Sofia, who would become my best friends. Aishya was a Palestinian Muslim, while Sofia, a Christian, was part Jordanian, part Italian. We were from three totally different cultural backgrounds but we grew to love each other dearly. None of us could speak Greek, so on occasion we would skip class and hide out by the athletics field. Some teachers spoke more Greek in class than others did, so we found it pointless sitting in their lessons. There was never a roll-check, so once you didn't bump into a teacher whose class you had skipped, you would never be found out.

It was in the Grammar School that, for the first time, a teacher told me, "Valerie, you can do anything in life, in whichever career you chose. If you apply yourself, then the possibilities are endless."

My new friends and I swapped stories on our different religious beliefs, learning so much from each other. I often went to Aishya's home for sleepovers. She told me that once she started menstruating, I wouldn't be able to come over any more. I learned a little of what it was like to be a woman in a Muslim world. I was raised in a home where women were viewed as equal to men; unfortunately, Aishya did not have that privilege. Her home was a loving and nurturing one, but she was treated totally differently to her brother Abdul. He was a year younger than her but he had an elevated position within the family, higher than Aishya, her younger sister, or even his own mother. Aishya's mother and father were first cousins and their marriage was arranged. She was expected to follow in the same path.

One night before the Islamic festival of Ramadan I slept over in Aishya's house. Her bedroom was opulent, with a large oversized white bed in the centre of the room. An expensive crystal light fixture hung overhead. We talked late into the night about our dreams and aspirations. Aishya was a ballet dancer and wanted to continue to pursue her dream of becoming a ballerina. But she knew that this would never happen. Once the dreaded period arrived, her life would change forever.

The following morning I woke to discover that my own period had started. A red stain lay on my side of the white sheet. Aishya's face went white as she looked at me with panic in her eyes. She swiftly ran to her mother, who raced down the long bright hall leading to Aishya's room, closing the door behind her. She yanked the sheet from the bed and pulled it to the sink at the rear of the room, where she began scrubbing it until her knuckles were raw and swollen. Aishya's family employed a Filipino maid, who was the father's eyes and ears when he was absent. She reported every minute detail of the family's activities to him. It was vital to get the sheet clean before she saw it. Once the sheet was washed and all traces of blood wiped away, Aishya's mother hid the sheet in a steel bucket. She told us that she would dry it later, once the maid had left to go grocery shopping. I felt a mixture of extreme embarrassment and confusion. A knot formed in the pit of my stomach.

Meanwhile Abdul was becoming suspicious outside the door, pacing angrily up and down the hall, shouting obscenities at his mother, ordering her to open the door of the bedroom. She told him to leave repeatedly but he began cursing and shouting at her. Once she composed herself, she slowly opened the door. Abdul stood brazenly in front of her and slapped her violently across the face. He then ran outside to the spacious veranda where he began tearing up all her beautifully decorated potted plants. I stood by, motionless, as I watched the tears spill from her large chocolate-brown eyes. It was at that moment that I truly realised that not all women in society are treated equally. I went home that day with my perception of the world we lived in altered for ever more.

During my first summer in Cyprus, I also got to know a young Turkish Cypriot girl, Yvriem. As my father worked for the United Nations we were permitted to travel across the border in Nicosia. We often visited the unspoilt hot sandy beaches along the coast of northern Cyprus, a world apart from the Greek beaches of Aiya Napa, which had imported sand. Tall slender Turkish soldiers walked the streets in their droves, dressed in dark green uniforms and linking each other's arms. The locals weren't used to seeing many foreigners and as I had red hair they would stare at me intently. Elderly women wearing black oversized dresses would often approach me, touching my hair to check if it was real. My parents would laugh but I found the whole commotion embarrassing.

Yvriem and I often went on shopping trips around the streets of northern Cyprus. We would sit in the local *souk* (shopping mall) chatting about clothes, music and jewellery. Her friends often accompanied us and made me feel like I was one of them. They were very modern young women; one of them drove a shiny black Mercedes. Some of them wore *hijabs* (head scarves) while leaving their homes, only to discard them once they sat in the car.

Unfortunately, Aishya's family were moving back to the Gaza Strip once the school year finished. As we said our goodbyes I knew that I would never see her again. Sofia was also moving but to a different school, the American Academy, the following year. I still got to spend time with Sofia in the summer of 1992 before my family returned to Ireland.

One evening at a disco in Nicosia, I met a young Ethiopian man named Solomon, who would remain my friend for many years. His father worked for the United Nations. We chatted away as young kids do, often meeting up on the base to go swimming and walking. Solomon phoned my house one day and asked me if I wanted to play a game of pool with him and his friends. He picked me up outside my house in his father's white Mazda 727 and drove me to the recreational room where he and his friends were playing pool. I was blissfully unaware that this room was located adjacent to the officers' mess. Only officers' families were permitted to use it.

I knew that there was a distinct difference between officers and other ranks but as I was so young I didn't comprehend the level to which it existed. We were just hanging out as teenagers do, having some harmless fun –

until an Irish corporal pulled me outside, saying, "You shouldn't be in here. Your father is not an officer; you are to leave at once." I was so humiliated and embarrassed that I didn't want to tell my friends. I simply told them I was fed up and asked if they would leave with me. It is a moment that I never forgot as it dawned on me that we were not permitted to mix. It wasn't seen as socially acceptable.

3

Becoming a Soldier

Our year came to an end very quickly and my parents decided that we should travel home across Europe in our new car. Once we arrived in Greece, I slunk into my hotel room. I ventured over to the balcony, my eyes filling up with tears. I gazed into the distance at the brightly coloured orange trees and watched as young Greek men swerved through the narrow streets on mopeds. My heart was filled with sadness. I wanted to go back to Cyprus and I didn't want to return to Ireland. I was fifteen years old but I felt that I had seen and experienced so much that my mind was that of a much older girl. I didn't know how I was going to fit back into the society I had left as a happy-go-lucky teenager a year earlier.

For almost two weeks we toured: Italy, Greece, Switzerland, Germany, Belgium and France. I arrived home in Ireland and for the remainder of the summer I found it extremely hard to readjust. I desperately missed the lifestyle in Cyprus. I missed the endless sunny days and I longed for my friends.

In September I started back at my old school. As I had been absent the previous year I had missed my Junior Certificate exams. I also missed my first subject options because the classes were already full. I was becoming fascinated with science and had studied all of the three sciences in Cyprus. I was bitterly disappointed that the biology class was full.

The year came and went without anything major happening. That year I also signed up to serve in the Reserve Defence Forces. I joined the reserve 1st Field Military Police in Collins Barracks, Cork. It seemed appropriate, since I had spent a year living on a military base. It was almost a natural progression. I was sixteen years of age when I signed up. I should have been seventeen to join up, but they never checked the finer matters like my identification, so I got away with it quite easily. I attended an army summer camp and submerged myself in all things military. I learned how to march and use weapons. As I was in the 1st Field Military Police I also learned the basics of crime scene investigation.

The following September I decided to change schools and repeat the year so that I could study biology. For two years I studied hard but there were times when I found it difficult to focus because I had grown to love Cyprus and travelling so much.

One day I stumbled across a book entitled *Price of Honour* by Jan Goodwin, which examined how Islamic extremism was affecting the lives of Muslim women. The book dealt with abuse against women by men in Muslim countries and restrictions placed on women in Islam. The topic of women's rights greatly interested me and I often wrote my school essays on such matters. I had been motivated to learn about these issues from what I had witnessed in Aishya's home. Not surprisingly, my parents were summoned to the principal's office and interrogated. My English teacher and the principal were often shocked at my subject matter, describing me as very strong-willed. I refused point blank to change my essays and my parents were proud, not angry, that my ability to spark debate landed them in front of my principal. I should have known better than to join the military, where I would have to follow without question.

As I loved science my mother wanted me to go to college to complete a course and become a laboratory technician. I was confused about my future and didn't know in what direction I should go. My first choice for college was to study Applied Biology in Cork Regional Technical College. However, I narrowly missed a place by fifteen points. My mother was devastated for me but I wasn't too upset. Instead I enrolled in Waterford Technical College to study Science.

I drove with my parents on the old road to Waterford. My mind was racing. It was a cold autumn day with grey clouds suspended in the gloomy sky overhead. When we arrived my parents enrolled me and set about trying to arrange my accommodation. It suddenly dawned on me that, if I became a laboratory technician, I would spend my days indoors, pacing around in a white coat. The prospect of spending the rest of my life in a laboratory did not excite me. I didn't dare tell my mother, as I knew how disappointed she would be.

At around the same time I became interested in the beauty industry. I had obtained a prospectus from the local College of Commerce and my mind became fixated on the beauty therapist course. Potential students had to have knowledge of biology and the course seemed extremely interesting. Studying beauty therapy would allow me to combine my love of science with my more creative side.

On the journey home I gently broached the subject of my future with my parents. I told my mother that I was considering studying beauty therapy. She looked at me flabbergasted and told me that the beauty industry in Ireland was only in its infancy, with relatively little employment. There were only a few beauty salons in Cork city. The salon that my mother frequented was a simple room divided by a shabby peach floral curtain. The words manicure and pedicure were almost unheard of.

My father intervened when he realised that I didn't want to study in Waterford. He seized the opportunity to try to persuade me to join the army, which was recruiting a platoon of thirty soldiers in December of that year, 1996. Over the coming weeks, my father spoke to me about it again and again. I came around to his way of thinking and decided that I would apply. I had enjoyed my time in the Reserve Defence Forces so once I agreed to sign up I began to get excited about my future. This was only the second platoon of recruits to be taken into the army in three years. There were over 500 applicants for only thirty places. During that time my father planned my interview meticulously.

It was pointless for me to attend Waterford Technical College to study if I was applying to serve in the army in Cork, so I enrolled in a bilingual secretarial course in the College of Commerce, as this was seen as a more fitting qualification for a member of the other ranks. I stayed in the College of Commerce until December so it would look good on my application form and during my interview.

My mother couldn't mask her disappointment. Once my father and I told her of my plans, she refused to speak to either of us for three whole months. Maybe she could see something about the way of life that I couldn't see but later recognised. She had her heart set on me going to college, but she finally came around. I saw the army as a way of travelling around the world. It had a steady wage and it was viewed as a secure job.

I rehearsed my interview with my father until I knew the answer to every possible question I might be asked. The day I arrived for my interview, my father dropped me off outside the conference block. After my initial nerves had settled down, I sailed through the interview, receiving word a few weeks later that my application had been successful.

I was thrilled but my excitement was short-lived. I had to complete a medical examination with all of the other potential recruits. It emerged that I and two other women were too short. Apparently the height restriction had been raised and I was an inch and a very important quarter below it. At that point I had built myself up mentally to a career in the defence forces and I was utterly disappointed. Still, I clung to the hope of a small miracle happening.

How could the army justify this decision, my father asked, when I had spent the previous three years in the Reserve Defence Forces? My father's attention to detail served me well; they couldn't possibly refuse me due to the fact that I had indeed served in the RDF. As a result, we all passed the medical. I was measured again but this time I wore three pairs of woolly socks, held my breath in and, sure enough, I rose the inch and a quarter that was required.

I will never forget the day in December 1996 when I was sworn in to serve in the defence forces. It was my nineteenth birthday. My parents dropped me off outside the conference block. I stood gazing at the barrack square. The tricolour was flying at full mast with the wind blowing gently, swirling across the square. The sky was dark and occasional misty droplets fell from the grey clouds overhead. As I walked through the wooden doors, I was met by the corporals, who hadn't seen fresh recruits in three years. They were circling like eagles, gliding in and out, seeking out potential prey or "heat seekers" – recruits who draw unwanted attention to themselves and their fellow platoon members.

I was quite well dressed the day that I signed up to become a soldier. I had begun to wear make-up and to style my unruly wild red hair. I was certainly in touch with my femininity. I knew some of the other five women to see, from the medical and fitness tests. However, when I entered the conference block, they made no attempt to talk to me. I was very bubbly and outgoing when I joined the army. Four of the women, strikingly similar in looks, stood together in a group that I couldn't filter into. Three had cropped black or brown hair framing their petite faces. One woman stood taller than the rest, with long brown locks neatly tied in a ponytail. Another woman floated past them now and again. They chatted loudly and excitedly amongst themselves while I made small talk with the other woman and some of the male recruits. The men whispered amongst themselves, tension hanging in the air. The corporals seemed tolerant, for now.

Each recruit was sworn in by an officer. I was ushered into the same room where I had completed my interview. I distinctly remember the room being quite bright. There were three officers in attendance and the room filled up quickly with potential recruits being sworn in, almost as though they were on a conveyor belt system. I was glad to see a female officer sitting behind the desk to which I had been sent. She flashed her eyes at me and motioned for me to take a seat. I placed my hand on the brown leather bible and repeated each sentence in full. I felt proud and my face lit up for the first time since I had applied to join the army. When the female captain realised from the application form that it was my birthday, her face softened. She wished me a happy birthday. Then, suddenly, a corporal swooped in to usher me out of the room.

As I stood in the main room of the conference block surrounded by my platoon, I smiled to myself as my father looked on proudly. Our platoon sergeant called the room to attention, informing us that we would be receiving a week off due to the Christmas holidays. He went on to tell us that we had a tough road ahead of us, that we would shed blood, sweat and tears. He wasn't wrong.

I left that afternoon with my parents, feeling a pang of apprehension flutter in the pit of my stomach.

A week later I found myself back at Collins Barracks. It had been an unusually cold winter, with no sign of the severe weather abating. The sky was blackened, with flecks of silver cloud hanging overhead. I cupped my hands, pulling them towards my face to breathe warmth back into them before reporting immediately to the training depot. I walked nervously through the dark corridor until I found the area where the other recruits waited anxiously. I gazed at the walls, mesmerised by the perfectly framed pictures of past recruit platoons staring back at me.

A petite female corporal brushed past me, her copper hair neatly tied in a bun, tucked just below her black beret. She greeted me in a formal manner and shortly afterwards we were joined by the rest of the female recruits. She led us to the stores where we were issued with our crispy white bed linen. The shabby floorboards creaked as I stepped on the stairs and the air was stale and musty. I was used to these buildings; as a child I had often accompanied my father to work on Saturdays. I was well accustomed to the staunch military atmosphere and the stern behaviour of the soldiers. I had grown up with it.

The corporal ordered the female recruits outside once we had received our sheets. She promptly fell us in outside the grey stony building. We were marched to our billet (accommodation), one arm swinging up in the air, the other holding the sheets. Once inside, she stood us in a line before boldly announcing, "What are we going to do with your wild hair, Recruit Sheehan?" A flush of red crept across my cheeks while I tried to explain that I had plenty of clips and hair bands.

I scanned the room. It was surprisingly clean and large, although extremely basic; the accommodation was of a substandard level. It had been divided into three by wooden partitions which had been splashed with a lick of cream paint. Each area had two standard metal army-issue beds and two old dated mahogany wardrobes. The floor was covered in thick grey linoleum which was greasy in patches. At the end of the room lay a wide open space in which stood a stiff old-fashioned ironing board.

That night as I lay in bed I closed my eyes, almost wishing that I was somewhere else. I was not sure what to make of my new life.

The following morning I awoke to the sounds of reveille, a soldier's early-morning wake-up call, echoing around the large barracks. I dashed around frantically, trying to get ready. The other women flew past me, all scurrying to reach the shower first. The bathroom could best be described as basic. Two toilets sat behind two whitewashed wooden doors. The tiles were at one time orange but had turned almost burgundy in colour. The square sinks had long lost their sparkle. The pipes running beneath the sinks, which rattled throughout the dark night, were covered in white paint peeling away in flecks, revealing areas of rust. The showers were the worst feature: two shower heads, balanced delicately on skinny copper pipes, barely allowed a trickle of lukewarm water through.

My platoon fell in that first morning and every other morning just outside the male accommodation. We were marched as a platoon for breakfast to the same dining hall where my grandfather had fed the troops for forty-four years. The men and women of my recruit platoon were drawn from all over Munster.

I was beginning to feel excited about my life in the army. After breakfast the orderly sergeant of the day marched us collectively to the weapons stores. The sounds of the army band rehearsing on the square fell on my ears and I felt proud that I had joined the defence forces.

The days rolled by quickly while my body almost went into a complete state of shock. Each morning I would wake up at around 6.00 a.m. I would neatly fold my itchy cream and grey army-issue blankets and the two crisp white sheets, squaring them off before showering, dressing quickly and falling onto parade.

The orderly sergeant would fall us in and inspect each of us meticulously. I often had to suppress a laugh as he scolded those who weren't up to scratch.

"Did you iron your trousers, Recruit?"

"Yes, Corporal."

"Was the iron plugged in, Recruit?"

Depending on the orderly sergeant of the day, things could go either way: quite good or very bad.

Our mornings were filled with outdoor foot drill classes. We had yet to receive our green combat jackets, therefore the wind would cut through our green woollen jumpers, sending shivers down our spines, the cold almost reaching the depths of our bones. Our afternoons consisted of weapons training on the Steyr 5.56mm assault rifle and general purpose machine gun (GPMG).

Each day our platoon had to go on physical training sessions (PT), which could last anywhere between a short hour and a few hours. On top of this, we were run everywhere, in section or platoon formation. (Our platoon of thirty was split for training purposes into three sections of ten recruits.) After meal times was the only exception to this rule. The sweat would roll profusely from my brow. I often became flustered trying to keep my hair neatly tucked into my bun and flimsy brown hairnet.

Every evening I would sit on the floor of my billet, spit-polishing my black boots, then ironing and starching my green uniform and preparing my notes for the next day's classes. The combination of early starts and not getting to bed until two or three in the morning soon had me consumed with exhaustion.

I began to feel physically sick at roughly the same time each day, just before PT. As a platoon we often went running in the "Camp Field", a large green field situated directly across from the barracks. I vividly remember one particular session. It had been snowing heavily and a blanket of bright white snow covered the entire field and the black tarmac track that ran around it. We ran a couple of laps. My legs felt like lead blocks trudging along beneath me. We then had to perform push-ups until my face hit the velvety snow and a mouthful lodged between my blue-tinged lips, the cold going deep into my body. Once I started to run again my mind and body went into autopilot, my legs sweeping along beneath me. I barely noticed the flecks of white snowflakes landing on my frozen nose. If I ever had the misfortune to fall behind I was made to run at an ever-increasing pace around the platoon while it was still running in formation. We were only just beginning and already my body felt like it was going to snap in two.

4

Recruit Training

A couple of weeks into our training, one woman dropped out, only to be replaced by another. Amelia joined our platoon and she was a breath of fresh air. She was very shy, softly spoken and, more importantly, extremely fit. The other women had not shown much interest in PT and I often wondered what they were doing in the army. I loved sport, so now I had a buddy, someone with the same interests as me.

I found it difficult to mix with the other women of my platoon. I seemed different and they had no problem pointing this out to me. I was from the city, the north side of Cork, and most of them were from the country. In the end I gave up trying to fit in because it was never going to happen, but I do remember how much it hurt. I secretly wished that the other women and I could put aside our differences; after all, we had met under extreme circumstances.

Battle physical training was particularly difficult. I was so small, as were the other women, and we had to wear the same cumbersome battle gear as the men. My green metal helmet sat on the bun at the back of my head, causing the front of the helmet to bang off my nose, which became inflamed and sore. My 5.56mm assault rifle was slung across my chest and on my back I carried thirty-pound rocket pouches. These are usually zipped onto the sides of the backpack but we could zip them together for battle runs and patrols. Our packs were weighed and if you were under by one pound you received five pounds extra for your mistake.

Our training sessions would start with the corporals, sergeant and platoon commander circling us like eagles, pushing us beyond our limitations in order to get us through a training session. This was called "beasting" and it was deemed necessary to ensure that a soldier was produced. The civilian was stripped down, her spirit broken and in its place stood a soldier. I didn't disagree with it, as I never found it to be derogatory or insulting.

I often struggled in those early days of my career, in particular during recruit training. I found the pace too fast for my little legs under the weight of my rocket pouches. I was often "beasted up" to the men and before long my soft calf muscles bulged, becoming rock hard. Searing pain would shoot across the small of my back as my body and mind were pushed further and further.

"If you don't want to be here, then get lost! Sign the papers and get out!" roared the instructors.

I wanted to be there and I managed to complete most of the runs. The roaring never stopped, spit from the mouths of instructors often spraying on our faces. A green army minibus followed behind the platoon. The shame was too much to bear if you ended up falling out and sitting on the minibus. I only ever got on it once.

Around the same time a new term was coined in our platoon for anyone who was showing signs of slackening off. "The Bastard Room" was located in the male accommodation. Fortunately for us women, we were never sent there. The male heat seekers frequently found themselves in their new home. If a male recruit fell foul of our corporals then they were sent to this room in an attempt to redeem themselves, as they had more inspections and life was a little tougher in general there. I knew nothing about political correctness, so I didn't see anything wrong with "the Bastard Room".

Different instructors had different methods of instilling discipline. One instructor had his own particular punishments, which were harsher than the rest. If a bed block was not folded correctly he would carry it through the long billet, howling and roaring, before throwing it down the stairs of the male accommodation. He often dismantled beds, hurling the metal components down the stairs after the blankets. He would then call the platoon on parade, usually at eight o'clock in the evening. There in the bitter cold he barked out commands and orders, leaving me confused and bewildered. Under his instruction we had to race to our billets, returning in full battle gear, complete with gas masks. The gas mask often left me gasping for air and unsteady on my feet as it fogged up.

The thin wisp of air that managed to get through would allow me to get some oxygen, which I would suck deep inside my lungs.

I would follow the woman in front of me, who would blindly lead me to the square. From there we had to pretend to make our bed blocks on the large open square and I would stagger back and forth whilst tidying my make-believe bed area. The pitch-black sky had stars which glittered but unfortunately there were no eyes peering out from any windows, so our punishment would continue. We were made to squawk like chickens, and flap our arms in and out frantically whilst lifting our legs.

Fifteen minutes later we would be dismissed, only to be returned immediately in our best uniform, which was usually kept for more formal parades. Fifteen minutes later it would be a parade in tracksuit.

This would continue for hours until my mind was as numb as my body.

On another occasion we had been in the camp field in full battle gear, running around and performing various manoeuvres. I was in dire need of the toilet but the same instructor told me that I was not permitted to leave under any circumstances. An intense pain formed deep in my bladder and I was unable to run anymore. I barely struggled to stand in the same position. I was also in the middle of my period. In these situations I was told that, if you want to become a soldier, learn to deal with it. Eventually the instructor told my buddy that he would have to perform push-ups on the black tarmac in full battle gear until I returned. We all had a buddy to encourage each other to complete runs. My buddy had been sick the same morning but he was not allowed to see a doctor. He was as pale as a ghost that morning; his appearance startled me. We had encouraged him to go sick. Finally he agreed, only to be told, "Get back out, you don't need a doctor."

Something happened to my buddy during that training session and later that day he passed out in the billets. An ambulance was sent for immediately and he was swiftly carted off to Cork University Hospital. Whispers of blame filled the long billets. Later that evening we heard that his condition had improved but we didn't see him back in the ranks of our platoon for a while. I couldn't help but feel guilty that maybe I had caused it by insisting that I go to the toilet. However, the finger of blame was pointing in a different direction. After that incident the instructors drew back for a while.

Each day we also had a room inspection. The orderly sergeant would pop on a white plastic glove, snap it into position and march through our billet, his eyes zoning in on any traces of dust or dirt. We scrubbed for hours every night but no matter what we did, the dreaded dust was always found and we had to do push-ups until the instructor deemed that enough punishment had been doled out.

One evening after late supper, Amelia and I raced to our room. I reached the partition leading to my bed space and then stood frozen, staring blankly, my smile evaporating from my face. The contents of our wardrobes had been thrown to the four corners of our little section of the billet. My clothes were strewn across my bed. Embarrassingly, my tampons were lying on the floor. Everything I possessed in that room had been tampered with. Amelia fared worse than me; her iron had been thrown and the water had spilled over her clothes, letters and shoes. She was very upset.

When we approached our orderly sergeant he wasn't surprised. "I did it. Both of your wardrobes were unlocked; you should have them locked," he said.

I was incensed. "I reported to the platoon sergeant last week that the locks on both of our wardrobes were broken. We're waiting for them to be fixed."

He apologised for his mistake, but his actions bolted me into the reality of army life.

It was tough to get through recruit training. I don't remember laughing much. Tension and frivolous bickering didn't help.

In 1997 the army was only coming to terms with women training with men, and this coloured the training. We were only the second group of women in Cork to train alongside the men. They didn't really know what to do with us. There were no rule books on behaviour towards recruits.

Looking back now, my recruit training, above all else, prepared me for the army. It was tough and on occasion I sobbed my eyes out, tears spilling uncontrollably down my cheeks. There were days after PT when my body was pushed to its absolute limit. I ended up on my knees, throwing up blood into the toilet of our block. Stabbing pains and constant retching left me feeling weak and out of my depth in the male world of soldiering.

Nothing ever compared to how hard it was. I often phoned my father in tears, unable to utter a coherent sentence. My platoon sergeant was right; I did spill blood, sweat and tears. I ended up in hospital once for nine days with inflammation in my Achilles' tendon. I secretly welcomed the injury and sat with my foot elevated in the large hospital room where old radiators rattled through the night. The lights of Cork city shimmered in the distance. The sterile smell of that place has never left my memory.

We had been training for weeks in weapons, map-reading, foot drill, judging distance and field craft and also performing our daily physical training sessions, all in preparation for the tactical phase of training. Tactical training is the military term for exercises carried out on the ground as battle preparation, such as section attacks, platoon attacks, ambushes and patrolling. We had received adequate instruction on the majority of modules; however, the finer details were absent. I later learned the skills to cope with tactics from the 4th Infantry Battalion. We weren't taught to pack correctly or told the correct items to bring. I was unprepared and ill-equipped to cope with my first-ever phase of tactics. I will never forget it and later in my military career I breezed through tactics, because nothing compared to what I was about to experience.

On a cold grey winter morning the green army trucks left Collins Barracks in a convoy, headed towards

Kilworth Camp, Cork, where the tactical training would be held. I sat in the back of one of the trucks, wind howling past me, feeling scared. Our female liaison corporal was present and on arrival she escorted us to our accommodation. I had been there once before in the Reserve Defence Forces; however, that was during a beautiful summer and this was an exceptionally cold winter.

The long wooden billet reminded me of a concentration camp. There is no other way to describe it. The floorboards creaked and were missing in parts. Rows of black metal bunk beds lined either side of the room. The brown wooden slats were damp, with green mould creeping out of corners beside masses of cobwebs. The mattresses were stained and damp. There was no electrical heating and a large black pot-bellied heater sat in the centre of the room. It had to be packed with turf and it often took hours before any heat was emitted from it. The army-issue blankets lay on top of each bunk, grey, itchy and uninviting. It was decided that we would sleep in our sleeping bags.

My body shook that first night, I felt the cold in my spine and my head throbbed. I wore two pairs of green woolly socks, a tracksuit, gloves and a balaclava on my head, as did the rest of the women. I didn't sleep much; I was afraid something would crawl over my face.

The men's huts were concrete rather than wooden, but they were all bad. Our bathroom contained two toilets, neither of which I ever sat on, fearing I might contract something. They were disgustingly dirty, the once-white bowls covered in green slime. Adjacent to the toilet area was our cramped shower, the worst shower I have ever seen. The walls were filthy and the shower curtain had murky brown and green flecks the whole way up to the top. The copper pipe barely worked and water often failed to make it through the large lime-scaled shower head.

As a result of having no adequate heating or drying facilities, I often had to put on soaking wet combat trousers in the mornings. We would desperately try to air our clothes next to the pot-bellied heater but only patches of the green material dried out. I remember feeling miserable, cold and often hungry during that two-week phase.

Each day was different but equally painful, physically and mentally. Our platoon was divided into three sections and we spent our days at the back of the camp, crawling over jagged rocks, through pools of muck and water. The long ditches offered both solace and pain. I basked in the breaks I received, lying against the wet ditches of Kilworth, but my legs and arms were often in agony as I crawled along them for hours that never seemed to end. Frost clung to the grass on the ditches and my fingers would freeze, often leaving me unable to pull the trigger of my rifle. My elbows and knees were covered in bruises and my shoulders were in constant pain that never subsided. The straps of the heavy rocket pouches would dig into my skin, leaving red indentations on my shoulders where bruises shortly followed.

Deep Freeze cold muscle spray kept me going as it rapidly cooled and numbed my shoulders and back each morning. Steam would rise from my green combat jacket and my back stung from the cold, but it was a better option than pain.

We nicknamed our platoon sergeant "Multi Bob" and "Bobbybananas" simply because he seemed to have a number of personalities. He was a very fair and reasonable man but if we were late or lost an item of ordinance, we suffered badly. The Cossack position was his favoured method of punishment. We would squat on the ground, legs apart, and walk in this position with the rifle held overhead. If you dropped your rifle you had to start again and again. If oil spilled or weapons were not clean, the Cossack or rifle PT was the punishment. Rifle PT is where a soldier is made to hold his or her rifle in a variety of painful positions, in one hand, straight out in front, to the side, overhead, or on top of it in the push-up position.

We performed section and platoon attacks on each other. On one occasion, I fell asleep in the middle of a section in attack. Sleep deprivation can be excruciating and when the opportunity arises a soldier may fall asleep anywhere out of sheer exhaustion. I lay next to the ditch where I had been stationed, in a pool of mud, my face submerged in the green grass, and I was fast asleep. I awoke to find my Section Commander standing overhead, laughing. It was a bit funny – how any soldier could manage to fall asleep in the middle of an attack! Yet I did. He didn't punish me; I think he felt sorry for me. My instructors were decent, fair men. Recruit training is meant to be hard; after all, the instructors have to produce soldiers.

We also spent a lot of time on the ranges in the torrential rain that fell from blackened skies, firing our rifles or machine guns and throwing grenades. I had an accident when I threw my grenade. A new instructor had arrived in Kilworth. He roared in my ear as I held the green grenade in my hand in the bunker. Startled, I dropped it just a short distance in front of us. The blast almost deafened me. Miraculously, no one was injured. It was a training grenade but I was never let forget it. I don't think anyone ever forgot it.

I found myself bonding well with some of the male recruits and there were times when we truly enjoyed training together. I made fantastic friends, some of whom remained friends for the rest of my career.

Our two-week tactical training phase was finishing up with a forty-eight-hour exercise in the Galtee Mountains. Our platoon formed up on parade on the square of Kilworth Camp on a bitterly cold Wednesday morning. We each received a forty-eight-hour ration pack, which consisted of two ready-made dinners, breakfasts, a few boiled sweets and biscuits. We mounted the trucks and were dropped off at the foothills of the snow-capped mountains.

My platoon climbed the mountains and over the hills until we reached the location of our patrol harbour or base camp, an area deep within the forest where we would set up camp for the two-day exercise. The patrol harbour was in good cover, away from habitation, with good routes in and out. The platoon was halted 200 metres from the area, taking up all-round defence. The patrol commander and his party went forward to complete a recce (reconnaissance). Once the platoon moved forward, each section was led in by our section commanders. Shortly afterwards the perimeter and communications cord were erected. Following this, the day routine, night routine and security were planned.

Each recruit was allocated a separate job. Latrines had to be dug and branches had to be chopped down with entrenching tools. Each section was situated separately along the triangular perimeter. I set up my area, pitched my camouflaged poncho as a means of shelter and absorbed the green surroundings of our camp. The scent of pine trees filled the air.

As we grew comfortable we took to sneaking away to the latrine area to smoke cigarettes, safe in the knowledge that we would not be discovered. Latrines were located in a position where they could be covered by a sentry. On that occasion, though, it was an advantage being a woman as our latrine was farther down the dirt track, so we could sneak in and out undetected.

Dusk fell quickly, with stars glowing overhead beside a gleaming silver moon. I was among a group of recruits detailed to carry out a water patrol. A number of patrols were sent out from our base camp each night – water patrols, recce patrols (where the objective is to gain information on the enemy), and fighting patrols (where the patrol attacks the enemy position). The patrol orders were given out and we headed cross-country to the area where we were to retrieve our water. As we marched over the uneven terrain a dense fog limited our vision. Immediately after we picked up the water, our section came under fire from the enemy element of the exercise. Flashes lit up the sky overhead and loud bangs blasted through my eardrums. Green and white smoke grenades engulfed each member of our patrol as we sprinted under the cover of pluming white smoke to a safe area. Once the attack ceased our patrol commander took control and doubled (ran) us back to a safe area, where each member of the patrol was accounted for. As I hiked up the uneven tracks of forest, the wet ground below my feet hindered my progress and I often fell, smacking my legs and hips off the rocks below me.

We were not permitted to take our boots off while we slept but I always did, to air my feet. We had to sleep with our rifles, never letting them go. We also had to name our rifles. I called my rifle "Betty" after my old family car. I never let go of that rifle, sleeping in a foetal position with the sling firmly around my wrist, the bronze buckle imprinting on my face as I slept. If I had let Betty out of my vision for even a split second, she would have been snapped up and I would have ended up in the painful squatting Cossack position. I slept on those nights to the sound of owls. The deep forest makes particularly eerie noises.

Throughout the long black night sentries were located at machine gun positions. After dark the only aid we had to guide us in and out of the harbour was the perimeter cord. The whole platoon was awoken just before light and we all went into stand to (all-round cover), because attacks are most likely at first and last light.

For the remainder of the day our platoon prepared for an ambush on the enemy. This particular ambush set the precedent for every subsequent ambush I was involved in. My platoon marched off that day, soaking, tired, sore and completely deprived of sleep. Once we reached the location for our ambush we formed three groups. We lay in wait of the enemy but as the minutes turned to hours, eyes slowly closed. Then, suddenly, we were jolted into action by the sounds of gunfire cracking through the crisp air. My finger refused to move as it had become stiff and frozen. Before I knew it, the ambush was over. I suspect that nearly everyone slept through a portion of it. It was deemed a success and we were pulled back to the area of our base camp. That night we followed the same routine as the first night and before I knew it I was back in Kilworth Camp, nearly a trained soldier.

I loved becoming a soldier. Outside the regimental confines of Collins Barracks, I loved my training.

Only one element of our training remained: scratch. "Scratch" is something that every recruit platoon goes through. It's a gruelling few hours of battle physical training. This word filled me with terror, but I gritted my teeth and prepared myself. We were marched, run and dragged over thick green ditches and under low bridges with our faces stuck in the muddy water. We ran for miles up and down hills with our gas masks on, in full nuclear battle combat gear. We crawled under barbed wire while smoke grenades were thrown near us. Then we were run up a long meandering stream in full battle gear, carrying rocket pouches weighing thirty pounds and each of us taking it in turn to carry a full sandbag. My back almost broke under the weight as my body was still not in perfect shape. Instructors roared out orders for what seemed like an eternity.

Finally it was over. I stood, almost astonished that I had succeeded. I was almost there, on the verge of becoming a fully fledged soldier.

A few days later I found myself in the familiar surroundings of Collins Barracks. We spent the following two weeks preparing for our passing-out parade. One afternoon all the women were summoned by the orderly sergeant. The men had all applied to serve in the 4th and 12th Infantry Battalions. We on the other hand were told we weren't allowed to. I was perplexed. Even though I had just completed sixteen weeks of gruelling training, my gender prevented me from serving where my heart wanted to be. I spoke about it to my orderly sergeant. Surprisingly, he agreed that it was wholly unfair. "Put your first choice down as the 4th Infantry Battalion. You have nothing to lose; all they can say is no," he said.

We weren't aware of any women serving in the infantry in Ireland at that stage. I wanted to become a combat soldier and not a typist. There's nothing wrong with being a typist, but it wasn't what I wanted. I held the white application form in my hand and with a blue pen I clearly wrote "4th Infantry Battalion" as my first option. My heart was racing, but once it was done I let out a sigh of relief. The infantry battalions were the last frontier of male machismo to be penetrated by other rank females in

Munster. On the eve of our passing-out parade I lay snugly in my bed, exhausted but jubilant.

The next day I marched proudly to the beat of the army band. My family were in attendance and even though I had lost a little bit of my femininity, I was thrilled to finally become a soldier. I thought that nothing could go wrong. All that remained was eight weeks of training and then it was on to our parent units.

5

Breaking New Ground

After our passing-out parade we received a much-welcomed two-week break. I went home to my mother, who tried hopelessly to change my mind about the 4th Infantry Battalion whilst my father, who had reservations about my first choice, still encouraged me.

He drove me back to Collins Barracks on a dark and dreary Sunday evening. His car pulled up outside my accommodation next to the command training depot and I sadly said goodbye to him. I pulled my green oversized army-issue bag from the boot and made my way up the two darkened flights of stairs to my bed space.

A wave of loneliness washed over me as I waited for the other women to arrive. I was looking forward to seeing Amelia, whose gentle nature always made me feel better. I made the decision to try to make amends with the other women, with whom there had been a number of arguments and simmering tension. I was surrounded by them every day and so it made sense for all of us to get along. However, fate was about to intervene and things would go from bad to worse at lightning speed between us women.

The following morning after breakfast our platoon was marched briskly across the barrack square to the conference block. Our platoon sergeant stood the platoon to attention and informed us that we would learn of our fate that day. We were to be interviewed by the 4th Infantry Battalion Commander and he would decide where we would be stationed once our training was completed.

A flurry of emotion washed over me. What if I was sent to signals or to an office, like the last women who had trained with the men? There were no vacancies in the military police so I became slightly apprehensive. I wanted to stay with the male friends I had made in recruit training and I wanted to be a soldier. I had never envisaged any other fate. The tension that hung in the air was felt by everyone, yet I clung to the hope of a small miracle happening.

As we entered the wide open room where we had attended so many of our lectures, all of the women were on tenterhooks. One of the women was summoned for an interview. Shortly afterwards, she stormed back, slamming the door behind her. The loud bang jolted us to attention and drew the close scrutiny of our instructors. She ran to the bathroom, followed quickly by the other women. Apparently she was to be stationed outside the barracks and could not mask her disappointment.

A few moments later it was my turn. A knot of nerves formed deep within the pit of my stomach as I made my way across the dark hall. When I entered the other room, the light atmosphere put my mind to rest. Three men – a colonel and two others – sat with their arms folded behind a long dark mahogany table. My body pulsed with emotion as I marched forward, saluted the board and sat down before their scrutinising eyes.

I was grilled at length about my recruit training and my childhood. I was brutally honest as I described how I had struggled at the beginning of my recruit training. My body and mind had gone into shock but towards the end, I felt I had excelled. While the defence forces never admits it, the fact remains that the civilian is initially stripped down to breaking point in order to be replaced with a soldier.

"Why did you pick the 4th Infantry Battalion?" asked the colonel.

"I applied for the 4th Infantry Battalion for the same reasons as the men," I told the board. "I want to be a combat soldier and I don't want to work in an office. I have completed my training just like the men and I don't think the fact that I'm a woman should stop me from working in the infantry." I also told them that my grandfather had served there for forty-four years and that his picture was still hanging in the military museum across the square. At that stage also, my father had been promoted to barrack quarter-master and was stationed in the Southern Command Headquarters. I had a strong military background and I was very eager to get this point across to them.

The colonel sat back in his chair and folded his arms across his broad chest once more. He took a deep breath before announcing that my application was successful. I was going to the 4th Infantry Battalion.

A smile beamed across my face as I stood up and saluted the interview board. At nineteen years of age, I didn't fully realise the magnitude of the decision. They gave me an opportunity for which I will always be grateful, which changed my destiny forever. However, it would also bring an amount of physical and mental hardship for which I had not prepared myself. I did not realise that the infantry battalions were the final frontier of machismo. The boys' club had never been fully infiltrated by a woman. Although I would be welcomed by many, I would also be ostracised by others. I would come across some draconian attitudes towards women – or, as they put it, the weaker sex.

I almost floated back across the hall. I was careful not to appear too jubilant, conscious of the feelings of others. When my instructors asked me where I had been stationed, there was an audible collective gasp when I announced "The 4th Infantry Battalion". Never before had women been accepted to serve within the other ranks of the 4th Infantry Battalion. Some were genuinely happy for me, although slightly confused as to why I wanted to go there. Surely an office would have been easier and more appropriate? Others couldn't hide their indignation and this was the trigger for an undercurrent of jealousy that would leave me sobbing uncontrollably most nights.

Later it emerged that Amelia was going with me, though as it turned out I would arrive there a few months prior to her. I was ecstatic, as was she. The other women were being sent to a barracks in Ballincollig, the 1st Field Artillery Regiment. Some whispered that my acceptance was prompted by my father's recent promotion. Either way, my odyssey through the infantry was going to be turbulent. I tried to brush off any feelings of negativity levied in my direction and set about concentrating on the task at hand: completing my training.

6

Out of the Frying Pan . . .

Before we were despatched to our parent units, we had another eight weeks of training left. During this 2–3-star training bloc, the physically demanding regime continued. However, the atmosphere became noticeably more relaxed between us young soldiers and our instructors. Our training comprised internal security, fighting in a built-up area (FIBUA) and defence in a built-up area (DIBUA), and nuclear battle combat (NBC) training, something that I grew to detest deeply. The mere sight of the black rubber gas mask sent my mind swirling.

The physical training became increasingly gruelling. Most of our training sessions by then had been battle PT, which involved running the endless tarmac roads as a platoon or down in the glen. Under the weight of my packs and helmet I often had a stinging pain in my lower back and would wince when I had to carry the machine gun. But I never gave up.

I had built up a solid endurance and my physical fitness was at an all-time high, but it did take its toll on my body. On many occasions I again found myself kneeling on the cold terracotta floor tiles in our bathroom after battle PT. My hands would grip the white toilet bowl as my stomach heaved and I coughed up a mixture of phlegm and blood.

My femininity was also affected by my pursuit of soldiering as there was little time for hair or make-up. As I was transformed into a combat soldier, I distanced myself from my femininity and my softer side. My personality also began to change; the bubbly, glossy-curled young girl was replaced with a colder, more distant and driven woman.

In the evenings we often finished early, but I had no escape. In a confined and controlled space, the uncomfortable situation in my room was taking its toll on me. I was performing better than ever during the day but this led to increasingly distant behaviour towards me by some. I would phone my father, begging to come home. The relentless sobbing often led to panic attacks, my head down, a brown paper bag around my mouth as I gasped for air.

The blood spewing from my stomach was becoming increasingly worse after PT and eventually I reported sick. I was admitted to hospital and a week later I emerged, completely relaxed and rejuvenated. The constant retching had stopped and my stomach had settled.

During 2–3-star training, soldiers complete a further two weeks of tactical training. This module was particularly difficult. I couldn't imagine how it could have been any harder than the last phase, but it was. We were again to spend two weeks in Kilworth.

To this day I still get goose bumps and shivers when I drive past Kilworth Camp on the way home to Cork. There's nothing on the outskirts of the camp but broad green fields. A thick, relentless mist often lingers in spring, complete with grey clouds suspended overhead. On approaching the army camp you're suddenly met with an abundance of green trees, cold grey buildings and lots of sheep. It's an awful, miserable place.

During this phase we were to complete a forty-eight-hour exercise called a "dig-in". We formed up as a platoon one unusually crisp spring morning in front of the waiting green army trucks. To reach our base camp a few miles away on the side of a hill, we had to tab it. Tabbing is when you march for extended periods of time in full battle gear. The men didn't seem to suffer as much physically because their physiques are designed for this equipment, whereas unfortunately female physiques are not designed for it.

I loathed my backpack in recruit training. The mere sight of it often filled me with fear. I stood at just over five feet three inches tall and my backpack would reach up to my waist. It usually weighed between eighty and a hundred pounds when packed for an exercise. The kit mat we were issued to sleep on was twice the length of my body and I had to keep it strapped to the top of my backpack. I also had to wear the green helmet and as usual it sat on top of my ponytail which, combined with a mass of clips digging into my head, drove me insane.

I slung my rifle across the front of my chest and often tried to hide when the machine gun was being allocated, but to no avail. The general purpose machine gun is usually called the mag. It's very big and very annoying when you're tiny. Over the years I found novel ways of modifying my combat gear to fit me more comfortably. I had no alternative or I just would not have been able to do it. Sometimes I went to army surplus stores and bought smaller, more compact items issued to foreign armies and wore those instead.

I covered my upper body in Deep Freeze again that crisp spring morning but I still didn't have the sense to take painkillers. We tabbed for a few hours over the harsh landscape of Kilworth. The ground always seemed to be wet, slippery and uneven. I inevitably ended up on my knees and bum a lot.

I started to like tabbing. Adrenaline rushed through my veins as I took each step and my mind tried to override the burning sensations in my legs and lower back. Like with any physical exercise, endorphins are released, which I would refer to as "happy hormones". I found myself becoming addicted to the rush, like a drug. I sometimes think that I became addicted to the pain. I felt exhilarated and strove to push my body beyond its natural capabilities, both mentally and physically. I would tell myself that the physical pain was in my mind and that I could overcome it.

It was during this phase of training that my love of all things military truly began. It's in my bloodline, as many a soldier would say. My grandmother Molly used to say to me, "I thought one of my grandsons would follow in your grandfather's footsteps. I never imagined that *you* would join the army."

We finally reached our base camp and started to prepare the frosty ground for the "dig-in". Standing on frozen grass on a sloping hill, I grasped my entrenching tool and, along with two of the men, banged down on the hard ground, starting the task of digging our own battle trench. We lifted the earth until beads of sticky sweat were rolling down our brows, almost hot despite the bitter cold winds. Ten hours later, we covered our trench with galvanising metal and a few brown ammunition boxes. I paused momentarily and stood back in admiration at our work. We had made our very first trench, and it looked pretty good!

I don't think any woman would be filled with joy at the prospect of lying in a trench for extended periods of time, grappling with a machine gun against the backdrop of roaring winds and downpours of rain.

Darkness fell over the hillside as I began to get used to my new surroundings. Initially as I lay in my new trench, it felt almost surreal, eerily like being inside a coffin. I lay on my green plastic foam kit mat and gazed overhead at the glistening stars. The smell of freshly dug earth engulfed my nostrils and the silence was almost deafening. It was actually a little warmer lying down so deep, but it took some getting used to. Flecks and occasionally chunks of muck would land on my face. The smell of the earth invaded my senses. It was a cold Friday evening deep within the heart of Kilworth and I thought about my friends at home. They would have been out dancing while I lay in a trench on the side of a hill.

The next day at lunchtime I set about brewing up my dinner, chicken curry. It took me almost twenty minutes to light the hexy tablet – a little white tablet you ignite and place under a mini-cooker. My hands were sore and swollen and I had to will them to move. Twigs and muck dangled from my once-glossy curls, which now looked more like tumbleweed. I had replaced my helmet with a soft green woollen skip hat, hoping that no watchful instructor would notice that my helmet wasn't on.

The curry tasted dreadful and instantly made my stomach churn. I grimaced as a mouthful travelled down my oesophagus and sat heavily on my stomach. Shortly afterwards I started vomiting and was sent to the medic, who told me I had food poisoning. It turned out that our ration packs were out-of-date.

I was summoned to the non-commissioned officer (NCO), and I wasn't just wearing green, I felt green. When I reached the NCO, I couldn't hold the vomit down any more. It gushed from my mouth, landing in a pool of partly digested canary-yellow chicken curry, just in front of him. The captain from the training depot had just arrived. The NCO started shouting, reprimanding me, "Private Sheehan, how dare you throw up in the company of an officer!" I felt so sick and thought to myself, *How can I stop myself from throwing up? Was it beneath the captain to see a human being throwing up?*

I was sent back to Kilworth camp with a brown paper vomit bag and spent the next few hours in the same filthy bathroom we had used in recruit training, my head stuck down the green and rusty toilet bowl. I decided to head back to my billet and sleep, hoping that I might feel better when I woke up. As I reached the wooden door of my billet and was about to open the black steel latch, I saw other members of my platoon filtering back into camp. Some were hobbling along carrying injuries while others had the same complaint as me: food poisoning. They looked as bad as I felt.

The regimental, uncompromising NCO arrived in camp shortly afterwards, without a fleck of muck anywhere to be seen on him. He swiftly sent for us all. He handed us bleach, a packet of blue cloths, grey steel buckets and mops and ordered us to clean all the toilets in camp. I still wasn't feeling very well but we all set about cleaning the toilets. They were so disgusting; to this day, I think they were the worst toilets I have ever seen.

The next morning I was feeling slightly better when I woke up quite early. I started to head over to the dining hall for some dry toast to settle my stomach. The NCO caught a glimpse of me and roared across the square, "Private Sheehan, where do you think you're going?" I told him and he replied, "You received a forty-eight-hour ration pack, so you're not allowed to eat in the dining hall." I tried helplessly to tell him it was out-of-date but he wouldn't listen. In the end I ate the biscuits, which were still in date – but which I knew caused constipation.

Later that day the rest of the platoon arrived and we prepared to head back to Collins Barracks. We had to clean all the weapons before we left. No matter how hard we scrubbed, the instructors would find grease and dirt up the barrels of the rifles and machine guns. I was still a bit nauseous and fed-up. Then, a few of us had a great idea – we decided to bring the weapons to the showers. We waited until no instructors were in sight and ran swiftly to the male showers, where we placed the machine guns under the shower heads and hosed them down quickly. We stood back in admiration at our work; they were sparkling.

At the next inspection, a corporal paced, hands clasped behind his back, up and down the length of the billet. He probed us about how we had managed to get the weapons so clean but none of us cracked. When he left our billet, looking totally confused, suspicious and paranoid, we burst out laughing.

7

. . . Into the Fire

The next day we all headed back to Collins Barracks. Tactics was over and all that was left to complete was FIBUA, DIBUA and internal security. I was so happy and relieved at the prospect of finishing my training. I wanted to get away from the stifling confines of my billet. The tensions between us women were invariably magnified within the claustrophobic walls of our room. I found it difficult to cope with this.

Towards the end of my training I found my mind totally preoccupied with what I ate. I didn't realise it then, but the way I coped with external conflict was to control meticulously what food my body consumed. There were days when all I would eat was a slice of toast for breakfast, fish for lunch and vegetables with a little piece of meat for dinner.

I hid this aspect of my life for a very long time, almost expertly. Inevitably hunger pains would stir in my stomach and on occasion I didn't have the willpower to abstain from food. This is when I would binge on food and purge afterwards. This was extremely destructive and it wasn't long before I started to develop a puffy face and swollen fingers. I often felt very weak.

I wasn't the only woman to fall into the vicious cycle where food became the enemy. Throughout my career in the defence forces, I regularly encountered women waiting for others to vacate the bathroom. As they purged into the bowl they would flush the chain to drown out the sound. Afterwards they would say they weren't feeling very well, that it was something they ate. For some reason I found the incidence of eating disorders very high within the female ranks of the defence forces. Maybe we couldn't control the environment we often found ourselves in, constantly pushing to excel and striving to be accepted. But we could control our eating habits.

This cycle of starvation, bingeing and purging followed me for many years. It surfaced whenever I was in turmoil, when my life, either professionally or personally, was spinning out of control. Soon my life was becoming a permanent binge followed by sleep deprivation. Long gone was the healthy glow I had arrived with months previously. Standing in Collins Barracks was almost a broken woman, a shadow of her former self.

Two weeks later we started the internal security module of our training.

Fort Davis is a beautiful, picturesque old fort located on a cliff-top overlooking Cork Harbour. It was built by the British as Fort Carlisle, and was presented to the Irish Government in 1938, when the official name was changed to Fort Davis. It is used today by the Irish defence forces for training. It is surrounded by a moat and lush green reeds. Standing on the edge of the square is an old church which still houses religious relics and ornate confession boxes. On the top level is a maze of tiny rooms, where we would later complete fighting in a built-up area (FIBUA) and defence in a built-up area (DIBUA). Underneath the top level is another labyrinth of tunnels and rooms.

Later in my career I would bump into my future husband at this very fort. Undertaking urban warfare training within the confines of an old army fort isn't a typically romantic scenario, but it's where I began to fall in love.

Riot training was part of the internal security module. Our equipment was basic, with a choice of either a large or a small shield. The large shield was at least two feet higher than me but I was allocated one as I was last in the queue. We were divided into two separate groups. Our instructors took on the role of rioters while we had to form a riot platoon to hold them back and bring the situation under control.

It was mayhem. The rioters hurled rocks and smoke grenades in our direction, often only narrowly missing us. The rioters were roaring aggressively and landing kicks and blows on our clear plastic shields. Red bricks used as weapons by the instructors peppered the skyline and green smoke billowed through the air from the smoke grenades that engulfed us. It became quite difficult to breathe. I couldn't see under my visor and helmet and everyone was choking and spluttering. We marched forward, at which point two members of the platoon were let through to take in a rioter.

The riot was becoming increasingly out of control. The blows were landing on my shield hard and fast and I struggled to maintain control. My little legs were buckling under the pressure. I was just managing to hold off the instructors who were landing on top of my shield. The plastic handle of the shield was cutting deep into my skin, leaving my arm throbbing. The pain became so overwhelming that I couldn't feel it anymore, yet still the blows and kicks kept coming.

I don't disagree with the methods used by our instructors. They had a job to do – to simulate a riot – and they executed it to perfection. Things may have spiralled out of control, but that's the reality of a riot in real life. So the riot training was practical and stood to us.

Eventually someone had the common sense to call a halt to the exercise. I stood deflated on the top level of the fort amidst a cloud of green smoke and began to remove my riot gear. My arms were covered in large fresh bruises and were red and swollen from my shoulders to my fingertips. I couldn't move one of my fingers.

I hadn't let my shield go but I was left with a broken finger. Over the next few days my arm turned a spectrum of colours, ranging from black to blue, yellow and green. The pain was excruciating initially but soon passed. I was unable to complete the FIBUA and DIBUA module due to my injury, but I stood on the sidelines along with a few others and observed. Injuries are common in riot training and I was lucky to escape on that occasion with just a broken finger.

With the end of training looming, we had more free time on our hands in the evenings. On one particular evening we had to go to the gym, which in 1997 was a tiny, shabby, rundown building, but it was neat and compact with a good staff running it. (A massive modern gym has since been built in Collins Barracks.) We had to be "bodies" for some soldiers who were training to be fitness instructors.

I walked in and spotted a very handsome young man. He had jet black hair, lightly tanned skin and wore loose grey tracksuit bottoms which showed off a cute little bum. My eyes fixed on it as he passed by. His name was Andy. He taught us aerobics and was quite good at it.

On each occasion that I met Andy a flurry of emotions would come over me. He was a pure gentleman, very sweet and quite shy. At the end of the session I approached him and wished him luck in his forthcoming exams. He gave me a chocolate and smiled at me. It was official: I had a crush. I felt an instant attraction to him, an attraction that would span a decade. He was a private in the 4th Infantry Battalion and I became even more excited at the prospect of being sent to the infantry after I met him.

The end of our training was only a few days away and we were informed that we had to complete a light infantry weapons course as a platoon. During the weapons course we would learn to use a 60mm mortar, the GPMG (general purpose machine gun) on sustained fire, and the 84mm anti-tank weapon.

However, the following day I was paraded and told that, because my finger was broken, I was being sent to the 4th Infantry Battalion immediately and that I would complete the course at a later date. I thanked God silently; I was never so happy to have a broken finger. I was finally free and let out a huge sigh of relief.

I raced to my room and packed my bag. It was a rare day in spring and rays of golden sunlight sprinkled through the window, bouncing off my bed. I stood alone to look one last time at the room where I had shed sweat, streams of tears and blood. I was overwhelmed with emotion but filled with relief. I had made it; I had survived my recruit training.

Around this time, I also decided to seek help for my eating disorder. I attended a support group once a week for a while, which helped me tremendously, giving me the tools to recognise why I was doing it and how to overcome it.

I truly don't know how I got through my training in one piece, completing exhausting physical training and juggling an eating disorder on the side. I did survive it, though, and finally started to get my eating disorder under control. I was aware that an eating disorder can return but I worked hard to overcome it.

8

The 4th Infantry Battalion

The following Monday morning I arrived at the doors of the 4th Infantry Battalion. My arm was in a sling, which wasn't how I had imagined starting my career in the infantry, but it would heal.

B Company was all locked up, as they were away on an exercise. So, I was told, was Support Company. I didn't know the structure of an infantry battalion at that stage and I didn't know what "B Company" and "Support Company" meant. As I would learn later, the battalion was split into different sections: three companies and a headquarters element.

I was bewildered and nervous. I went to the end of the grey concrete block and walked up two flights of stairs. There was a narrow corridor to the right through which I ventured until I found a little office. I cautiously peered around the door and was greeted by a startled sergeant. He told me that the majority of personnel were away on an exercise.

Confused, he asked me, "Are you sure you're meant to be here?"

"Yes," I replied and told him what had happened.

He asked me to wait for a moment, turned on his heels and went to speak to the captain. Eventually, he returned to tell me that I could work with him until my finger got better and the other companies returned. I would then be sent to B Company, but for the moment, I remained within the safe confines of the 4th Infantry Battalion orderly room.

I spent the next three weeks delivering letters and making cups of tea. I was told to look busy. I had to walk around constantly with a brown envelope in my hand addressed to a colonel. I learned how to file documents and letters and how to answer the phone.

The men I was working with were lovely. They were very helpful to me and on occasion very funny. The sergeant was a kind man and always did what he could to guide me and help me. This warm, relaxed, friendly atmosphere was a pleasure to work in and in stark contrast to what lay ahead.

One afternoon I was sitting at the desk in the office when I heard loud footsteps thumping up the hall. A non-commissioned officer (NCO) appeared around the corner and shouted at me, "Private Sheehan, you're meant to be in B Company and not up here." I clung to my seat and didn't dare answer him back.

The sergeant whom I had been working with spoke up, "Come on now, B Company was away and I said she could work in here."

The NCO stormed off in an angry huff and later reappeared, this time with the B Company commanding officer by his side. There was a tug of war as to where I would be sent, and eventually I had to go to B Company. I didn't mind. It's where I wanted to go, but I had enjoyed my time in the orderly room. I was sad to say goodbye to the sergeant and his kind manner.

For the next few weeks I lined up on parade in the morning with the men. I again met Andy but he was very shy and found it difficult to talk to me. Luckily, I can talk for Ireland, so I approached him a few times.

Our mornings in B Company were spent cleaning toilets. The men had new accommodation, with huge steel lockers, hot showers and the best of facilities. The women, on the other hand, were not extended the same treatment. I was allocated a tiny wooden locker in an already-cramped locker room in my old building, which was shabby, run-down and lacked hot water.

On Monday mornings, B Company personnel went swimming. Andy offered me a lift to the pool. I had arranged one already and I think he was disappointed. I was unaware that he had a bit of crush on me too.

One weekend I escaped with Andy and some of his fellow soldiers to the sanctuary of the Support Company office. The atmosphere was much better there and we were chatting and messing about. The company sergeant came marching down the hall and stood at the door, his piercing eyes staring through me. He told me I was going with the company on a ten-day exercise to the Glen of

Imaal in County Wicklow and Fort Davis. After officers complete their college education they have to do a month-long course called a young officers' course. I was to be one of the other ranks soldiers they would have to command as part of their training.

"Do you think you can handle it?" he added.

"Yes, of course," I replied.

It must have been hard for him to deal with me; I don't think he knew what to do with me. I was a test case in the 4th Infantry Battalion, I suppose, but I just wanted to be treated the same as the men. Of course, you're never just one of the lads when you have a ponytail.

It was the middle of summer and I felt a surge of excitement and nervousness rush through me. I arrived on parade the following Monday morning, prepared to leave for the exercise. The entire ordinance was handed out and signed for, and we mounted the trucks. I was the only woman on the exercise. We were headed for the Curragh military camp in County Kildare to form up with the rest of the troops; from there, we continued to our destination in the Glen of Imaal.

One of the instructors who had trained me was also present. I got on brilliantly with him and he treated me and viewed me as equal to a man. On the first night we had to set up a base camp; a female officer asked him, "Would you make out my orders and set up my bivy [where she would sleep]?" We looked at each other as if to say, *the audacity of her!* He did it for her because he was a bit soft. As he did so, he explained the different steps to me.

The days rolled into the nights in quick succession. Each day we would fight for hours, completing gruelling section and platoon attacks. We tabbed over the hills for hours, drenched in sweat and laden down with backpacks and ammunition. One of the men in my section, Glen, was over six feet tall and top-heavy. He was marching directly in front of me. He was a constant source of both encouragement and amusement. When we reached the top of the hill, he had vanished. I looked around but couldn't see him anywhere. I turned quickly to another soldier and asked, "In the name of God, where did Glen go?" Then we suddenly heard his cry for help. He had sunk down a bog hole and was up to his waist in muck, his rifle barely visible above his head. I couldn't help him out because I had fallen to my knees in a convulsion of laughter. Eventually we managed to rescue him, but he wasn't amused.

We reached our destination shortly before dusk. One by one we filtered into the dense green vegetation of a thick forest. After marching under the strain of my backpack for hours, I was exhausted and overheating. I lay my backpack beside me and lay down to recover. After a while the sweat turned cold and a chill ran through my body.

Glen had been saturated and had his own ideas for keeping warm. He got a large fire blazing and was happily munching on a packet of crisps. The flames were crackling and sparks were jumping out around the toes of his black boots. A young officer made the brave decision to approach him – something not many people would do.

"Are you for real, corporal?" said the officer. "We're in the middle of a base camp and you're after lighting a fire and now you're eating crisps! Put out that fire immediately."

"I tell you one thing now, boy, if I was you I'd go back over where you came from. I'm fucking soaked and in danger of getting hypothermia. So no, I won't be putting any fire out – unless you have a tumble-dryer handy," said Glen.

"But you'll give our position away to the enemy."

"There's no fecking enemy, you eejit – it's a mock exercise." It was hilarious and the young officer walked away like a meek little mouse.

That night the temperature dropped rapidly. Around ten o'clock I was sent to the top of the forest to act as a runner – someone who would deliver messages between the platoons for the officers. They told me to deliver a message to a platoon commander. I had to head deep into the forest and follow the glow sticks hanging on the trees. The forest was pitch black and I couldn't really see in front of me. It wasn't long before I was lost. I was walking among the trees and couldn't see a glow stick anywhere.

Suddenly I came across an obstacle – a few trees had fallen and the only way past them was to jump over them. I stood back and made an attempt to jump over them, but I slipped and my rifle became lodged under one of the trees. The rifle's sling was tight around my neck, choking me. I lay gasping for air, barely able to breathe. I had to work my fingers underneath the sling in an effort to breathe and managed to ease the grip on my neck, but I still couldn't dislodge the rifle from under the tree.

I was stuck, without anyone in sight. I realised that it could be a very long night and resolved that I should just try to keep my spirits up and stay warm.

I must have been lying there for about two hours before I heard another soldier passing. I called out loudly, my voice echoing through the trees until he eventually found me. He helped me to dislodge the rifle and set me free. At that point he was also very lost. After going around in circles for another hour we eventually found our platoon. I passed on the message and headed back to my trench, deflated. I could have been lying there all night and no one would have noticed.

We were a good few days into the exercise and on one of the nights we were allowed to go to the local pub. A few of the soldiers I was with bought bottles of Jack Daniels, hid them in their rocket pouches and took them back to the trenches with them. I was freezing in my trench and went to the trench nearest me. It was more like a house than a trench. The lads were all drinking from the bottle of Jack Daniels and offered me some. "Come on, it'll keep you warm and you'll sleep," they said. I took a few swigs and settled down in my sleeping bag between the three lads, our body heat keeping us all warm. I'm sure that, with my camouflage cream and filthy hands, they did not find me attractive. Those days were simple; I was accepted as a soldier and my sex didn't play a part. I was just one of the lads.

I awoke about two hours later to hear one of the others getting sick outside the trench. He was on his hands and knees, heaving up into the dirt. I think he had drunk way too much of the Jack Daniels.

The following day a few patrols were sent out. I was sent down to help clear a track and Andy was there. Andy and I began moving large tree trunks. I was beginning to really like him. There was an instant chemistry between us. He stood next to me, leaned in closely and whispered softly into my ear. I got goose bumps and couldn't focus on anything except him.

I followed him around the whole day like a lost puppy. I'm not sure if he found me attractive at that stage. I hadn't washed in a few days and I was just piling more and more camouflage cream onto my face. My hair was a mess of tangled curls interwoven with twigs. I smelt of dirt and sweat.

The day passed quickly and we began preparing for the exercise that night – something called a NATO T. I didn't know what it meant at the time but I went along with it and did exactly what I was told.

We mounted the trucks in preparation for the night ahead. We were dropped at the bottom of Camera Hill in the Wicklow Mountains. It was pitch black, but the scene was surreal. We were to fight right through the night to the top of the hill, with the Reserve Defence Forces playing the part of the enemy. The exercise was under the control of the directing staff (DS), instructors from the military college.

We moved up the hill in tactical formation and immediately came under fire from the enemy. A member of my section was informed that he had been killed by enemy fire. It was right at the start of the exercise so he was laughing, delighted that he didn't have to fight the whole way up the hill. I followed the instructions of my section commander to take cover and return fire. The sky was lit up by thunder flashes and smoke grenades going off all around me. The exercise pushed farther up the hill.

I was relatively fit and so I was managing well. When you're in the midst of an attack you get an adrenalin rush that keeps you moving. It was wet and misty in parts and the terrain was boggy and uneven. The hill was littered with big rocks, but I had invested in a pair of Mendel boots and wasn't falling on my bum half as much as before.

The weight of my ammunition-filled rocket pouches and my rifle was taking its toll on my body. At that stage half of my section had been "killed" and I was still going. Halfway up the hill, I fell to my knees, smacking them off a rock. The pain seared across my back. I couldn't get back up. I thought to myself, *If you don't get up now, then you're a failure*. My tiny frame wasn't built for such manoeuvres but my mind would have to overcome it. I had hit "the wall", and I just felt like I couldn't go on. My mind went back and forth – *Give up, keep going*. After what seemed an age, I rose to my feet and struggled on.

We finally reached the top of the hill six long hours later. When I eventually got there I was told to dig another trench. I was so sick of digging bloody trenches. All I wanted was a nice warm bath with bubbles, followed by my own bed. My section commander and I were the only people still alive at that stage in my section. He had to pretend he had received shrapnel wounds to his leg. He put on a great show, screaming at the top of his voice as I bandaged his leg with my field dressing. He was hilarious.

Just then, a DS approached me and said, "You're dead."

I lay there thinking, *He kills me now, six hours later, when it's all over? What's the point in killing me now?*

We set up a defensive position on top of the hill. The exercise finished and we all headed back down the hill. This took another hour and a half and I was shattered but also very excited about the fact that I had done it and hadn't given up. We headed back to the trucks and back to the dig-in site where we withdrew and prepared for the next phase in the exercise: FIBUA and DIBUA.

We were again headed to Fort Davis for this phase of the exercise and I was excited. I loved Fort Davis. We boarded a naval ship to ferry us over to the fort. On the ship Andy approached me again and we started chatting. We were getting on very well but he seemed quite shy. We probably clicked because I never shut up and he never talks much.

We disembarked onto black sea riders, which brought us to the fort. It was my first time on a sea rider and I felt strange but very excited as it traversed over the waves and the water sprayed across my face. The salty air filled my lungs and I could feel my skin getting a good exfoliation. Everyone was quiet in anticipation of the upcoming exercise.

We started fighting immediately, taking cover and quickly manoeuvring up the hill. Thunder flashes were flying in all directions and we moved under the cover of smoke grenades to advance on the enemy. First we had to clear the lower levels, which took hours. Each room had to be cleared. The fighting went on well into the night until blackness engulfed the entire fort.

I managed to get close to Andy and stuck by his side for a few hours. I wasn't supposed to be in his section but I managed to manoeuvre myself into it deliberately. Never underestimate a woman with a plan, especially in matters of the heart. He was trying so hard to impress me with his military prowess and I was behind him every step of the way. He gave me orders, which I followed without question.

At one point in the night Andy said to me, "Wait here, Val, while I clear this room." Then he disappeared. I heard a loud scream, followed by a loud smacking noise. I realised that the railings on top of the steps leading down into the room were missing. Andy lay sprawled on the ground below us. He had fallen a good two metres and smashed his knee off the ground. He was in agony.

I had just managed to get close to him and now he was being carted off in an ambulance. I was left with my platoon to finish the exercise. I couldn't believe it – Andy was gone and my heart sank. I didn't know when I'd see him again.

We lay deep in an underground tunnel and were told to wait for a while. We were exhausted, all whingeing and moaning, as soldiers often do. I fell asleep in a mucky puddle next to a big rusty boiler and awoke to the sound of gunfire, which was our signal to move.

As dawn approached we had cleared the lower level and moved to the top of the fort. The platoon cleared the top level and as the exercise drew to a close I found myself staring out at the breathtaking views of the sea. It was a beautiful scene and I felt both elated and exhausted.

I asked after Andy and was told that his mother had collected him. He was on crutches when he left.

We headed back to Collins Barracks. I had completed the exercise and I was proud of myself. My father was very happy that I had finished it and I knew I had made the right decision in applying to serve in the 4th Infantry Battalion.

The following Monday morning after parade, an NCO said to me, "You finished the exercise, Private Sheehan – there was a bet between the senior NCOs to see how long you would last. Nobody said you would finish it, but you did. Well done!" I just shrugged it off.

I was paraded again. "Private Sheehan, you did very well on the exercise. Would you like to work in the office now?" I gave the same answer as before and was dismissed again to join the lads on the lines.

A few weeks later I was told I was to rejoin my recruit platoon to serve on the border with Northern Ireland during the BSE outbreak. We were joined by another platoon that had joined the army three months after ours. There were more women in this platoon, which I was happy about.

When I arrived in Dundalk I shared a room with the five women from the other platoon and it was great fun. I got on well with all of them. I struck up a good friendship with one of them, Lisa, a softly spoken, well-mannered woman with a mischievous glint in her eye, a heart-shaped face and chestnut brown eyes. Some of them were "girly girls" like me and two were from the north-side of Cork, just like me. I knew instinctively that nobody would call me a Norrie.

We all went out to the local pubs and nightclubs a few times, including one night in Castleblaney with some other soldiers with whom I had trained. Unfortunately, my nights out with my comrades were having quite a bad effect on my waistline. One morning I tried to put on a pair of tight black trousers but the zip wouldn't even close. I lay on the floor, rolling around, trying in vain to stretch them, when the backside burst wide open. *That's it*, I thought; *I have to stop drinking pints with the men or I'm going to end up looking like a beached whale.*

In the afternoon I headed over to the gym and started working out. I met a very enthusiastic physical training instructor (PTI). He made out a programme for me and I stuck to it rigidly for the remainder of the trip.

I also came across a copy of a book called *Bravo Two Zero* by Andy McNab. He was a British soldier in the SAS. I found myself engrossed in the book and started to think seriously about my future. I set my mind to training and training hard. I didn't want to just pass anything any more. I wanted to be the first woman to pass the army Ranger Wing selection course. After reading that book and meeting that PTI, the army started to become my entire life.

I finished out the tour and returned to Collins Barracks in Cork. There I was told that I was being sent to Clonmel to complete my light infantry weapons course with the platoon that had come in after my one. I was thrilled that I was going to be with the women from that platoon, as I got on so well with them. Life seemed good all around.

9

Clonmel

Winter was fast approaching when I arrived in Clonmel Barracks to commence the weapons course but I felt comfortable in my new surroundings. Lisa and I shared a spacious room which was bright, airy and smelt of fresh paint. The other women were just down the hall.

Clonmel is home to Support Company of the 12th Infantry Battalion. The light infantry weapons course is designed to train soldiers in the use of the 60mm mortar, the general purpose machine gun on sustained fire (GPMG SF) and the 84mm anti-tank weapon. The instruction we received on each weapon was very professional and I found the atmosphere relaxed. Gone were the days of relentless screaming and roaring during recruit training. I had carried a lot of tension around with me over the course of the previous months but gradually I felt it slip away. I was no longer a raw recruit but a young soldier. Nevertheless I remained cautious under the watchful eyes of our instructors.

Our days were spent training on the weapons, learning how to employ them in a tactical environment. We became very proficient in the use of all three weapons. After a full day's training I would head out on the long stretches of desolate road that ran around the outskirts of Clonmel. My favourite running routes were among the steep winding hills. I lost myself in the green landscape, trees swaying gently along the path, wind blowing in my face.

I spent a lot of my time running alone, listening to my walkman. My running seemed to be improving slowly, but I often found that I couldn't keep going, my skin and lungs burning from the cold air. My calf muscles would often seize up. I'm no Sonia O'Sullivan and endurance running was far from my strong point. When I was younger I was a very good sprinter but never a long-distance runner. In the quiet stillness of those hills, I strove to push myself physically further with each passing day.

I tried to keep my mind focused on my long-term goal – to be the first woman to pass the army Ranger Wing selection course. At the time I knew of only one woman who had tried but failed to pass it. A few male members of my platoon had expressed an interest in doing the selection course. The pass rate is only ten per cent and the idea of women passing the course was and still is scoffed at. I saw this as a challenge and something to aim for. I didn't tell anyone because I didn't want to be ridiculed.

Andy's cousin Michael, who was in my platoon, had told me that Andy had started the selection course. I had got talking to Michael before our morning parades. I thought about Andy a lot when I was in Clonmel. I had almost become consumed with thoughts of him. I had never felt like that before about any man. I found myself asking Michael about him, at first subtly, then more blatantly. I didn't know at the time that he was reporting my growing interest back to Andy.

The weather was becoming so cold that most mornings the gravel square of the barracks was almost frozen over with ice and occasionally flecks of snow fell from the sky. Icicles hung from frosted panes of glass. My cold nose had a purple tinge each morning as the course sergeant paced up and down the ranks, his breath almost visible in the cold air as he gave out orders. My lips became permanently chapped, from which I still have a slightly visible scar.

Nonetheless the parades were relaxed and our dress code had also relaxed considerably. Lisa and I were becoming inseparable and we shared everything, from clothes and make-up to green woollen balaclavas and thick knee-length army socks, which proved very cosy during that long winter. We both found comfort in our friendship and where there was one of us, the other usually followed. Some evenings we would venture down the town, wandering around the bustling narrow laneways scattered with clusters of little shops. Christmas wasn't far away and the Spice Girls had released a new single. I bought their CD and often blasted it on in our dorm if we were getting ready for a night out.

One Thursday evening some of the women decided to go out clubbing. It was the night before the "day shoot" in

Kilworth, when we would have to make use of our weapons training, which we had now completed. I told Lisa that I didn't want to go because drinking alcohol would interfere with my training. She really wanted to go out with the others but they didn't want her to. She sat in their room as they discussed their plans for the night and also passed sweets around, but deliberately cut her. In that environment, where you spend most of your days and evenings with the same people, it can be quite hurtful to be left out of the main group. She gently left their company and came back to our room. Her tiny frame stood solemnly against the door, her eyes welling up, tears cascading down her cheeks. She was very vulnerable and very hurt. Her chestnut-coloured eyes looked empty and hollow. I told her not to worry.

Half an hour later the other women flew past our door, wearing wedged high heels and carefully applied make-up, handbags swinging in the air behind them, their faces all dazzling smiles. I got on quite well with them but I didn't like the way Lisa was being treated. I stood on the sidelines, impartial for a while, before finally deciding to help her.

"That's it, I have a plan," I said.

We waited patiently to ensure that they had left the barracks before creeping into their room, where we changed their alarm clock setting to 7.30 instead of 6.30.

It was pitch black and freezing cold as our platoon stood on parade at 7.30 the following morning – ready to travel to Kilworth for the day shoot. Stars were still clearly visible overhead in the blackened sky. Our platoon sergeant was pacing frantically up and down the length of the platoon, waiting for the other women to appear. Eventually they had to be woken on the orders of the platoon sergeant, but they didn't have time for breakfast, to make their lunches or to pack their combat gear properly.

They arrived on parade on that icy morning flustered, feeling the full wrath of our platoon sergeant. Spit flew from his mouth as he berated their tardiness. The women stood open-mouthed, not uttering a word, almost frozen to the spot, pale white faces and rose-tinged cheeks staring blankly at the platoon sergeant.

Lisa and I both knew it hadn't been a nice thing to do, but we giggled silently to ourselves.

During the course of the day shoot the 60mm mortar was constantly misfiring. There were murmurs of dissatisfaction between the ranks at the level of misfires as it was highly unusual and unsettling.

We spent the day moving between different weapons and dodging gusts of wind. My hands ached constantly from the frosty air nipping at them, but I had grown very accustomed to this. As darkness fell, the shoot came to an end uneventfully and we returned to the barracks.

We were nearing the end of the course. All that remained was the night shoot, which took place at a later date. The evening sky was greying over as the night shoot began. I once again found myself kneeling behind the machine gun in soggy muck, combat trousers soaked to the skin, knees embedded into the ground. I was placed with two other soldiers on the Mag SF (sustained fire) group and was preparing to fire the gun, which was mounted on a large black steel tripod. It was my favourite weapon and I enjoyed using it.

The shoot was progressing well. A mixture of live ball and tracer 7.62mm rounds whizzed by in the distance, peppering the skyline, interspersed with the tracer rounds whose red flash lit up the darkened sky. The cracking of gunfire flooded my ears. As a platoon we were spaced out in a straight line for the shoot. On more than one occasion the shoot was stopped, once again because of misfires on the 60mm mortar. It was a bitter night, with the cold air biting at my skin, leaving my nose dripping wet. When I was firing my body and mind reacted simultaneously and I found that I got a kick from firing the SF.

Farther down the gun line, there had been no fewer than eighteen misfires on the mortar. There was a lot of commotion surrounding the mortar group and everyone was becoming fed up. By any standards, eighteen misfires is an unusually high level of stoppages.

As I knelt on my knees, willing my frozen fingers to release their grip on the trigger, my mind drifted back to Andy. I hadn't so much as kissed him but I felt drawn to him, which was very new to me.

I was snapped back to reality when the young officer with my group leaned over and spoke to me. I couldn't understand the muffled sounds through my double hearing protection. I lifted my ear muffs to make out what he was trying to say: "Listen, can you hear that screaming?"

It was then I heard her piercing cries echo across the gun line. I was gripped by fear and felt a sudden wave of nausea roll over me. I still think back to that moment. There was no break from the screams. Within seconds everyone was pulled back fifty metres from the firing line.

There had been an accident. It was Lisa. When she had dropped her mortar round into the barrel of the mortar, there had been an explosion and the barrel had split like a banana. Some of the group received injuries. But Lisa's hands had been placed at the end of the barrel. She had lost her left hand in the accident.

One of the women who had trained with Lisa had done a medics course instead of the weapons course. She passed it with flying colours and this was her first duty as a medic. She did an amazing job in calming Lisa, who couldn't feel anything as her body went into shock. The medic cut her out of her combat equipment. Lisa kept asking if she was going to be in trouble over her combat gear. She was rushed to the hospital along with the other injured personnel.

I was in a daze about what had just happened to her. Lisa was so young and so beautiful, with her whole future ahead of her. Now she would have to change that future.

I returned to our room to pack up Lisa's belongings, filled with a sense of loneliness at her absence. Our once-bright and airy room seemed empty and gloomy without her. I missed her infectious laugh, which usually rippled around our room.

The following afternoon I was cleaning the rest of the mortars with Michael and we were looking intently at the barrels. It was obvious how old they were from their weather-beaten appearance. They were etched with grooves and dents from years of firing.

During the weekend I went to visit Lisa in the hospital in Cork. As I made my way up the elevator I felt that familiar wave of nausea roll over me again. I stepped into her room to see her lying helplessly with the white cast on her arm. Her sallow skin looked pale, almost eggshell-white. They had tried to save her hand but unfortunately could not. She looked so fragile, with a deep sadness in her eyes, yet she still had the sweetest smile on her face. We spoke and I tried to utter words that would console her, but I knew that nothing I could say could help her with what she had to face.

As the months passed, Lisa came to terms with her loss and carried on as best she could. But her irrepressible exuberance diminished and she found it hard to muster the strength to carry on. There were days when she looked broken, glistening tears tumbling down her sallow cheeks. Lisa had a gentle nature and a beautiful soul. She found it increasingly difficult to deal with the reality of her loss and eventually left the army in favour of motherhood.

I had my own coping mechanism. Even then I had the ability to compartmentalise my emotions. I should have talked about my feelings but I never did. I never discussed anything; instead I opted to bury my feelings and submerge myself deeper in my training. Maybe I should have cried but I refused to allow myself to cry, which I later found to be destructive. I was becoming cold.

I would pound the roads relentlessly while a flurry of emotions and thoughts raced through my mind. By the end of each run I would feel totally exhausted and detached. On reflection, I should have faced my own feelings but instead I found comfort and solace in my running.

10

Portlaoise Prison

On the last day of the course I was told that I was being sent to serve in Portlaoise Prison. I had only seen the soldiers guarding the prison from a distance. I was apprehensive at first but began to look forward to what would be another new experience for me.

Another woman was also being sent into the prison; together we would be the first female other ranks soldiers to do so. (Female officers were permitted to serve in the prison.) We arrived in Portlaoise Prison the following Monday morning and I was immediately sent to the prison commandant, who happened to be a woman. When I greeted her I was surprised at how glamorous she looked. Her silky blonde hair lay on her shoulders and she was wearing a rich red lipstick. Her polished accent was very welcoming and immediately I felt more relaxed.

She gave me a brief account of the prison and its inmates. It housed some of Ireland's most notorious men, including the "the Border Fox", Dessie O'Hare, the INLA gunman who was serving a forty-year sentence for the 1988 kidnapping and mutilation of Dublin dentist John O'Grady. Portlaoise Prison is one of Europe's most secure prisons. Our job as soldiers was to patrol the rooftops, perimeters and gates. When we were patrolling the rooftops we would have to monitor the activities of the inmates during their yard time. The IRA and INLA were housed on different floors of the high-security block. Each different faction had its own yard time. The common criminals were housed in a separate block.

I found our duties tedious and monotonous. We had to complete twelve-hour shifts followed by twelve hours of rest time. I divided my time off duty between catching up on precious sleep and training. I worked out in the prison's small gym and ran around the narrow black tarmac track that surrounded our compound for a few miles most days.

I became very run-down and very thin due to a combination of a poor diet, training and duties. My cheeks sank hollow into my drawn face and I began to feel my hips protruding visibly through my black cotton running pants. To make matters worse, the water that ran from our showers was filled with lime which caused an unsightly irritation to break out on my skin in the form of boils on my back and face.

I discovered that Andy was also stationed in the prison but unfortunately he was not on my shift. I would have to make do with catching fleeting glimpses of him running past my post when I was on duty. He had acquired a slight limp since the accident at Fort Davis. He had also just attempted to pass the selection course to join the elite army Ranger Wing unit. He didn't pass it on that occasion and was a bit disgruntled when I broached the subject with him.

"How did you get on during the selection course for the Ranger Wing?" I eagerly asked him, trying to be flirtatious.

He just stared at me coldly and said, "I'm here, aren't I?"

He put his head down and turned on his heels. I could feel my cheeks flushing with embarrassment.

I tried to engage him in conversation a couple more times in those weeks, but failed miserably.

Soon afterwards I learned that Andy was being relieved early from the prison. He was being posted to the Curragh where he would complete a non-commissioned officers' (NCOs') course just after Christmas. I was left feeling dejected and had almost given up when fate steered events in my favour.

When the trip to Portlaoise was drawing to a close the platoon had a much-anticipated night out in Cork city. We arranged to meet up in a pub called the Old Oak. Familiar faces propped up the long shiny brass and oak bar, which exuded a lively atmosphere of warmth.

My mind again lapsed back to Andy. I was hoping he would still come to the platoon's night out even though he was due to go to the Curragh after Christmas, as most of his friends were going out. I was hoping that I would bump into him, but I discovered that unfortunately he had gone to a different pub with a few of his friends. I decided to enjoy myself anyway. I had bought new clothes for the occasion – a black figure-hugging top with a lovely pair of tight black shiny pants, which I hoped I wouldn't burst out of. My hair was girlishly loose and I wore a shade of rust lipstick. It's strange to think back now, but in those early days I was still in touch with my femininity, to some degree at least. I felt very free and was really beginning to enjoy my life.

Later that evening we went to a nightclub called Mangan's. I stood patiently in the queue for the cloakroom when I noticed a man staring at me intently. I was a little startled and slightly unnerved by his persistent stare. Through the darkness I could vaguely make out his raven-coloured hair. He intrigued me. I tried to move gracefully towards him but stumbled unsteadily a few times on my black suede platform boots.

As he lifted his head up slowly, I suddenly realised that it was Andy, looking all dark and mysterious. My heart raced and my stomach flew into a knot, so much so that I couldn't utter a word. I felt a mixture of confusion and embarrassment. I tilted my head slightly, half-smiling, leaving us both feeling relaxed.

We spent the rest of the night talking. We spoke of our dreams, our aspirations and our goals in life. I was full of dreams in those days. I didn't want to live my life full of regrets, with broken dreams. I admired his ambition and his drive to succeed. He was just so sweet. We shared similar passions in life, which drew me closer to him.

I think back to that night sometimes. It was the first night we truly got to know each other. It took me by surprise. We started dating straight away. We never left each other's side. Over the coming weeks we became best friends and I truly believed that I had found the love of my life, my soul mate. I started to fall deeply in love with him.

11

Decision Time

After the monotony of the prison I decided to study part-time at the weekends as a fitness instructor. Over the following months I immersed myself in books and fitness, both of which were my passions. Andy encouraged me enthusiastically so I fell into the routine of studying and exercise easily. My company sergeant facilitated me with weekends off duty and before long I was happily coasting through military life.

Andy introduced me to his world, fresh from the country, and I whisked him into my group of friends. One evening he took me to the opera house for a performance, which I found very posh, but I forgot my glasses and so we travelled back to the barracks for them. The barracks was almost pitch black, with only single lights illuminating the darkened doorways to each block. I walked into the locker room and peered around tentatively. My equipment lay strewn across the thickly carpeted floor.

Decision Time

I silently gathered up my belongings before heading back to Andy's car. He was surprised but told me not to worry. He was touchingly tender towards me at a moment when I was feeling particularly rejected. Sometimes I felt very much on the outside and this incident just clarified my position. The picture became very clear to me; I was acutely aware that I had chosen a life among the men. The following morning I informed my company sergeant, simply because my gas mask had gone missing. It was a serialised item of equipment and its loss would have resulted in my being charged. He informed the company commander, but I never got my stuff back. I never again went into the recreation room.

I worked away on the lines each day with the men, alongside Amelia, who had joined B Company shortly after me. Every morning there was a cleaning detail. We had to scrub the toilets, mop the cold tiled floors and vigorously sweep outside the block. I would find myself kneeling on the grey stained carpet of the company office, scrubbing teabag smudges from the walls under the scrutiny of the clerks. It was official: I was at the end of the pecking order in terms of my rank. I didn't mind, as I had chosen not to go down the clerical path. I would have felt confined and stifled.

At least when I was finished scrubbing I could go for a run with the men. I worked away diligently on my fitness instructors' course and trained when I had the time. Most of my time was spent perfecting my aerobics techniques.

To relax and escape every second Sunday, Andy and I went hill-walking, inhaling crisp fresh spring air as we disappeared into the snow-capped Galtee mountains. The craggy rocks and the narrow winding paths offered an atmosphere of freedom. We would pack our rocket pouches, throw on our green waterproof gear and head high up into the hills. Andy was infinitely more experienced than I was in the mountains. His stride was that of a mountain goat and I struggled to maintain his pace. Occasionally he would stop dead in his tracks to quiz me on my map-reading skills. Once he looked at me in total disbelief when I picked out a reference point.

"There, that white thing over there – I'll use that as a reference point."

"Valerie, seriously, I know you're half-blind but that white thing over there is a sheep. You can't use a sheep as your reference point because it moves."

When we would reach the top we'd take cover behind a boulder to eat ham rolls and drink piping hot tea. Then we would sit wrapped in each other's arms. The cold mountain air was silent and still and I was in love. Those days evoke such warm memories for me. It was so simple, yet so wonderful.

Our company sergeant informed the company one chilly Monday morning that names were being taken for the forthcoming UNIFIL tour of duty to Lebanon. I seriously considered travelling as it would prove an escape from the daily grind of barracks life. I saw it as an opportunity to travel and experience the reality of soldiering in a war-torn country. I never really considered how it would affect my relationship with Andy. I was still at a stage where I didn't feel I needed his permission or approval and, as he had completed two trips already, I didn't think he would mind. I didn't need much persuasion to put my name forward.

Andy seemed startled when I told him of my decision, his green eyes narrowing and a deep furrow forming on his brow. I knew it meant leaving him behind but it was an opportunity that I felt I couldn't pass up. Although Andy seemed positive and supportive he remained quite subdued for the remainder of the journey home.

The following Monday morning after our early morning parade I headed for battalion headquarters and nervously walked up the dimly lit flights of stairs to the company office. The musty stale air always lingered on those stairs, taking me back to those times in my childhood when I went to the barracks with my father. I knocked softly on my company sergeant's door and he gestured for me to come in. I sat on the orange plastic chair and placed my sweaty palms on my knees.

My company sergeant instilled fear in me like no man ever had before him – which was his job. He was a fair man. I gulped down a deep breath before telling him that I wanted to serve in Lebanon. He snapped his head up and creased his brow. He looked at me closely for a while and then said he would do what he could to facilitate me. He questioned me about Andy. I told him I had no intention of letting my personal life interfere with my professional life, that I wanted to travel to further my own career. I suspect he found me difficult, a handful to manage. I don't think he fully understood why I had chosen to stay on the lines with the men.

He told me that, as a woman, I would not be permitted to do most of the regular duties carried out by Irish soldiers in Lebanon. I had but two choices open to me – either to serve as a waitress in the officers' mess or to work in the comcen (communications centre). I was told that, because Lebanon was a predominantly Muslim country, female UN peacekeeping soldiers could not operate on the checkpoints or in the outposts, and were not permitted to carry out mine sweeps or form part of the infantry platoons.

I wondered if all of this was true or just a convenient way for the hierarchy to justify placing us there as waitresses or signalwomen. The male soldiers, some of whom I had trained alongside, were permitted to carry out every duty.

Later I was told that I could not under any circumstance be placed on a checkpoint as Muslim men would not deal with women. However, there is another side to this argument. Muslim women were largely forbidden from dealing with male soldiers and, for that purpose alone, we could have carried out these duties. I was also told that I could not serve on any observation posts because there were no toilet facilities or accommodation for women on these posts.

My final exams on my fitness course were looming and I studied at every available opportunity. I remained highly focused on my goals as I wanted to prove myself and to better myself. I completed my exams with little drama and had to wait a couple of weeks for the results.

During this interlude, I continued hill-walking with Andy each weekend. As we returned to Cork after a day's climbing, I lay in his little green Peugeot, almost in a haze from exhaustion. Andy seemed unsettled and suddenly announced that he too wanted to travel to Lebanon. A long silence filled the car. I took a deep breath and paused before telling him that I was thrilled.

We drove home that day, my mind swirling back and forth about our relationship, but I resigned myself to the simple fact that I loved him and wanted to stay with him.

A few days later, Andy asked me if I would like to travel on holidays to Canada with him before the trip to Lebanon, as we would be on leave. I was apprehensive initially at the prospect of travelling for three weeks around Canada with him, but I agreed.

Later we found out that we had both been selected to travel to Lebanon. We were to be sent to serve with B Company in the village of Haddatha in southern Lebanon. Andy would be stationed in a rifle platoon while I would serve in the radio room, known as the comcen (communications centre). I had really wanted to serve as an infantry soldier but women did not have equal opportunities to men and I was very lucky to be even going. I was filled with apprehension; I wasn't a signalwoman and had received very little training in the area, but my father reassured me that I would receive full training prior to my departure.

I swiftly moved my mind to my holiday. We had chosen Canada because my sister Lynda had moved there a few years previously and had married her French Canadian boyfriend, who was by now serving in the Canadian navy. For three weeks Andy and I backpacked our way around British Columbia, hitchhiking, camping out in the vast open forests, white-water rafting in the great rapids of British Columbia, and growing closer than ever before. I sat in the boat that took us through the clear river waters and raised my hands high above my head to inhale a deep breath of warm air. Basking in the warm summer sunshine, I had never felt so free or so happy. I began to feel confident and secure again; I was truly carefree.

I was blissfully unaware that at the pinnacle of my happiness, life was about to drop me down to a new low with a jolt.

12

Trouble Ahead

It was a warm evening late in August 1998 when we returned to Ireland. A few days later, I found myself standing in the long hallway of my mother's house, soft summer rays creeping through the net-curtained window. I glanced over at the long polished mahogany hall table and noticed a white envelope with my name clearly marked on the front. I instinctively knew that it was the results from my fitness instructors' course. I nervously opened the envelope. I stood breathless when I realised that I had received an all-over distinction. I knew that I had worked extremely hard but never imagined I would do quite so well. I was thrilled.

That month was spent preparing for the impending tour of duty. I was extremely nervous about going overseas, especially being one of only two females going with B Company. Also, I had not had six months' training as a signalwoman, which left me unprepared for what lay ahead. We were based in Kilworth for the duration of our preparatory training. From there we often travelled to the Curragh and the Glen of Imaal for other aspects of our training. During the evenings in Kilworth I would review my recruit training signal notes in a desperate attempt to get to grips with my new job. Andy spent hours guiding me and testing me.

I was beginning to feel slightly unsettled by some of the comments passed by fellow soldiers about the fact that I was a woman. But I didn't react in those days. I was simply too embarrassed and therefore chose to walk away. There were times when I felt extremely uncomfortable and I truly didn't know how to cope with certain situations, as I had never encountered them before.

I think, in general, that my presence was viewed with suspicion and, in some quarters, contempt. I was exposed to the raw daily life of soldiering among men and all that it encompassed – the screaming, the relentless roaring and the sexual innuendo. Most days it flew over my head without much impact. Other days it reduced me to tears. I would hide behind the white door of the toilet cubicle with my head in my hands, sobbing uncontrollably, before composing myself to face the day again.

My smile faded with each day. In the end I found myself concealing my femininity in order to fit in. I wore less and less make-up and my clothes became duller and more conservative. I strove to be accepted so much that I began to adopt male mannerisms. Every second word that came out of my mouth was almost explicit. Yet I still could not escape the fact that I was a woman in a man's world.

A series of incidents involving a small number of soldiers happened over the course of the following weeks. One particular corporal pointed out to me that he did not approve of my relationship with Andy, nor did he approve of Andy himself. I felt uncomfortable with these comments but tried my best to ignore them.

On a chilly wintry afternoon I stood outside the guardroom having been tasked with bringing the .5mm machine gun into the stores. It is a large black weapon which is extremely heavy. I was lifting it with another male soldier when the same corporal shouted out gruffly, "Look at you, you're too weak to be carrying that gun. All her fitness training and she's still too weak to carry a machine gun." Andy's friend was standing nearby, which left me feeling embarrassed. I didn't react; instead I left to find my friend Melissa.

Later that same day in Kilworth camp the corporal walked over to me, placed his hands on my shoulders and rubbed them. I could feel my face flush red instantly and I forcibly shrugged him off without saying a word. Other soldiers just stood by in silence.

These and other incidents made me feel uneasy about our forthcoming trip to Lebanon.

The following Tuesday the company travelled in convoy to the Curragh, where we would observe checkpoint exercises and complete our battle inoculation training, which formed part of the mandatory preparation for overseas service. I had decided to brush aside the incidents of the previous week and concentrate on my training.

On a grey blustery Tuesday afternoon, we were standing on a long narrow road which ran around the outskirts of the Curragh Camp, not far from the United Nations training school. Tall lush green trees lined the road, branches draped across the black tarmac, leaves swaying under the influence of strong winds. Some distance away a battle exercise was taking place. I stood observing the exercise with the rest of the company.

Suddenly, the corporal grabbed my arm in front of numerous other personnel. Squeezing my arm tightly, he muttered in a sarcastic tone, "Did you get a fright there? You jumped," before laughing out loud. I looked at him coldly, gesturing for him to release his tight grip.

Afterwards, I stood surrounded by my company but keeping to myself, autumn leaves flooding the ground. We had been waiting for the army bus to take us back to Kilworth camp. The corporal started singing "The Things You Do For Love" whilst fixing his stare on me. He was leaning back, one hand in his pocket, the other hand pulling on a cigarette. He then gestured for me to walk towards him before sitting down on a low red-bricked wall, requesting that I do the same. He told me that Andy was to be kept out of my room or "I will give you some bollocking". At that stage Andy had never stayed in my room, nor I in his.

On the trip back to Kilworth, I was careful to sit a few seats ahead of the corporal and some of the others to avoid their scrutiny. Andy tried to alleviate my concern but my mind was whirling. I gazed out bleary-eyed into the distance as droplets of rain streamed down the window. I could hear laughing and comments aimed at me being shouted in the background – there was mention of the pill, tampons, period pain tablets.

One soldier said to another: "Hey, I forgot to tell you that you're fucked when we get to the Leb, because you'll get caught to do all the jobs."

"Why's that?"

"Ah, you know yourself – the girls won't be able to do anything. They can't do manual labour, for God's sake; they can't even do press-ups on their toes."

The other soldier sniggered.

A knot of anxiety formed in the pit of my stomach and I sank further into the seat, fearing that this was only the beginning. Andy gently put his hand over mine, squeezing it tightly, reassuring me that things would be okay. The bus was full to capacity with male soldiers and only one other woman. Teardrops brimmed on my eyelids but I tried to hold them at bay in an effort not to display any form of weakness. Still a tear trickled down my cheek but I managed to remain composed.

As a woman I was made to feel that I was privileged even to be there. It certainly was not the general view that I had the same right as my male colleagues to be there.

I began to lean on Andy at this time for emotional support. My father was also a source of constant wisdom and understanding. I wanted to make him proud of me. He seemed to understand me and knew that I simply wanted to be a soldier.

The following Monday morning I found myself sitting outside the target shed in Kilworth. It was a small grey concrete building with large brown wooden doors surrounded by green country fields, endless ditches and wide open spaces. I had a radio set in my hand and was practising with the other woman, Melissa. She was a little taller than myself, with elfin-like features, extremely pretty, her blonde hair always tossed up into an unkempt ponytail. The wind was blowing across our faces but we laughed as we endeavoured to learn our new job. We were quite capable of managing the radio set. However, the same corporal who had been giving me grief before approached us and made remarks about my "squeaky" voice, telling me I couldn't do my job. I chose to ignore him.

That evening I put on my black trackster bottoms and old battered Nike runners before heading out on the narrow winding roads of Kilworth with Andy. The smell of clean fresh country air filled my lungs. It was my escape on that cold night when I was feeling particularly down. Andy pushed me physically whilst nurturing me emotionally. We talked until the quickening pace would not allow us to hold a conversation any longer. A multitude of thoughts raced through my mind – recruit training, my weapons course and Lebanon all tangled up. The wind whipped at my legs but I refused to stop until my body stopped, until I was barely able to move. I felt that running breathed life back into my soul. It released my emotions in an environment where emotion was frowned upon.

As I entered the camp I passed the canteen. Most of the soldiers were inside drinking from crates of beer, singing raucously. In those days a heavy drink culture existed in the Irish defence forces. The majority of evenings were spent drinking late into the night. That was a different era, when the older soldiers were known as "old sweats". We, the younger soldiers, were known as "yellow packs". The army was changing gradually but for a while both young and old crossed paths. We were seen as inferior because we had to complete various courses, travel overseas regularly and pass our medical and fitness tests in order to renew our contracts. The older soldiers did not have to adhere to such stringent guidelines. This created tension between the younger and more seasoned soldiers.

That weekend we returned home and I seriously contemplated pulling out of the trip. I didn't want my first trip overseas to be a bad experience. My instincts were telling me that it was going to be extremely difficult. On Saturday evening, I lay in bed, my heart beating fast, rain washing down my window. I peered up at the darkened sky where stars twinkled brightly, wondering what to do. The previous two years began to feel like a fuzzy dream. I had gone from being a carefree schoolgirl to a woman, a soldier travelling to a war-torn country in the company of hundreds of men, seasoned soldiers. In the end I decided that I had to go. While there were other women accompanying us on the trip, the majority were being sent to Battalion Headquarters at Camp Shamrock, to serve as waitresses.

I found it difficult to say goodbye to my family and friends. At that stage my relationships with my civilian friends had become distant. Our lives were worlds apart.

They talked endlessly about clothes, make-up, shopping and holidays. I, on the other hand, was consumed with thoughts of rifles, machine guns, signal equipment and overseas service. My femininity seemed to be slipping away, and in turn my lifelong friendships began to slip away.

I had one loyal friend in the army whom I truly valued, Amelia. She had been at my side from the very beginning and I felt a kinship with her. To my delight she too was chosen to travel, but she was being posted to Camp Shamrock to serve as a waitress. She was a combat soldier from the 4th Infantry Battalion and also a member of the Irish athletics cross-country team, but was being given the job of waitress. She wasn't outwardly perturbed by her role as she was a quiet, gentle girl. I knew I would be unable to see her much as Camp Shamrock was a few miles from my camp, but her presence still comforted me.

The morning we were due to leave for Lebanon I woke up early, unaware that my life would never be the same. I tried to remain positive but deep within I knew obstacles lay ahead. The smile on Andy's face temporarily relieved my anxiety. I wanted him to hold me, to reassure me, which he did. Suddenly I didn't feel so alone. Looking back I can now see that moment as a pivotal turning point in our relationship. I almost became co-dependent on him. I felt that I needed him to protect me. I realise now that I should have broken free and stood on my own.

That night I waited in line to board the plane that would take us to Lebanon. I was nervous but also excited. I banished all negative thoughts from my mind. I knew that this was a good opportunity to travel, to experience a new culture and to further my career. My natural instincts told me different, but I chose to ignore them and travel anyway.

I had my inoculations, was wearing my new overseas green uniform, golden suede army issue boots and, most importantly, my blue United Nations beret. I felt ready as I made my way up the steel steps to board the plane that would take us to Beirut. On the final step I briefly turned around to take one last look at the place I was leaving behind, Ireland.

13

Highs and Lows in Lebanon

Our aircraft touched down in Beirut late into the night. As I emerged from the plane I felt a light wave of heat brush over my body. Although it was October it was considerably warmer than in Ireland. Lebanese soldiers guarded the perimeter, rifles slung across their broad chests, hands tucked into their deep pockets as they slowly monitored our arrival. Along the perimeter sat oil drums with flames crackling inside, bright orange sparks landing on the warm tarmac below.

I formed part of the orderly queue behind Andy to be issued with our United Nations identification cards. Diesel fumes filled the air, a smell that would linger in my senses over the coming months.

"Are you okay?" asked Andy.

"Yes, I'm fine," I replied.

"I'll be here for you, so don't be worried," he told me softly.

I stared a little bemused at the back of the white UN trucks waiting for us nearby, where teddy bears dressed in red Santa suits dangled. The soldiers preparing to leave Lebanon all wore red Santa hats. They flickered past us, merrily singing Christmas songs, even though it was just October. This burst of Christmas cheer was aimed directly at the incoming rotation of troops, as we would be away from home that Christmas. Their jovial mood quietly eased my anxiety and a smile stretched across my face.

I had always wanted to serve in Lebanon, and here I was. My mind drifted back momentarily to my childhood when I was only six years old and my father was serving here. I was overwhelmed to think that I had followed in his footsteps, and in the footsteps of thousands of Irish troops before me.

We mounted the white trucks and drove off amid a cloud of rising dust from the track below. The journey was marked by a sea of potholes and badly lit, uneven roads. In the sea of cars, Lebanese civilians blasted loudly on their horns. I soon began to realise that the Lebanese were an animated people, preferring to use hand gestures than silent diplomacy. We were on our way to Haddatha, high in the hills of southern Lebanon.

At one point in our journey the stillness of the night was interrupted by the cracking of continuous gunfire and the whistling of artillery rounds, followed by the explosive deafening sound of their impact in the distance. The diesel truck came to an abrupt halt. Andy protectively put his arm out to prevent me from hurtling forward. I was glad of the darkness at that moment so I could hide my startled expression. The convoy had been grounded until the latest shelling subsided. I was used to the sound of gunfire in a controlled environment but not on active service in a war-torn foreign land. Although I had heard the sound of gunfire countless times before, here it felt very different. Finally, though, it eased off and we were on the move again.

As we neared our destination, the trucks climbed up the crests of hills before tilting forwards in anticipation of the steep downward descent, sweeping through small wadis along miles of narrow dusty roads. Sparse trees starved of nourishment whipped the trucks as we passed. Suddenly, large whitewashed rectangular boulder slabs loomed in the headlights, painted boldly with the numbers "638" in black. We had reached our destination. As we dismounted, I felt Andy's shoulder brush past mine and he flashed me a smile which relieved my nervousness.

I wiped the sticky sweat from my forehead and peered around the camp in an attempt to find my bearings. Under the gleam of the moon I could vaguely make out my new surroundings. My ears absorbed the dull throb of the generators in the background. A young soldier paced back and forth on a rooftop behind a white concrete balcony. As I watched him pacing, rifle slung at his side, I reflected on how each and every Irish soldier who served in Lebanon puts their lives at risk daily. The personnel from our camp were drawn from the battalions of Cork, Limerick and the Curragh, each volunteering to serve in this hostile land. The outgoing soldiers were all tanned, beaming broadly, in stark contrast to our pasty pale skin and nervous faces.

A young female soldier, long blonde hair scraped into a tight ponytail and a mischievous glint in her eye, whisked me and Melissa to our accommodation. She was nearing the end of her six-month stint in the comcen. She looked about the same age as me and appeared full of confidence, eager to impress us. She told us to report to the comcen at 8.30 the following morning after breakfast, before leaving us to settle in.

I pushed open the large blue metal door to find a characterless room but thought to myself that we could make it cosy. We each had a metal bed complete with multi-coloured duvet and two soft white pillows. At the foot of my bed stood a grey metal wardrobe next to which sat a small white fridge. I was pleasantly surprised to see a modern TV and video recorder resting on top of the fridge. The walls of our room were painted antique white with a marble-effect speckled floor. A green curtain lined the sliding glass window, which was covered with a wire mesh to protect us from mosquitoes.

We settled into our room, stuffing our green army-issue bags under our beds. Before long I lay my cheek against my soft white pillow and fell into a dreamy sleep.

Sometime before dawn had fully broken I stirred in my bed, hearing the muezzin call to prayer from the mosque near our camp. The rhythmic music echoed throughout the valley. This music was familiar to my subconscious mind, because I had heard it from the many mosques scattered all over northern Cyprus when I visited there as a teenager, so I soon drifted back to sleep.

Some time later another familiar sound forced me awake. My ears were flooded with the continuous racket of gunfire interlaced with tracer rounds and heavy artillery bombarding the hills and wadis surrounding our small UN camp. I jumped up straight in bed, my back against the wall, tightly gripping my duvet close to my chin. Melissa had a similar reaction as everything around us shook. Her petite body lay, barely able to move, as our door rattled and so did we. Nothing quite prepares you for streams of gunfire waking you from the safety of your sleep.

On that first night we didn't go to the bunker because the shelling was deemed too far away to raise the camp siren that would implement "groundhog", when all troops would immediately have to make their way to the safety of their bunker. Shortly afterwards I fell asleep again, finally waking at 7.30 a.m. I dressed quickly and came out of our room. The camp looked very different under the splashing rays of the bright Lebanese sun in a clear blue sky. A UN flag flew in the gentle breeze.

I immediately set about finding Andy, only to be told that he had just left for Hill 880, an Irish compound overlooking our camp perched on a rocky hill about two miles away. I felt my heart sink. I didn't know when I would see him again. This was to be the beginning of our long separations while on our tour of duty in Lebanon.

Personnel stationed in our camp, B Company headquarters, usually spent two months on an observation post, referred to as a compound, before being rotated to another post for a further period of two months. Finally they would spend two months in camp. While in camp the infantry soldiers carried out daily mine sweeps, foot patrols, camp guard duties, checkpoint duties and shotgun escorts. The Irish compounds were located around the rugged mountainous terrain of southern Lebanon, often only a few hundred metres from SLA (South Lebanese Army) compounds. Their duties there were to report any movements or shooting in their area, relaying it to the communications centre (comcen) in B Company headquarters. Movement reported was usually the SLA or Israeli Army travelling between compounds by tank or carrying out foot patrols and mine sweeps.

I headed towards the dining hall, which was situated below the officers' mess, adjacent to the comcen. It was the same compact concrete building I had seen the night before, the roof of which was patrolled continuously by Irish soldiers. I made my way down the cold steep steps into a narrow corridor. Outside I noticed the thick whitewashed walls and the gabions – a wire mesh cage filled with jagged uneven rocks, to protect the building from mortar rounds and the heavy bombardment of artillery fire.

I walked into the brightly lit spacious dining hall and spotted a few faces that I recognised, quietly talking amongst themselves. Shortly afterwards, the corporal who had been bothering me before swaggered into my line of vision. I had mulled over our situation in my mind for some time. I thought that we might be able to solve our problems respectfully. He told me that the dining hall also acted as the camp bunker/ bomb shelter whenever the camp went into groundhog. However, during groundhog

I would have to report immediately to the comcen cell.

After breakfast I went to the comcen where Melissa, who rarely ate breakfast, stood waiting patiently. The comcen was tiny, barely stretching sixteen by eight feet. A single crude light fixture was suspended overhead. To the front was a large dusty window pane which served no purpose, since a concrete slab was erected right behind it. A selection of military report books sat neatly on a long dark wooden table, alongside a single microphone which was used for announcements. The rest of the room contained different sets of radio and signal equipment. The 77 radio set was our main radio, used to contact Camp Shamrock, the central camp in IrishBatt, and the surrounding outposts. In the corner sat a musty old brown tweed chair. We were given a quick run-down of our responsibilities before being shown the way to the generators, which sat in a large door-less corrugated steel shed on the edge of the long road running through our camp. The generators also fell into our role of responsibility. I stood on the flinty grey gravel in the cool shade of the shed, feeling slightly confused. I had never seen a generator before and when I asked for further instruction I was refused. Without learning the correct procedure for operating the generators, I could have ended up shutting down the electricity for the entire camp. In the end I had to ask another soldier in camp for help.

I busied myself for the remainder of the day, becoming familiar with my role in the comcen and the camp. We were issued our rifles along with other military ordinance and I briefly spoke to my company sergeant, who displayed a quiet authority. He told me that I could go running every day at 3.00 provided the camp wasn't in groundhog. He showed me the way to the makeshift gym.

Later I wandered around the camp to familiarise myself with the area. Our camp was surrounded by a circular barbed-wire fence. All around, the once-barren dry red earth was replenishing itself after a summer where the soil crumbled under the blistering summer sun. Dense green fir trees and bushes ran perpendicular to the uneven damaged road.

As I wandered around the camp I noticed a cluster of shops just outside the gates. Most locals warmly welcomed the Irish soldiers because of their long proud history of peacekeeping in the region. Over the years the local economy had come to rely heavily on the presence of Irish troops.

After lunch I ventured into one of the mingy shops to escape the midday heat. Inside was a pleasant Lebanese woman with sallow skin, her hair well hidden behind her coffee-coloured *hijab*. Her deep-set brown eyes were shadowed, almost sunken, in her long, drawn face. Her name was Raniya. Her little shop was at the heart of our trip to Lebanon, as she sold a vast selection of CDs, videos, jewellery and electrical equipment.

She shuffled behind the counter and pulled out some old catalogues displaying the most exquisitely designed gold, white and diamond jewellery, including engagement rings.

"Why you no married?" she asked softly, a cheeky grin etched on her face.

"I'm too young to get married."

"I am twenty-six, am married with four kids."

"I'm only twenty and have no intentions of getting married," I replied, giggling.

Marriage was never something I had thought much about. I had never imagined myself wearing a fancy wedding dress. But as we chatted I found myself thinking about marriage and all that it encompassed. I forced the topic from my mind.

Raniya was amused at my frizzy hair; to my disappointment, the only toiletries she sold were shampoo and conditioner. She told me that if I wanted my washing done she would happily oblige for the sum of six US dollars per large bag. She allowed me a brief glimpse into her life, ushering me towards her small home, which lay hidden behind tall freshly plastered walls. I looked around the garden at the intricately woven carpets scattered outside the white wooden doors. Hanging plants were draped around the entrance, evoking an exotic feeling of her little world. This was somewhat spoiled by the military uniforms drying under the Lebanese sun. Raniya's young daughter was sitting cross-legged in a slice of shade on a carpet, eating pilau rice with her hand. A scent of jasmine filled the air from an incense stick burning in a small carved wooden box perched on a narrow window ledge. Scenes from my own life flashed before me, when I had been a guest in my friends' homes in Cyprus.

I went to bed early that night feeling jet-lagged and overwhelmed. Before my head hit the pillow, a blaze of gunfire ripped through the air. It was the Hezbollah attacking the SLA compound only a few hundred metres from Hill 880, Andy's post. The alarm was sounded, echoing loudly throughout our camp. Melissa and I quickly clambered for our green 5.56mm Steyr assault rifles, blue UN helmets and heavy flak jackets, immediately making our way towards the comcen. As I ran breathlessly across the road I glanced up at the low stony hills, feeling agitated.

In the comcen, the surrounding B Company observation posts reported any rounds, whether artillery, mortar or machine gun fire, and an approximate estimation of the amount that landed around their area of observation. Immediately afterwards each report was radioed through to the communications centre in Irish Battalion headquarters, Camp Shamrock. I stood observing, occasionally taking over, learning quickly how to operate the comcen effectively and efficiently in this tense atmosphere.

Outside, the Hezbollah guerrilla fighters carried out their relentless attacks on the SLA compounds high in the hills. The SLA and Israeli army immediately retaliated, bombarding the area with 120mm mortar rounds and peppering the skyline with .5mm heavy machine gun fire. The deafening thud of 155mm artillery rounds could also be heard throughout the surrounding wadis and hills.

Inside the comcen, reports were coming thick and fast. Each Irish observation post also reported if they had a firing close, meaning a mortar or artillery round landing near their compound. Movement of any description, whether by tank or foot, was also radioed into the comcen. This information was then quickly reported to Irish Battalion Headquarters.

Groundhog would usually stay in place for one hour after the attacks had finished. This level of shelling would continue most days for the remainder of our trip, just before dawn or just after dusk. After a while I grew used to the daily bombardments of the hills, even becoming immune to the roaring sounds.

The local Lebanese had spent a large part of their lives in this battleground. I often saw the women return to the fields to work shortly after a morning of heavy shelling.

The Hezbollah movement operated as a *de facto* government in southern Lebanon, one of its objectives being to combat Israeli occupation. They operated a fully dedicated resistance. The Hezbollah had the full support of the local people for its guerrilla warfare. Throughout the years Hezbollah helped to rebuild the region, giving its people access to education, medical care, agriculture and a basic welfare system. While much of the Arab world regards Hezbollah as a resistance movement, it is seen as a terrorist organisation in several western countries, including the US.

I quickly settled into a daily routine. One afternoon I glanced up to see Andy. Our eyes met as I watched him run towards me. I was relieved to see his handsome face smiling back at me.

"Do you want to go for a run?" he asked.

"Yes, of course I do," I eagerly replied.

Most days if there was a lull in shelling a few soldiers from the surrounding observation posts were brought into camp so that they could go running or use the gym in camp. On these days I would be greeted by Andy's smiling face. We would run beside each other on the designated route. The pitted black tarmac road twisted along the hills, passing small brightly coloured houses where groups of Lebanese men sat smoking and drinking thick black coffee from small white cups. Occasionally they would greet us with the Arabic word "Marhaba", meaning hello. Lining the road were colourful posters of Hezbollah's martyrs and large placards erected on wooden slats showing Hezbollah's Shia leader, Hassan Nasrallah, who mobilised and motivated the rank and file of Hezbollah on the battlefield.

I always wore thick black trackster bottoms and a modest T-shirt, as I had been told that under no circumstances was I allowed to wear shorts. I grew accustomed to the climate, almost gasping at the thin air, sucking it deep into my lungs as I panted heavily, my legs running mile upon mile. We regularly covered up to ten kilometres on the Tibnin run but there was always an escort present in the form of an armoured personnel carrier for our protection. I really enjoyed that time of day. I thought about my ambitions and knew that if I gave up without trying my best, it would mean spending the rest of my life in the knowledge of my failure.

Andy tried to push me physically further on our runs but, overwhelmed by our long separations while on our tour of duty, I found myself stopping, doubled over with laughter, simply longing to hug him.

"You are not taking your training seriously."

"I am! I just missed you," I replied jokingly.

He leaned across and wiped my sweaty forehead before kissing me softly. "Come on, you have to push yourself," he whispered.

I glanced above at the grey clouds and felt a droplet bounce off my cheek, shortly followed by a bout of torrential rain. The rain danced across my face, and I felt alive. For a fleeting moment happiness filled my heart. I ran especially hard that day, all the while knowing that winter was setting in high in the hills of Haddatha. We arrived back in camp utterly exhausted and shivering, clothes drenched to the skin. However, being cold and wet is something every soldier soon gets used to. Andy pulled me in closely, squeezing me tightly before saying goodbye. I stood quietly, watching his silhouette disappear into the distance.

In those days a strong drink culture prevailed overseas. Each night crates of cheap beer were sold in the camp canteen, which inevitably led to wild drinking sessions, during which a bodhran was usually whipped out and a trad session would ensue. I was told to mix more and so every now and then I would find myself drinking happily with the lads from our camp in the canteen, which was a long rectangular Portakabin. To the right of the bar a soldier's poem had been hand-painted in yellow handwriting on an emerald green wall. Pine wooden seats rested against the walls and low wooden tables were spread across the linoleum floor.

One night as I sat next to a friend of mine, he asked, half-jokingly, "Can I have a shag?"

"What? I'm not shagging you!"

"Ah go on, no one will know. I'm starved of female affection," he said, laughing.

"I'm not shagging you, so just forget it."

"Out the back there's an empty Portakabin – we could do it in there."

"Will you fuck off! I'm not shagging you!"

"Ah, it was worth a try. No hard feelings."

We both doubled over laughing. I knew instinctively that he was serious but also that his intentions were not malevolent. To be honest, I respected his direct approach. He was single but it was then that I fully realised how hard it must be for a man to be away from his wife or girlfriend for extended periods of time. In the macho environment of overseas service, there is no escape to the confines of a woman's sensitivity.

Later that evening I bumped into another soldier, whom I shall call Colin (who has died since). He was one of those who had passed insulting comments about me previously. He stood facing me, eyes flashing.

"You are a whore and a slut. I know you are with other men," he shouted.

"How dare you call me a whore?"

"You are a whore! I worked with a whore overseas before and now I have to work with a whore again."

This tirade of comments left me feeling both shocked and hurt. In the beginning I felt my relationship with Colin was at least respectful, but that no longer seemed to be the case.

Colin did not get along with Andy. On a previous trip there had been a nasty altercation between one of his friends and Andy. I felt that this incident greatly contributed to the growing tension I felt from some of the soldiers. Andy by now had the protection of his rank as a corporal, but I was left in camp to feel some of the wrath from this incident, as I was his girlfriend. Later I received an apology from Colin, which I accepted, hoping that things would improve.

Late at night, once the shelling had subsided, I usually passed the long hours in the comcen alone, watching a movie or reading. On one particular night I leaned over, pressed the "play" button on the video recorder and suddenly caught a glimpse of a pornographic movie which had been deliberately left for me to see. Startled, I scrambled for the "stop" button.

As time passed I became quite accustomed to pornography overseas and even began to see it as an integral part of the working environment. On reflection I realise that my perception of "normal" was somewhat obscured by the unusual working environment in which I found myself.

There were days when I found life in Lebanon quite tough. I was frequently being relieved late from duty, sometimes by up to an hour, by which time breakfast would be over. I broached this subject with a superior but the issue was not resolved. That same afternoon we had a company commander's inspection, whereby he inspected the company's best uniforms on parade. Afterwards I was told I had a mere six minutes to change into work fatigues. I dashed towards my room and dressed quietly, mindful that Melissa was sleeping after completing her night shift. I suddenly heard an announcement over the loudspeaker: "Will Private Sheehan report to the comcen sometime today." I quickly raced back, only to be told that I was not allowed to go running anymore.

At times I wished desperately to be a man, so I would not be singled out constantly for being a woman. My only release was my running but even this was now apparently to be taken from me. Thankfully my company sergeant later told me that no such restrictions or limitations could be put on me. I was much relieved, as every other soldier in camp was permitted to go running.

I tried to tell myself that the only thing that mattered was getting through the trip. I knew that if it was happening at home in Ireland, such behaviour would not be tolerated. Maybe common sense evaded some overseas.

The fact that I had spoken to my company sergeant was not appreciated and I was made very aware of this. It was later suggested to me that I could be sent home or to work in the officers' mess as a waitress or to work in the office, and that I could easily be replaced with a man.

I was made to complete an extra shift of work on top of my own, the fourth one in as many weeks. The previous week I had requested to be covered while I took part in a basketball tournament with some of the male soldiers from B Company. The reaction had been predictable: "What the hell do you want to play basketball for? Basketball is a fella's game."

However, I was eventually allowed take part in the basketball tournament. This was a welcome break from camp.

I was uplifted each day I received a letter from Andy. The envelopes were always the same, white with a blue and red rim, inside which was a cream page penned with blue ink. In his scribbled handwriting he poured out his feelings for me, leaving me warm with love.

I often sat with Raniya in her little shop. Her husband, a short wiry man with weathered olive skin, would flit in and out. She would smile at him, only to be brushed off with a grunt. I felt sorry for her. In his presence she became quite submissive, ensuring that not a strand of hair was visible from behind her coffee-coloured *hijab*. I had heard a story from some of the seasoned soldiers in our camp about her. Apparently, Raniya's husband had once found her talking to a male Irish soldier. She wasn't wearing her *hijab*. He had dragged her from the shop by her hair, beating her violently up and down the village. She was seven months pregnant at the time.

She worked all day, every day in the shop, washing clothes for soldiers and taking care of her young family. I had read many books on women in Islam. On occasion I had seen for myself what life was like living under the laws of Islam, under the veil. I thought about how lucky I was to have been born in Ireland.

Occasionally the soldiers from the outposts were driven into camp if there was a lull in shelling. On those evenings, Andy would sneak into my room. We would spend a few hours watching movies, including my favourites, *Titanic* and *City of Angels*, which fuelled my desire to spend a lifetime with him. From the moment I had clapped eyes on Andy, I knew he was the one for me. There were moments when I yearned for a life of happiness, even children. I longed to escape from the confines of military life. I was beginning to feel extremely walled in.

We often talked about our future together. We started to discuss marriage a lot. When I arrived in Lebanon I never expected to get engaged. Eventually he asked me to pick out a ring. I was overjoyed at the prospect of becoming his wife. We created our own world, away from the canteen and the glare of prying eyes. When he returned to the hills I found myself becoming miserable.

I remembered one ring that glittered magically, shining out from the glossy pages of Raniya's catalogues. The rings in Lebanon were the most exquisitely handcrafted rings I had ever seen. They displayed a typical opulent Arabic style, which I loved. Raniya's rings were very expensive by Lebanese standards, so I carved out a plan of action. One cool night when Raniya wasn't looking, I took the magazine to Mohammed, the proprietor of the other shop. He had known my father when he had been stationed in B Company as the company sergeant. Together we drew out a copy of the exact ring. He was asking only half the price that Raniya was asking. I made a few changes to the arrangement of the diamonds and thick yellow gold band before racing back to Raniya's with the magazine. My ring was ordered from Beirut.

I was overwhelmingly in love, but this was often overshadowed by my life in camp. I found my working atmosphere overbearing at times. I found some of the things being said about me very distressing but I tried my best to ignore them. I was acutely aware that if I did not get a good report from overseas, this would damage my future promotional prospects and any application to serve overseas again. A bad overseas report can often destroy a career.

Meanwhile, my eating disorder reared its head again. I began to write down everything I ate and exactly how much I trained. In the evenings I would spend hours in the gym, trying to wipe out my frustration by lifting weights and running miles upon miles. I became consumed by both food and exercise. Soon I began to feel very tired.

I realise now that I had chosen to shift my unhappiness at my working conditions to the back of my mind. I could not control my environment, but I could control what I ate. If I ate a portion too much at dinner I would go to the bathroom and purge. Soon enough it didn't matter what I ate because I knew I would purge. For a fleeting moment it dulled my emotions. Afterwards I would sit on the cold floor in the small bathroom, eyes closed, feeling sad and empty. I would convince myself that this was the last time.

I had so far managed to keep my eating disorder hidden from Andy but inevitably he would find out. It was my secret coping mechanism, where I shifted my attention to my body. Bulimia is relatively easy to hide. A person will often appear to have a normal body weight, but their immune system is greatly affected by their lack of daily vitamins and nourishment. The only visible sign is the appearance of swollen cheeks and fingers, caused by water retention, the body's response to the constant purging. I was always careful to eat a banana afterwards, conscious of the damage being caused to my heart by the constant purging. Bananas contained magnesium, which I knew was good for my heart.

Deep inside I was aware that the vicious cycle was beginning all over again. I willed my mind to overcome it. Some days I succeeded, but not every day.

14

Christmas in Lebanon

Christmas was approaching and I began to miss my family at home. Melissa and I decorated our room with streams of red and blue tinsel. We hung large red Christmas stockings along the walls with strings of Christmas lights that twinkled brightly in the dark. We decided to immerse ourselves fully in the Christmas spirit even though we were in Lebanon.

Andy was having difficulty getting into camp due to the level of shelling that was taking place. I decided to relax my training and enjoy myself. I had a friendly relationship with most soldiers in camp, especially a few of the cooks. One in particular took me under his wing, always keeping a watchful eye out for my welfare, which was of some comfort to me.

Melissa and I worked on opposite shifts so I didn't get to hang out with her much. She hailed from the barracks in Limerick and her group of friends were young Limerick lads. Sometimes I would come off duty to find herself and her friends merrily drinking and singing Christmas songs in our room. We would stay in our room drinking late into the night, until a flood of soldiers was heard spilling out of the canteen, singing loudly. The guys would then have to make a quick dash to their rooms, along the same route which Andy used to sneak in. We were very aware of the fact that if a man was caught in our room, we would all be charged and found guilty. We skirted around the rules sometimes. There were only two of us women. If one or the other was on duty, it would have been very isolating. The lads usually congregated in each other's rooms watching movies, and sometimes in our room. At that point I had a good relationship with most of the soldiers, both the young and more seasoned ones.

As I settled into a routine I tried to get out of camp as much as possible. I struck up friendships with some of the drivers, who often allowed to me to accompany them on their water truck detail when I wasn't on duty in the comcen. We would fill the truck with water from the well at Tibnin Bridge, later distributing it to the various observation posts. I would act as shotgun escort, wearing my flak jacket and helmet and carrying my rifle. It was an opportunity to see Lebanon, in particular the more secluded villages including At Tire, a strategic village which the Irish occupied. It also afforded me the chance to see Andy.

The drivers often stopped in the larger towns, taking me around various mingy shops, introducing me to locals. Lebanese women greeted me with a soft kiss to each cheek before whisking me to the cool shade of their shops. They delighted in showing me the latest fashion trends, displaying a dazzling selection of silk garments used as dressing gowns and more intimate garments, known amongst our Irish troops as "kinkies". I was shocked to find that these local Muslim ladies were far more open sexually amongst themselves than we were at home. It allowed me a brief moment to feel feminine during a time where I was increasingly losing all sense of my femininity.

My flaming red hair had started to grow out into a tangled mess and my blonde highlights were rapidly fading. So, after one such trip I asked my company sergeant if it would be possible for me to go to the local hairdressers. "Valerie, we're in the middle of a war zone and you want to go to the hairdressers?" he joked. I pleaded with him for days before he eventually relented. "I'll have to send an armed escort with you – but you are not to tell anyone," he said.

My good friend the driver took me along the dusty route, dropping me off at the local hairdressers, which I had discovered on my daily runs with Andy. Another friend waited outside, acting as escort. The shop front was blackened out because of Islamic restrictions. Inside, the women sat on comfortable black leather chairs, happily gossiping in Arabic. A selection of large posters displaying Arabic models were splashed beside wide mirrors and white wash basins at the back of the shop. The salon would not have looked out of place in Ireland. All *hijabs* were hung neatly on an ornate coat stand.

The hairdressers greeted me warmly before setting about fixing my frizzy hair and eyebrows. A young

Lebanese woman with dark kohled eyes leaned me back gently. She held a long string of thread in one hand and attached the other end to her tooth. She threaded my eyebrows in the traditional Arabic fashion. She coloured my hair and dipped my head in the cold white basin to rinse all traces of hair dye away. When she was finished, my blonde highlighted hair and perfectly groomed eyebrows stared back bright-eyed at me from the mirror.

Suddenly my escort burst in. "In the name of God, how long does it take to get your hair done?" The hairdresser ran towards him, screaming and brandishing her fists boldly in his face. It was unheard of for a man to see a Muslim woman in the absence of her *hijab*. He timidly scuttled out of the shop amid screams from the local women. I will never forget the expression on his face. I think he was genuinely scared. We all laughed and I said my goodbyes, not wanting to leave the comfort of the salon.

Andy and I were due to go on a sixty-hour leave pass into Israel. I had always wished to return to Israel one day. I had been there with my parents as a teenager when we lived in Cyprus. We decided to go to Tiberias, a city on the shores of the Sea of Galilee. I silently wished my ring would arrive beforehand so that Andy could propose to me officially on our short trip, but it didn't.

We mounted the back of the small white UN soft-top truck. The driver put his foot down and sped away. Andy and I exchanged smiles; I was feeling so excited. The canopy flapped against gusts of wind in the silence of the surrounding hills. The summer months were long gone and a chill filled the air. It was a sunless grey morning but inside I felt my heart race as I was finally free of the boundaries of our camp.

We travelled for a couple of hours, passing open plots of land with tobacco crops, animals grazing nearby behind shabby wooden fences. Little shops occasionally dotted the roadside. We noticed a sprawling mansion with oversized white stone pillars at the entrance. Standing in a small plot of land next to this fabulous mansion was a small house made from grey corrugated tin sheets. Some Lebanese lived in a world of luxury in comparison to most people's living conditions.

We swept down out of the hills along the dusty roads until finally we arrived at UN Headquarters in the coastal town of Naqoura on the Lebanese/Israeli border. We passed through the Israeli checkpoint after a thorough security check by the border guards.

The Israeli town of Nahariya lies approximately two kilometres from the border. It is a favourite haunt for Irish soldiers on sixty-hour leave passes. It also has the distinction of being one of Hezbollah's favourite targets, with its inhabitants living under the constant threat of rocket attack. From here we had to take a bus to the city of Tiberias. By the time we arrived at our little hotel, it was very late, with the sun setting in a rainbow of bright orange and red.

We had a sprawling bedroom suite with a seafront view. I quickly slipped into my cream pants and white lace top before we headed out to eat. We walked the long winding streets hand in hand, lush green palm trees gently swaying in the warm breeze among the many tourists who flocked to the city. Narrow streets led to open cobblestoned courtyards where the scent of aromatic dishes wafted through the air. I felt like a girl again. I felt relieved to be away from the stifling confines of my camp; all that mattered was that I was with Andy. Everything else back in Lebanon would work itself out.

We sat on wicker chairs at a glass table underneath a green umbrella and ordered food. My mood shifted and I felt agitated, as I often did at meal times. I knew that if I ate, my stomach would bloat as it was not used to retaining food. Andy ordered us pizza, which I ate reluctantly. In my mind I battled with the notion of keeping it down.

Later that evening, when Andy was tucked up in bed, I crept into the bathroom. I was terrified he would uncover my closely guarded secret. I slowly turned on the tap to drown out the sounds of my bulimic purging. Then I heard Andy outside the door, trying to come in.

"What are you doing, Valerie?"

"Nothing – I'll be out in a minute."

"Let me in now!" he yelled.

I was filled with panic but I refused to let him in. Eventually I emerged from the bathroom. He was sitting quietly on the bed. "I know what you were doing," he whispered gently. "You are not fat."

"I know I'm not fat."

"Then why are you hurting yourself like that?"

I struggled to hold back the tears that threatened to tumble from my eyes. I knew that I needed help. I knew it hurt him to see the woman he loved doing this to herself. I told him everything, asking him for his help.

"Of course I'll help you to get better – but you cannot keep secrets from me," he told me.

I told him that when I focused my mind on my body and food, it forced it away from what was happening in camp. Andy looked at me with his thoughtful green eyes, pain etched on his face, pledging to help me get better. I felt an emotional weight had been lifted from my shoulders.

The following morning we sat outside in the hotel courtyard for our breakfast. Israel was full of courtyards. Exotic colourful flowers draped the stone walls in the morning sunshine. Andy served me up a buffet of fruit, vowing never to order me pizza again. We waited a full hour until my body had digested the breakfast. We sat there chatting while the warm winter breeze blew softly against our legs.

"You are going to have to be strong," he said. "From now on, ignore them; write down everything you are feeling instead of blocking it out. If I am not in camp ring my post anytime you feel down or you get the urge to get rid of your food." I knew that with his help I could start to overcome my eating disorder.

We spent the day visiting museums, Tiberias being one of the four holy cities of Judaism. We haggled at the markets with the many Israeli vendors jostling for our custom. We smiled at each other like any young couple.

After a small dinner that evening Andy led me to the pier and we strolled along the long wooden railings under a canopy of glittering stars. Andy looked slightly agitated.

"What's wrong?"

"Nothing's wrong," he assured me. "Let's go back to the room."

My heart sank; I thought that perhaps the revelation of my eating disorder had put doubts in his mind over our relationship. Maybe he didn't want to get married to me. Back at the room he led me to the balcony, which had a breathtaking view of the Sea of Galilee. I could almost taste the salty air.

I was immersed in the scenery when I noticed Andy bent down on one knee.

"Will you marry me?" he said softly. "I was trying to ask you on the pier, but I couldn't get the words out. I wanted it to be perfect."

Tears welled up in my eyes. "Are you sure you want to marry me?"

"Yes, I want to marry you."

"Well then, yes, I will marry you."

He hugged me tightly, squeezing me in close.

"Everything is going to be okay in Lebanon, I won't let anyone hurt you," he whispered.

I rubbed the tears from my eyes and thought of something more practical: "Did you get my ring?"

"No, it didn't arrive yet. But I didn't want to propose to you in Lebanon; I wanted to do it here."

It was a magical moment that I have never forgotten.

Our trip ended all too quickly. I settled into camp life again, the happiness from Israel fading fast. Shortly afterwards, it was insinuated that I had stolen or misplaced some money from the camp headquarters building. However, there was no evidence to support these allegations. As a result I was no longer permitted to leave camp, either to go running or perform shotgun escort.

I was deeply hurt by the accusations and also by the fact that I could no longer go running. Every other soldier in camp was allowed to do so. I again spoke to an NCO about the matter but this led to the situation worsening. I was scared of losing my job as a result of these accusations. I had done nothing to warrant this and was deeply upset by the whole matter. I spoke to Andy, who was perturbed by the whole situation. I was advised to speak to an officer about my job in camp.

The next day I stood to attention in front of the officer and saluted him. He sat behind a dark wooden desk and asked me what was going on. It was a daunting experience, where I felt little sensitivity was shown. I told him that I did not want to work as a waitress, the only other job available to me as a woman in B Company. I tried to outline the continuing problems I was having with some of the other soldiers, but he told me he wasn't interested. He flicked his hand in the air, dismissing me, and then bowed his head immediately to his work. I left his office, my mind whirling. I felt that he could have at least listened to me.

The following day I was told that I was too emotional and could not handle criticism. However, it was decided that we would all start with a clean slate. I became extra-vigilant in my work, for fear of being removed from my job. I was later allowed to continue with my running and shotgun escorts.

After that particular incident I followed every procedure meticulously in camp. I became extremely cautious about everything I did in the comcen for fear of being removed, as that threat hung over me constantly.

For a few brief weeks my life improved, allowing me to carry on with the task of being a soldier, which was all I had wanted from the beginning.

Most mornings before daylight had fully broken the local Hezbollah put in a dawn attack on the surrounding SLA compounds under the shadow of darkness. Almost immediately afterwards the SLA compounds opened fire, sending bursts of .5mm heavy machine gun fire in the direction of their enemy, obliterating the ground around them. Tracer rounds intermittently sprayed across the skyline, as did the heavy 120mm mortar rounds, which bombarded the dark surrounding valleys and hills. Clouds of brown dirt swirled high in the air as members of the Hezbollah dived to the ground, taking cover behind shrubs and barren vegetation.

If I happened to be on duty in the comcen I immediately pressed the siren to alert the camp that we were now in groundhog. The noise of the screeching siren sounded throughout the camp, jolting all troops from their beds. They grabbed flak jackets, helmets and rifles before racing to the safety of our bunker, gunfire all around warning them of the impending danger.

Inside the comcen I took in a flood of reports, filling out pages alongside the company sergeant and company commander. I pressed the black radio receiver against my cheek, often for over an hour, as each post sent in its latest report and I passed them on to Irishbatt headquarters in Camp Shamrock. Even when all firing ceased, we still had to remain in the bunker. Usually an hour was required before groundhog was lifted from our camp. By this time the local Hezbollah would have made their escape in time to begin their day's work.

It was a well-known fact among troops in our camp that one member of the local Hezbollah worked in our kitchen. Once he was dropped at his front door, having completed his early morning attack, he would then make the short walk to our camp to prepare the morning breakfast alongside our cooks. This routine was followed most mornings and some evenings.

I hadn't seen Andy much, as the level of shelling prevented him from coming into camp. It was hard to believe that Christmas was looming. Every soldier serving overseas misses someone at home, especially at Christmas. Many of the men were fathers desperately missing their wives and children during this festive period.

On Christmas Eve morning Melissa went with some other soldiers to Tibnin orphanage, a short distance from our camp. The orphanage was created by the local people but greatly helped by the Irish troops serving in Lebanon. The Irish soldiers often brought supplies, especially at Christmas. This helped to lift the young orphaned children's mood during this festive period. I was disappointed I couldn't go but was thrilled for Melissa, who was delighted to be going.

I was putting the last notes in the log book after completing a night shift. There had been a brief lull from the constant bombings. Andy suddenly popped his head around the comcen door. His stint in Hill 880 had come to an end and he was now stationed in camp on guard duty. He was hiding something behind his back.

"Close your eyes."

"Why?" I giggled as I closed them.

"Now open them."

My eyes blinked open. He was holding a baby-blue G-Shock watch, and also every Madonna CD he could find in the local shops.

"Happy Christmas."

A smile beamed across my face. "Thank you, I needed a lift," I joked.

"I'll meet you in the dining hall for breakfast once you're relieved."

"Okay, I shouldn't be long."

After breakfast we went to my room. It was cold outside but it was almost Christmas.

"Close your eyes," Andy said again.

"Why?"

"Just close your eyes."

"Okay, okay, they're closed."

"Open them."

My eyes widened when I saw the neat red velvet box shaped like a rose in his hand. He clicked open the box to reveal my engagement ring. I was absolutely thrilled. I had guessed that I might get it for Christmas but when he didn't give it to me in the comcen I feared I might not. My eyes were immediately drawn to the enormous sparkling diamond, with three small diamonds running diagonally along either side of it. Andy gently slipped it on my finger. I glanced up and saw the happiness in his eyes. I silently thanked God for delivering such a kind man as my future husband.

Christmas came and went quickly, the almost daily bombings serving as a permanent reminder that we were not at home. I spent my twenty-first birthday in Lebanon. Andy arranged a little party for me. Our friend the cook supplied the cream birthday cake. The company sergeant gave me a full crate of free Almaza beer, which I passed around.

He also gave Andy some Coca-Cola, believing he didn't drink. In fact, it was just beer Andy didn't drink. The cook had a bottle of whiskey left over from the Irish coffees served at Christmas, and he sneaked this to Andy at the party. Spirits weren't available in the canteen so Andy had to sneak the whiskey into his cans of Coke. The company sergeant watched a little confused as Andy got fairly drunk, not having had any alcohol in over two months.

The men in camp were lovely to me on my birthday and most congratulated us on our engagement. I truly believed I had reached a turning point and that things were going to be all right.

A short time later it was decided that to boost morale we would hold a "beach party" in our canteen one night. Each soldier dressed up in summer clothes, golden sand was strewn across the canteen floor and beach balls were blown up. Outside, torrential rain bounced off the tarmac and trickled down my face as I made my way towards the canteen wearing an oversized heavy green jacket and a pair of trendy black sunglasses – under the jacket I wore a pair of black shorts and a black t-shirt.

I mixed happily with the men that evening. Some were absent, having returned home on leave for the Christmas period. A warm atmosphere filled the canteen as we played games and drank the cheap local beer. I had finally settled into my life in Lebanon, finding an inner peace and happiness that had previously eluded me.

15

Under Fire

One day in the comcen a voice crackled over the 77 radio set. "Zero, zero" was called repeatedly. I asked for the call sign of the person on the radio set but instead heard the words, "You are a dog! Shut up, you bitch" roared back at me. I was given a false identification and bunker number. However, after a few months in the comcen I knew everyone in the company by their voice. I rang the soldier in question and told him never to behave in that manner again.

The 2 I/C (second-in-command) of the camp had been out in his Land Rover, which also had a radio set. He heard the individual calling me a dog and a bitch. In fact, many soldiers had heard it. Each soldier was paraded the following morning and informed that if I was ever called names again they would be charged and found guilty. Most soldiers didn't mind, as it was common knowledge who had said it.

On Saturday evenings an armoured personnel carrier (APC) usually brought troops to Camp Shamrock so they could go drinking in the canteen there. One Saturday evening when I was on duty, the company sergeant informed me that the trip to Camp Shamrock was full. Shortly afterwards Colin entered the comcen to put his name forward for the trip. I told him that the company sergeant had said the trip was full. He leaned in towards my face and shouted: "Whether or not I go is none of your business."

"I'm just passing on a message to you; you'll have to ask the company sergeant," I replied.

An officer who was present followed Colin outside and told him that he was never to speak to me in such an aggressive manner again. I couldn't understand Colin's behaviour towards me.

Some nights when the camp was silent and most soldiers were sleeping deeply, I would sneak around the back of the camp to Andy's room. I would set my alarm for 2.00, safe in the knowledge that nobody would catch me. Andy was only in camp for about a month, as we were due to go on leave during his time there, so I didn't do it often.

Our female toilets were located at the end of camp, beside the male accommodation. There were two rows of male accommodation, one facing the road which ran through our camp, the other facing the toilets. As luck would have it, Andy was in the row that faced the road. This was infinitely more difficult to get into, as the soldier who patrolled the rooftop had a clear view of his row. I would quietly peer around the corner, waiting for the patrolling soldier to turn his back before moving quickly. At that point I would sprint to Andy's room; he would have left the door unlocked.

At two in the morning one Sunday in early February I came to Andy's room. On Sunday mornings, if I wasn't on duty, I didn't have to be up until eight o'clock. I fell asleep almost immediately, exhausted from the never-ending stream of duties. Some time before dawn, the silence of our camp was interrupted by the sound of gunfire blazing overhead. I had become so used to the shelling that it rarely startled me anymore. Most soldiers wouldn't move until they judged the rounds were falling nearby. By now most of us could easily sleep through the racket of gunfire in the distance.

I nudged Andy and rolled my eyes, which were puffy from sleep deprivation. I muttered, "For God's sake, I'm so sick of them. It's my only day off."

"You'd better have a look out the window, it might be far away," replied Andy.

I tumbled out of bed, peeled back the duvet and slid the green curtain back slowly. As I gazed sleepily out the window, my eyes suddenly popped wide open. Bursts of red tracer rounds were passing directly overhead. Then an eerie silence filled Haddatha.

"God, Andy they flew right through our camp!"

"Don't be ridiculous, they couldn't be attacking our camp."

I stood nervously for a few minutes, waiting for the sound of more gunfire, but nothing happened. I sensed that something was wrong but Andy was adamant that it was finished as silence filled our camp. "I told you it would be okay. They rarely attack on Sundays. Get back into bed," he said groggily. I slipped back under the duvet and snuggled next to Andy.

My eyes were closing again when I heard a furious whistling sound. "Oh my God, I told you, they're attacking the camp."

We both jumped from the bed, scrambling to get dressed. The thud of mortar rounds exploding was followed by streams of relentless gunfire which peppered through our camp. The windows next door were shattered, shards of broken glass spread across the floor. Soldiers flew from their rooms, grabbing their helmets and running for cover, crouching down to evade the heavy machine gun fire ripping through the air.

Suddenly I realised my own situation. I shouldn't be in Andy's room. Not a single soldier knew I ever stayed in his room or he in mine. Andy only came to my room when Melissa was on duty, so she wasn't even aware that he stayed overnight.

"I'm trapped! How am I going to get out?" I asked.

"It's okay, I'll wait with you until everyone is gone."

Once the full row of soldiers had evacuated I tore around to the back of the billet. I caught glimpses of fallen trees. Then a vicious whistle deafened me. I froze, covering my ears, shutting my eyes tightly and crouching down towards the ground. I was filled with terror; I thought that I was going to die. Directly across my path a 120mm mortar round landed near the male toilets, sending plumes of smoke high in the air. I ran to my room, quickly snatching my equipment. Outside I noticed other soldiers who were trapped, a look of fear across their faces. "We can't get across the road," they yelled.

The attack had intensified, long bursts of heavy .5mm machine gun rounds bouncing off the black tarmac road, ripping it open. By now the sun had risen, allowing us a clear view of our camp. Another terrifying whistle filled the air and clouds of brown dirt and white smoke swirled high above the ground as another 120mm mortar round exploded.

We stood still, bracing ourselves to sprint across the road to the safety of our bunker. We were filled with fear. Another roaring whistle reverberated throughout camp. We waited for its explosion and then ran for our lives. Most billets were empty but in the distance I caught sight of soldiers still running for our bomb shelter. Andy found himself in a similar position to me, trapped, waiting for a brief lull in the firing before dashing to the bunker.

Once inside, I rushed to the comcen where I immediately helped to take in a flood of reports. A tall slim soldier appeared inside the comcen carrying his rifle in his hand, blood staining his forehead. He looked dazed. "We need a med-evac (medical evacuation) immediately. There's a soldier badly injured." I radioed Camp Shamrock for a med-evac but they could not send one in. A medical evacuation of a single soldier can endanger the whole team. It was too dangerous to send one until the heavy bombardment subsided.

I later learned that the Irish soldier had been standing at his post on the rooftop when a 120mm mortar impacted on the sandbag position only metres from where he stood. It tore open the 7.62mm machine gun which was mounted on a heavy black tripod. He received shrapnel wounds to his legs and arms. Shrapnel from the mortar round peppered his post, sending chunks of concrete to the floor. He had been stumbling for cover down the stairs when he had met another soldier who had gone to check on him. He was carried to the kitchen where camp medics assisted him, but we could not evacuate him.

The lethal 120mm mortars were still ripping through our camp. The SLA was putting down heavy .5mm machine gun fire. As soldiers we could adapt to this environment. However, this was my first experience of coming under attack. We were a sitting target, unable to defend ourselves. It was felt that we were outgunned and it would appear that the policy was to not retaliate.

Outside, the continuous racket of gunfire refused to stop. Suddenly all communications went down. We braced ourselves for the worst.

Inside the bunker, another soldier was injured. He was running for the safety of our bunker when the 120mm mortar round impacted on the machine gun position on the roof directly over his head. He was knocked to the ground when the heavy sandbags and masonry from the roof fell on him. He lay still, unable to move, while other soldiers attempted to pull him from the rubble and carry him to the safety of the bunker. Miraculously, he survived. He was a giant of a man and the backbone of the company tug-of-war team. His height and strong build probably saved his life.

News quickly filtered through the ranks of our company that the Hezbollah had used our camp as cover to launch an attack on the SLA compound overlooking Haddatha. The SLA had retaliated immediately.

Finally the firing stopped, but we remained in groundhog for fear of another attack. Darkness filled the comcen and a deathly silence hung over our camp. There was nothing we could do but wait.

We left the comcen and headed towards the kitchen. To our relief, all soldiers were accounted for. It was a miracle that no one was killed. Soldiers and medics helped those injured while we waited. Andy too had made it to the bunker. He told me how they were running up the long black road when a mortar round had landed in an embankment just outside the camp but they escaped unharmed. Over an hour passed, silence still filling B company. After a long period of inactivity, groundhog was lifted. We were safe, but shocked that the SLA had deliberately attacked our camp.

A Lebanese television crew were filming amid the scenes of general chaos. Suddenly, a group of us noticed a yellow Mercedes travelling through our camp. One of the kitchen staff sat in the back seat cradling an RPG (rocket-propelled grenade launcher). They brazenly drove through the surrounding chaos. The Hezbollah had learned that the camera was more powerful than the gun. They usually filmed their attacks, later distributing them for sale in the local shops. I knew that their latest attack would be widely available in our area of operations within a few days.

Myself and my sister Deirdre. I was going to a dancing competition.

Christmas 1992, Ayia Napa, Cyprus.

With my parents in
the Lebanon, 1992.

During training in the Glen of Imaal.

The morning we were attacked in Lebanon, 1999.

The sandbag position was obliterated during the attack on our camp; Lebanon, 1999.

Best overall soldier, 2002.

On duty in Eritrea, 2002.

Eritrea, 2002.

On duty in Eritrea, 2002.

Local Ethiopian kids in Sheraro on our patrol.

Receiving our female team medal having completed a fun run for charity, with Colonel Prendergast in Eritrea, 2002.

My wedding day in 2004.

With my sons in Cork before our move to Kildare.

With my two boys, Alex and Christopher.

From soldier to beauty therapist - the new me.

16

Bad to Worse

The following morning I reported to the officers' private dining quarters. On top of my duties in the comcen, I was also by now working as a waitress in B Company while some of the other personnel were on leave. During my teenage years I had held down a number of part-time jobs while I attended school; being a waitress was never one of them. The officers in B Company headquarters had their own dining area above the main dining hall, so they never mixed with other ranks personnel. Inside, a large window overlooked the sandbag position which had been obliterated the previous morning by a 120mm mortar round. Shards of broken glass had been swept into bundles all around the linoleum floor.

One of the officers sat silently reading a newspaper as I hovered about in the tiny kitchen next door. "What would you like to eat, Sir?" I asked. "I will have a cup of tea and a bowl of cereal," he replied. He had his own personal cutlery placed neatly in the kitchen. I filled up his white cup slowly and placed it next to his Corn Flakes. He banged his fist on the table, almost spilling the milk from his bowl of cereal. "Where is my saucer?" he yelled. I was unaware that he also liked a gold-rimmed saucer beneath his cup of tea.

I stood back, slightly bewildered. I stared around the room at the shattered glass lying on the floor, thinking of the attack the previous day. It seemed all he was interested in was a gold-rimmed saucer. I dashed to the kitchen, panicking momentarily when I couldn't see the saucer; eventually I located it in a cupboard above the sink.

Later Andy bumped into Colin and confronted him. "Will you just leave her alone? What has she ever done to you?"

"Go on, boy, thump me, go fucking on. Give me a dig – do what you did to that fella on the last trip," replied Colin. "See those stripes that you're wearing? I'll have them ripped off your arm."

For a fleeting moment Andy seriously contemplated thumping him in the face but because he was a corporal and there were witnesses also present, he just walked away.

A couple of nights after the attack on our camp, I could hear a party going on in the room beside mine. I knew many of the soldiers there – Colin's friends – had been drinking heavily earlier in the evening and had taken a crate of beer back to the room. I was alone so I went to ask Andy to stay in my room with me. Around 2.00 a.m., Andy came in and locked my door behind him.

I was sleeping soundly when suddenly I was jolted upright by the sound of loud continuous banging on my wall and laughing. It was around 4.00 a.m. Andy advised me to ignore it. I was also aware that if Andy was caught in my room I would have found myself in a world of trouble. We fell back asleep but were woken again about three-quarters of an hour later. I could hear shouting outside as Colin shouted to be let into his room, but was refused. Suddenly I could hear banging on my door. Andy disappeared under my duvet while Colin proceeded to slide open my window. I froze, closing my eyes and pretending to be asleep, hoping he would leave. To my relief he did.

At 6.00 a.m. I awoke again to the sounds of banging on my wall. It was early morning and Andy was fearful of being caught so he sneaked out and returned to his accommodation. Outside the sun had risen in the blue dawn sky. I climbed out of bed and slipped into my uniform before heading to the toilets to freshen up. Splashing cold water on my face, staring at my reflection in the mirror, I felt tired, lonely and fed up.

After our morning parade I headed towards the headquarters building as I had arranged to go to the dentist. I met Colin and told him that I was going to the dentist. He said that I wasn't allowed as I had to perform a cleaning detail. I was so tired and upset that I could feel hot tears threatening to spill down my cheeks, but I managed to hold them back. I told him that I had to go the dentist as my bridge needed to be fitted. Exhausted, I began to walk away, but then I turned around. I felt that

I had to stand up for myself, as the situation in camp was becoming unbearable.

"Do you realise what you did last night?" I asked Colin softly.

Jumping to his feet he quickly walked towards me. "What I did? What I did?" he roared aloud.

"Yes, what you did. You were banging on my walls and my door and you opened my window," I replied firmly.

"I wouldn't lower myself to open your fucking window. Anyway, you slept in your own room last night. It makes a change from where you usually sleep," he barked.

"You probably don't even remember last night," I said. "You were locked. You were drinking until six this morning. You were probably locked going on duty."

Suddenly a senior NCO came into the room. He asked me if I wanted to make a complaint but I said I just wanted to be left alone and I returned to my room.

Fifteen minutes later I was called back to the headquarters building. Colin was there. He became very aggressive, leaning his head in towards me.

"You have made a very serious allegation against me," he said. "Do you remember the last trip here in the Leb? Remember that girl – you know her and I know her. Well, if you don't take back what you said, everyone will turn on you and ignore you, just like they did with her."

The senior NCO was present but this did not deter Colin. I backed away as he lunged towards me. The NCO caught hold of his arms, physically restraining him, grabbing him by the shoulders and forcing him up against a wall. Colin was still screaming at me, with his arms outstretched and fists clenched. I quickly raced towards the door, fearing he would attack me. Inside, he was restrained and told to shut up four times. I told the senior NCO that I did not want to make a complaint, but he referred the incident to the company commander anyway. The company commander then immediately reported it to the military police.

Wildly exaggerated stories circulated throughout the camp at an overwhelming speed, ensuring that I became completely ostracised almost overnight. The MPs were called in, even though I hadn't made a complaint. I was interviewed by the military police until I felt completely drained emotionally. I had never intended it to come to this. I certainly could not tell them that Andy, who had witnessed everything, was in my room that night.

The MPs asked me if I wished to make a formal complaint about Colin. It was unheard of in those days for a woman to make a complaint of harassment in the defence forces. Since I was forced to speak with them, I decided to think about the situation carefully. I felt that this behaviour would not have been tolerated at home. Later, I was told that I was accusing Colin of sexual harassment. If I am honest, I did not even know what sexual harassment meant up until that day.

After that incident I was transferred to the officers' private dining quarters on a full-time basis, where I was made a permanent waitress. I was removed from the comcen.

This was to be my new assignment for the remainder of the trip. I felt humiliated.

The following evening I went to the canteen with Andy. He looked at me with his warm green eyes. "You are going to walk in there with your head held high. Do not let them break you," he whispered gently. The cook also chipped in. "Valerie, I am here too, so you have nothing to be afraid of."

We sat at a table with men whom I had considered my friends. They immediately got up and left, glaring at me while sipping on their Almaza beers. It was apparent that only a handful of the men would talk to me, and then only in private, never in public. I was being ostracised for speaking to the military police, even though it had not been my choice.

We decided to leave when suddenly a soldier, one of Colin's friends, passed a comment aimed at us: "Yeah, go on, get out. Two's company, three's a crowd."

I turned around just in time to see a glass bottle being hurled at my head. I quickly ducked out of the way and it whizzed past my temple before smashing on the floor next to me.

The cook yelled at the soldier who fired the bottle. "You are not only stupid, but you are a shithead!"

Shocked, I left the canteen for a moment, but I had had enough, so I decided to face him. I turned around and walked back into the canteen, stopping in front of the man who had fired the bottle.

"If you were a man, you would have said it to my face instead of yelling it when my back was turned and firing a bottle at me," I shouted. "What kind of a man fires a bottle at a woman when her back is turned?"

He jumped to his feet and lunged towards me with his fists clenched tightly, rage spreading across his face. Andy quickly intervened and a scuffle broke out, fists flying in the air. Andy was pulled back and restrained while the men roared at him. He was pulled from the canteen and outside I became extremely upset.

I was later pulled aside by the orderly sergeant, who had heard about the incident.

"Why are you doing this? He's a decent fellow," he said.

"You don't know anything! They just fired a bottle at my head."

"I didn't hear that any bottle was fired at you."

"What? When I was leaving, they fired it directly at me."

"I think you should drop this. I know your father – what would he think?"

His words stung me. What would my father think? Would he have liked his daughter treated in this manner?

By this stage, I hadn't eaten in a few days. My appetite had vanished. At that point I just wanted to go home. In my room at night, I lay alone in bed, crying myself to sleep, dizzy from lack of food. In the quiet darkness of my room I often felt a rush of anxiety. I began having panic attacks, hyperventilating, unable to breathe. I tried to wipe the tears from my eyes but they just kept coming.

Most of the other soldiers had become extremely cold and distant towards me, no doubt fearing for their own careers. Some of the older men would pass snide comments to me. I flushed with embarrassment, choosing to ignore them, even though they were intent on condemning me. Andy was extremely supportive, encouraging me to finish the trip. "I know how hard it is to be a woman in this environment, but you have to stay strong. Don't go home, don't let them drive you away."

I continued to waitress, but felt inadequate. I hadn't joined the army and gone through months of physically gruelling recruit training and weapons courses to become a waitress. I wanted to be a soldier.

17

Home, Back, and Home Again

On 16 February, the company commander informed me that I was being transferred to Camp Shamrock for my own protection. A blanket silence filtered through the camp, as I was completely ostracised. At that stage I had been questioned again by the military police. I was weak, tired and humiliated.

As I packed my bags, preparing to leave, Andy came to say goodbye. Melissa was present. A male soldier passed the door.

"Is he affecting your privacy?" he barked at Melissa.

"No, he's not. He is just saying goodbye to her," she replied.

"Their relationship is affecting you – I am reporting them."

He later made an official complaint to the company 2 I/C but nothing came of it.

My heart throbbed as I said goodbye to Andy, not knowing when I would see him again. I took one last glance at the room which I had made so cosy. It had almost become soulless. My heart filled with a deep sadness as I closed the door quietly behind me.

Those days blended into one another. Inside Camp Shamrock, I was kept away from everyone. The camp was quite large with blocks of accommodation. However, I was given a transit billet of my own away from every other soldier. The small rectangular Portakabin was pleasantly bright and airy but became bitterly cold during the night. I was surrounded by men, some of whom had been my friends, whom I had drunk with in B Company on occasion, but I was an outcast. They stared at me boldly, never flinching in their gaze. I honestly did not know how to cope with the situation. I thought perhaps that there was something wrong with me. I was so insecure; I wished that I was a man.

Amelia was also stationed in Camp Shamrock. She quickly befriended me, as did another woman and a male sergeant. Nobody else would speak to me. There were quite a few women based in Camp Shamrock but most refused to speak to me. Stories circulated indicating that women would never be allowed to serve overseas again because of what had happened to me in B Company and another incident on a previous trip to Lebanon. I was being blamed for women never being permitted to serve overseas again. However, I was very grateful for those few who stood by me.

Those women showed me great kindness, and I felt safe in their company, but they were unable to protect me fully. Late into the night I would curl into the foetal position in the icy cold transit billet, blankets wrapped tightly around my body. I had brought my CD player with me. Trying to fall asleep, I tossed and turned as my favourite music played softly in the background, my heart beating fast. Eventually I would drift off into a dream world, allowing my mind to take me elsewhere.

For two days I hardly emerged from that room, preferring to isolate myself. I went to the dining hall on a few occasions, either in the company of the two other girls or alone. If I was alone and went to sit at a table, the men would immediately stand up and sit elsewhere. I found this treatment humiliating.

The military police investigation continued. I had lost my job and been transferred to Camp Shamrock, so I decided to tell them everything that had taken place throughout the entire trip, as I had kept a diary. I felt I had nothing more to lose. I did not want to spend my entire career putting up with this treatment. I remained subdued but I signed the full report outlining everything that had taken place. I simply wanted to be treated fairly and to continue with my job.

I had come to love soldiering, I loved training every day. I thought these traits would carry me through. It never dawned on me that my sex would stop me. Maybe I would have felt differently if I had grown up in a family where I was told that I was less than a man, but I hadn't. In my whole life, I had never been told "you cannot do this because you are a woman". I stupidly believed that women were treated equally to men in Irish society. In all of my schooling, I was always told that I was equal to a man but it seemed in the Irish defence forces I was not viewed as equal. I think it was this naivety that caused me to become so strong-willed in the end, following through on principle despite the treatment I received as a result.

Meanwhile, Andy and I were due to go on leave for around eighteen days. I like travelling to new places. I was never one for sun and beach holidays. I prefer to visit new countries and experience different cultures, so we decided to travel to Kenya. I had booked and paid for my tickets. In the end, though, because I was feeling so low, I decided to travel home to be with my family.

The evening arrived for us to travel home. Andy was in the back of the vehicle waiting for me. He decided to look for me when I didn't show up. I was in the transit billet packing my bags. I had been crying. As I popped my head up, he immediately noticed my reddened eyes. He was carrying two furry white teddy bears hugging each other closely with a large red satin heart in the centre. This made me smile.

Our driver turned out to be one of the men who had been paraded over the radio incident where I had been called names. He hadn't spoken to me since. I was blamed for reporting this incident too, even though the company 2 I/C had heard this for himself. I sat in the back of that Jeep travelling the same road to Beirut by which I had arrived underneath the moonlit sky. The enthusiasm I had felt standing on the warm black tarmac of the airport just a few months ago had faded. Even the diamond from my engagement ring seemed to have lost some of its shimmer. Neither the driver nor the escort would speak to us for the entire trip, so an awkward silence filled the vehicle. Andy looked at me protectively, reassuring me. We caught glimpses of cars whizzing past on the dark roads, flying red, yellow and black Hezbollah flags out of their windows. The same large colourful posters depicting Hezbollah's martyrs and leader lined our route.

Once we reached our destination the driver came to an abrupt halt. I thanked the men but they refused to acknowledge me.

Inside the brightly lit airport was a flurry of multinational activity. Muslim women flew past in full black floor-length burqas. I noticed their hands were covered with black satin gloves, decorated with fabulous diamonds. The only visible parts of their bodies were their eyes. They were Bedouin women, denoted by the black steel bar running down over their noses. We boarded our Middle Eastern Airline plane, bound for Ireland. I was exhausted. The large airplane was relatively empty, allowing me to stretch out and sleep, but thoughts of Lebanon often lifted me from my dreams, distracting me.

The following day I arrived at my mother's front door, bone weary. She extended her arms out to greet me, and pulled me in close. It felt good to be home with my family, to be held and to feel loved.

"Valerie, I can feel your ribs. When is the last time you ate?" she asked.

I later asked Andy, "Do I look awful, Andy?"

"Well, I still love you, but you have looked better," he replied.

I glanced at my father and suddenly the realisation of what had happened fully impacted on me. I felt that I had let him down. I hadn't been strong enough.

Over the following days, my family supported me emotionally, encouraging me to return to complete the trip. Andy also urged me to return to Lebanon. He took me shopping around Cork city and I started to smile again.

One evening we sat in Scotts, one of our favourite bars in Cork. Sipping on our drinks, we spoke at length.

"Finish the trip," Andy urged me, "but then leave the army, Valerie. It is no place for women."

"Why should I leave just because I'm a woman?" I replied.

"You're not a man. You will never be fully accepted. You can fight the system but you will never win. Is this what you want from your life – to serve as a waitress?" I hadn't been told what my appointment would be if I returned to Camp Shamrock. Since most of the Irish female soldiers worked as waitresses in Camp Shamrock, I assumed that this would be my appointment.

"Of course it's not what I want. I want to be a soldier, Andy."

"A soldier. I know you can do it, but you will never be accepted. You are intelligent, outspoken . . . they don't like these qualities, Valerie. Go back to college; make something of your life."

I shook my head. "God damn you, Andy, I will not leave! I will not allow them to drive me out!"

162

"So you'd rather bite off your nose to spite your face," he said sternly.

The waitress took our order but I didn't even notice her; I was consumed by Andy's words. Maybe he was right; maybe I should return to college. But I couldn't bear to leave the army under such bad circumstances, leaving a bitter taste in my mouth. The majority of Irish soldiers were decent, honourable men. I felt that I had been ostracised due to peer pressure. I felt the blanket silence fell into place because the decent soldiers were afraid to speak out.

I knew that I had to stick it out, suck it up. Andy's words fell on my ears but it was too late; my mind was made up.

I was going back to Lebanon and I refused to leave the army. I felt that I had to stand my ground. If I ran then, I would always end up running. In the end, I would return on principle. I believed women to be equal to men. Of course I suffered greatly for my naivety. If I had accepted my job as a waitress earlier, maybe my life would have been much easier.

I returned to Lebanon in early March against a growing tide of resentment towards me. Travelling back, I had a gut-wrenching feeling in the pit of my stomach. I was put to work immediately in the communications centre in Camp Shamrock, which I was grateful for. At least they hadn't placed me in the officers' mess as a waitress.

A young female officer offered me kind words of wisdom, which I have never forgotten. Her words were unexpected but greatly appreciated. She went out of her way to advise me and to help me, but discreetly, which I was appreciative of. She was very dignified – an officer and certainly a lady. Her advice kept me going. She took care of me, along with another male officer. They often pulled me aside, asking how I was bearing up. They weren't much older than me. They were a new breed of officer, willing to accept other ranks females within the defence forces. Together with Amelia and another woman and man in camp, they kept me going.

One sunny afternoon an NCO in the comcen pulled me aside.

"Why did you come back?" he asked. "If I was you I wouldn't have come back."

"And let them win? I will not be driven away by them."

"Look, Valerie, I like you, and I will deny that I ever had this conversation with you, but you are not wanted here. Go home."

"I didn't do anything. I will not go home; I am staying and that is the end of the conversation," I replied.

"You reported that man in B Company?" he asked.

I told him what had actually taken place. He understood the army rumour mill, how it had twisted the story to form a new one. I knew him to be a decent man and he was simply trying to advise me, but I thought he had no right to tell me to go home.

I tried to carry on as normal, so I went running most days. The weather was improving, warm Lebanese rays beaming down from a perfect blue cloudless sky overhead. The daily run in Camp Shamrock was only a few miles, with few houses lining its route, most of them unoccupied.

The female officer had sought permission for us collectively to wear shorts, due to the heat. Her application was approved. I passed a group of female soldiers on the route, all wearing shorts in the bright sunshine. Their pace was too slow for me so I extended my stride, running a few hundred metres in front of them.

A male soldier who was senior in rank to me came running from the opposite direction. He drew to a sudden halt in front of me.

"Private Sheehan, get up to attention now!" he said. "How dare you wear shorts? Do you realise that you are offending the locals? This is a predominantly Muslim country. You look like a whore. I am reporting you immediately when I reach camp."

I wiped my eyes in stunned disbelief, the glare of the sun slightly blinding me.

"I was told that I could wear shorts," I replied. I told him that the female officer had been granted permission by the battalion commander for all of us to wear shorts.

"I don't believe you! How dare you?" he snarled.

I knew that he would pass the other women wearing shorts and realise his mistake.

This wasn't to be the last incident. A few days later I was sitting in the recreational room with Amelia. A female soldier asked us to leave so that she could use the phone. Around forty-five minutes later my name was called over the loudspeaker.

"Private Sheehan, contact the switchboard."

I walked down the dimly lit corridor and entered the recreational room. The other woman was still on the phone, so I asked her if I could use it. She became abusive so I returned to Amelia's room immediately. Moments later she flung open the door of her room and went in search of her friends. She then began screaming.

"Where is that fucking bitch?" she yelled. "I'll go over to her transit billet and tear her out of it."

"Yeah, give her a box," her friend replied. "Actually no; we'll go to the company sergeant and say that she was causing trouble in the female billets. We'll get her thrown out."

"I'll give her a box."

I tried to escape from Amelia's room but they caught sight of me. She raced towards me.

"Have you a fucking problem with me?" she yelled.

There was no mistaking her anger. She clenched her fist tightly and punched me violently in the eye. I fell to the floor from the force of the punch and held my hands to my head to cushion the blows. There were other women present at that stage. I was kicked in the head and ribs. I found it hard to distinguish where the blows were coming from. I was screaming at them to stop. Eventually it did.

I managed to stagger to my feet. As I tried to leave the billet one of the women said to me, "Don't report her, please."

"I heard you encouraging her to give me a box, saying ye would get me thrown out."

"I was only messing, I didn't mean it."

166

"You were not messing," I said.

"Let her go," yelled the woman who had punched me. "We all know what she's like for reporting people, after what she did in B company."

My eyes filled up with tears, a searing pain flashing through my head. I decided to go to the doctor because the pain was quite bad. On my way, the company commander of Camp Shamrock was headed in my direction. My black eye was quite visible where she had punched me. He noticed that something was wrong.

"Are you okay, Private Sheehan?" he asked.

"Yes, I'm fine."

"Private Sheehan, what has happened?"

I began crying as I told him what happened. He ordered an investigation.

A few days later I travelled to Naqoura, UNIFIL HQ, with a couple of other soldiers. One of the NCOs had allowed me to go with them in order to get me out of camp because of the tensions there. In Naqoura, he said to me, "I have told you this before, but I have to say it again. Most of the men hate you – they have said that if you put a foot out of line, you will be charged. I'm only telling you this for your own good, giving you a heads-up, so please don't say I told you. I will protect you but I cannot be there all the time."

I appreciated his help and his honesty but I was deeply hurt. With so many openly admitting to hating me, I began to hate and loath myself. My eating disorder returned as a non-expression of my feelings. I would gaze in the mirror at my reflection, examining my body for flaws, pinching excess flesh anywhere I could find it.

I had had enough. I phoned my father because I wanted to go home. I was suffering internally. I didn't know that my father later phoned a senior Irish officer. I don't think any father would tolerate his daughter being treated as I had been, whether I was a soldier or not. Following this I was paraded before an officer. He sat in a small office behind a plain desk, hands clasped tightly, fingers interlocked, flanked by other officers standing at his side. He was a middle-aged man with greyish hair and a stern face.

He spoke directly to me. "Do you realise that you are a soldier? You cannot just phone your father every time you have a problem. This is a United Nations peace-keeping mission, do you realise that, Private Sheehan?"

At that moment, after all that had happened, I just wanted to go home. My whole life had changed unimaginably.

He went on: "You cannot go home."

"But I can't eat, I can't sleep, I am having panic attacks and I have chest pains. I want to go home," I replied.

He looked straight through me and shrugged. "You cannot go home; you are a soldier."

"I have been called countless names for months; I've had a glass bottle fired at me; been physically assaulted; hardly anyone will talk to me. I just want to go home. If I don't go home it's going to get much worse." I had become scared for my own safety after what had taken place. I wondered what was going to happen next if I stayed.

"The only way you can go home is through a medical repatriation," he went on angrily. "Go to the doctor and ask him to sort it out for you, because I can't."

I wouldn't allow myself to cry in front of him. I had done enough crying.

I went alone to the doctor that day, feeling deeply upset. He examined me before arranging for my repatriation home. He was very understanding, and didn't seem to care whether the other officers liked it or not. He refused to be told how to do his job. He prescribed me sleeping tablets each night. When I closed my eyes, everything seemed to drift away. I finally began to sleep on my tangled mop of blonde curly hair. At that moment in time, I felt that my military career was over, completely dead. I felt demoralised.

A few days later I was flown home with a medic, which is standard procedure when returning on a medical repatriation from overseas. I spent a few days in a dull unattractive grey military hospital, which again is procedure. Andy remained behind in Lebanon, ringing me every night. He stood by me, comforting me during such a horribly dark period in my life.

The doctor at the hospital interviewed me at length. It seemed that certain officers from overseas wanted me silenced but he remained objective, refusing to be side-railed. He issued me a clean bill of health before discharging me, completely fit for duty. The female soldier who assaulted me was eventually charged by a military court and found guilty.

However, I have never been officially told the outcome of the investigation into what had taken place in B Company. But once I was back in Ireland, Andy told me over the phone what he had heard. Apparently, Colin was only found guilty of being drunk and disorderly and was sent to serve in an observation post.

The memories from that trip have never truly left me. They shaped my future. I buried them deep within but they surfaced regularly in the form of anger and ambition. I often found the two were interlinked, ambition born out of anger. On reflection I think it is anger that pushed me later on in my career. I vowed never to let anyone treat me like that again.

At night I often woke thinking I was back there, clenching and grinding my teeth to the point where my bridge cracked. In those days I found it incredibly difficult to be a woman in the army. As the months had passed, all traces of my femininity gradually slipped away. I found myself becoming distinctly cold and distant. In the end I just stopped crying. I had fallen to my lowest ebb after Lebanon. I began to insulate myself from my own feelings.

A few years later, I was told that some called me the "Ice Queen". I think I created her to protect myself from being hurt.

18

Should I Stay or Should I Go?

I spent the following weeks at my parents' home recovering from my experiences in Lebanon. I had a month's leave but decided to take extra time off to contemplate my future. Part of me wanted to stay in the defence forces but part of me wanted to leave. My parents and family encouraged me to stay. They always had my welfare at heart, believing that I should stick it out. They didn't want me to run away from the problems, but to face them. It was an extremely miserable period in my life, which I found difficult to overcome.

To my relief, Andy returned home from Lebanon a few weeks later. I met him in Jury's Inn in Dublin, where he arrived late one night. When I opened the door of my hotel room he dropped his green army bag and flung his arms around me. I had missed him so much after I came home. We spoke for hours that night.

"Valerie, you are going to be my wife. How are we going to have a family with both of us in the army?" he asked tenderly. He had such a loving heart sometimes. I reflected that maybe it was time for me to accept my role in life, hang up my army boots and settle down. Maybe I should stop chasing my dream of being a soldier on an equal footing to a man.

In the end, the soldier in me wanted to stay. The army was in my blood. I wanted to live my dream despite the difficulties I had faced. This was compounded by the fact that I was a female soldier in a man's world. But I was not ready to let it go yet. I could not leave the army with such a bitter taste in my mouth. Eventually I decided to return to work, having regained my sense of perspective. I felt that I had to give my career another chance.

In May 1999, shortly after Andy returned home, we decided to move in together. We rented a cosy, compact little bungalow in Midleton in County Cork. I filled our little home with pictures and souvenirs from the countries we had visited together. I was madly in love, almost bursting with joy at our first home, which lay a short walking distance from the town centre. I had also, for a time, conquered my eating disorder with Andy's support.

Back at work, I was offered a position in the barrack accountant stores. Initially I was disheartened at the prospect of working in an office; from the beginning, I had tried to avoid being tucked away in a clerical position. However, I accepted the offer when I was told it was only temporary and I was guaranteed that I could leave whenever I wanted to return to the infantry lines. I thought working in the stores would allow me time to heal fully after the previous year. In a few months I could return to the infantry.

Greatly embellished stories still circulated about what had happened in Lebanon. Each day I found it difficult to face people but as time passed my confidence grew and I regained my strength surrounded by my family, friends and Andy.

My life in Collins Barracks began to settle down. I worked alongside three privates and a company quartermaster, all men, in the stores. They were the funniest most accommodating men I had ever worked with. I looked forward to going to work every morning in the large grey two-storey building, which had a very warm friendly atmosphere. We shared responsibility for all jobs equally, under the guidance of our company quartermaster. I helped manage the barrack laundry account and waste disposal account. I also helped with filing, general office chores, distributing supplies to each unit and stock-taking. They never judged me or asked me what happened in Lebanon; they simply accepted me for who I was. I became one of the "men", working each day and enjoying myself in the process. Once all my work was complete, I was permitted to go training and never once stopped. For a while I found myself feeling happy again. I found an inner peace and contentment in both my professional and private life.

At home, Andy and I began to plan our wedding. We arranged to get married the following summer in Christy's Hotel in Blarney, now known as Blarney Woollen Mills. It was nestled in the picturesque village of Blarney set close to beautiful wooded countryside. I wanted my wedding day to be unforgettable.

I sifted through an endless array of wedding dresses with my sister, as I wanted to find my dream dress. I knew that the minute I set eyes on my perfect dress, I would know it. Finally I found it, in a tiny wedding shop tucked away in an old shopping centre called "The Queen's Old Castle". It was a white satin fitted dress with a mermaid skirt and sweetheart neckline. Platinum embroidery and Swarovski crystal detail covered the bodice, flattering my figure perfectly and minimising any flaws. I had never been happier.

The months passed quickly and Andy was delighted that I had settled down in work and in life. His career was going well; he had completed numerous military courses and was due to start instructing on a potential non-commissioned officers' course. A few members of my own recruit platoon had also been selected to complete the course.

During this period I again began to question my own career. Although I loved the barrack accountant stores I didn't want to stay there forever. I too wanted to be promoted at some stage. I wanted to climb the ranks. I had recovered from my experiences in Lebanon – on the surface at least.

On a beautiful late summer's day, I asked an NCO from the 4th Infantry Battalion, which I was still attached to, about my future. He told me that I had to stay in the stores, but that meant I would never get promoted. I could easily have coasted through the next few years in the stores but I wanted to further my career. It seemed that what had happened in Lebanon held me captive in many people's eyes.

A number of other women had also joined the 4th Infantry Battalion while I had been in Lebanon. I watched as younger soldiers started to pass me out for promotion. I began to feel frustrated.

Andy could not understand why I couldn't be happy with an office job. Cracks began to appear in our relationship.

"You knew when I met you that I wanted to get promoted some day and attempt a selection course," I told him.

"But we're getting married. Why can't you just stay in the stores? Why do you have to try to fight the system again, Valerie?"

"I have as much ambition as you," I replied. "I joined the army just like you. I want to progress. I want to be a soldier. It isn't fair that I'm tucked away in the stores. I did nothing wrong in Lebanon. I want to try and get back to the infantry."

In the end, it became a battle of wills.

On reflection, I realise that Andy simply wanted a wife who would immerse herself in that role. I think that, subconsciously, he was also trying to protect me, to shield me, maybe from myself.

I loved him so much but we began to argue as I saw his career take off when mine was effectively deemed over.

"I cannot go through this again, Valerie. I'm not sure that I can marry you," he told me. "I'm not going through what happened in Lebanon again. You always have to compete with the men. If you don't want to stay in the stores, leave the army – go to college, make something of yourself."

"Except, Andy, I don't want to go to college! I want to go back to the infantry and I want to get promoted, just like you. Why can't you understand that?"

"Just leave the army, Valerie," he told me.

I became extremely disheartened. My military future looked bleaker than ever. My aspirations of becoming a corporal in the infantry seemed lost. I realised that Andy could be right. Was it worth the hassle all over again? Maybe I should just leave?

Andy remained steadfast in his decision: either I stayed in the stores or left the army to return to college. Fighting for a career in the infantry was not an option he entertained. If I had made either of these decisions, then he would still have married me. Thinking back, I think it's reasonable to say that Andy didn't want a wife running around the mountains with a rifle in her hands. He would have preferred a more traditional wife, with a more traditional career.

I felt like I had an angel on each shoulder, pulling me in opposite directions. One voice told me to choose my fiancé, my best friend, my training partner, and ultimately my soul mate. The other voice told me to pursue a military career in the infantry battalion, despite the odds stacked against me. It was my magical Swarovski crystal wedding dress or my 5.56mm Steyr assault rifle. It seemed I couldn't have the two. I mulled over my future for many days, torn in two.

In the end I chose Andy, my dream wedding gown and marriage. What was the point in fighting the system again at the risk of losing my fiancé? So I resigned myself to becoming a wife. I decided to leave the army.

It was a cold blustery day with thick black heavy clouds overhead when I told my father that I wanted to leave the army. He couldn't understand how I felt, begging me to reconsider.

"I am not staying there forever. I wanted to get promoted, to be an active soldier. I didn't join the army to count fish knives all day," I replied.

I handed in an application form to be discharged from the defence forces to my company sergeant and informed my boss in the stores. He urged me to reconsider. I expressed how grateful I was to him for taking me under his wing, but I couldn't stay.

I was on leave before my discharge. Over the following days I pored over job notices in the papers. I still felt totally confused. I even went so far as to apply to work at a leisure centre at the Maryborough House Hotel in Cork. I completed my interview and was offered the position. I started work the following Monday morning, before my discharge, at the elegant hotel set on acres of gardens and woodland.

A few weeks later the phone rang on the reception desk; it was my father. "Valerie, the colonel wants you to come back to work," he said softly. Ironically, this was the same colonel who had initially accepted my application form to serve in the 4th Infantry Battalion.

"I am not going back so that I can be tucked away in the stores forever," I replied.

"It's only temporary, Valerie. In a few months, if you still want to leave the stores, I've been told that you can, but the colonel won't process your application for discharge. He doesn't want you to leave."

I hung up the phone that day and immediately handed in my notice at the hotel, which I had been working in only a few weeks. During the short period of time that I had worked there, I had come to realise that Andy was sacrificing nothing. His career continued to bloom while I began to shrink inside. I was offered a flicker of hope, that I could head back to the infantry, so I grabbed it.

Later that evening, I told Andy of my decision. His reaction stunned me.

"Our relationship is over," he yelled. "I want a wife, not a woman who will compete with me for everything. What was wrong with the leisure centre? You could even have gone to college."

"That's not what I want; I want to continue in the infantry someday," I shouted back defiantly.

I stood frozen in shock as he swept passed me, walking out the front door and out of my life, distancing himself from me as he never had before. Fear spread through me quickly. It felt like barbed wire had gripped my heart, crushing it to pieces.

That weekend I lay in bed, sobbing and wailing. My heart throbbed so much that I was almost hyperventilating. I desperately missed waking up lazily beside Andy, gazing into his strong face. He refused all my calls, my desperate pleas to reconsider. I had fleeting moments where I thought I had made a crazy mistake, but it seemed it was too late. The previous few months, especially Lebanon, had taken their toll on our relationship. I knew I would probably never a love a man with the intensity with which I had loved him. He made me laugh, he made me cry. He was my soul mate. We fit perfectly together. I couldn't eat, I couldn't sleep for weeks. Had I thrown away the love of my life for the army?

I knew I had to let him go despite the pain because if you love somebody you have to set them free. I felt that if he truly loved me, then he might come back, so I lived with hope.

Time passed and I returned home to the delight of my mother and also to the army, where I remained working in the stores. I dreaded the prospect of bumping into Andy each day. It wasn't long before I passed him in the gym. He was pumping weights, sweating profusely in a grey singlet top. He glared in my direction before saying hello. I acted cool and aloof in an attempt to mask my heartbreak, but in the end I failed miserably. Instead I found myself begging him to reconsider once more.

He was adamant. "I want a strong woman, a wife, not someone who cries all the time," he snapped. "I hope you are happy with your career, Valerie, because we are over."

I ran from the gym, gulping down a lump in my throat, my heartbreak quickly turning to anger. I ran lap after lap of the camp field until my muscles burned, begging to stop. When I did eventually stop, I noticed that my muscles were burning a bit too much. I was out of breath, with an unusually hot sticky sweat pouring from my forehead. I was extremely fit and thought it was unusual for me to be so exhausted.

It suddenly dawned on me that while I had been nursing my broken heart, I had overlooked the fact that I hadn't had a period in some time.

19

Becoming a Mother

The following afternoon I stared teary-eyed as three consecutive pregnancy tests turned positive. I had been feeling a little tired in the mornings but never suspected that I was pregnant. I spent the next few hours oscillating between total despair and happiness.

I texted Andy to say I needed to speak with him. Later that day he approached me at the office in the barrack accountant stores. I assumed he would reject me and my unborn child. I finally built up the courage to tell him shakily, but a worried expression flashed across his face. I bowed my head, waiting for his reaction, but there was none – instead he arranged to meet me later that evening. For the next few hours the sickening fear that he may not want us never left me.

I sat in a dimly lit corner of a glamorous bar waiting for him to appear. I was so scared, knowing that I was pregnant, but I was also unexpectedly happy. I knew that my unborn baby was precious to me and I accepted that, no matter what Andy would say, I was going to raise my child. I made sure that I looked attractive, trying to project an image of togetherness, being in control, making a huge effort with my appearance.

I hadn't noticed that Andy was standing at the long gleaming bar until he turned towards me. Suddenly he was sitting next to me, holding my hand and rubbing my cheek. Rather than add to my worries, he gently eased them away.

"You look really nice, Valerie. Pregnancy suits you," he whispered.

He gently placed a hand on my stomach as I twitched in my seat. A smile eased across my face; it had felt so long since he had held me. I wondered if this was just a false intimacy. Would he leave me again? He displayed an understanding that took me by surprise, assuring me that he would stand by me and our unborn baby. Only the previous day I had a broken heart. Now I was carrying his child and we were planning our future. We decided to keep our news a secret until I was three months gone.

A few days later I started to bleed quite heavily at my parents' house. Of course, I had to tell them of my pregnancy then. Although they were a bit upset, they gave me their full support.

My father brought me to a local maternity hospital. On arrival at the hospital, the bleeding had intensified, and was even showing through my clothes. I almost miscarried, but thankfully the bleeding stopped and all seemed fine. However, I had some horrible experiences at that hospital, and decided to change to a different hospital.

My sister had given birth to her second child in the Bon Secours Hospital under a very kind gynaecologist. It was a private hospital which was quite expensive but I had my own private health insurance and some savings. My sister immediately booked me under her gynaecologist in light of what had happened at the other hospital. Two weeks later I arrived in the Bon Secours bleeding again, but this time I received immediate care. My doctor told me to rest for the next few weeks, reassuring me that my baby was fine.

I returned to work two weeks later. The fact that I had chosen to have my baby in the same hospital as female officers was not liked. The army dentist congratulated me and gave me a few tips on pregnancy, as she herself was a recent mother. She didn't seem the slightest bit disgruntled that a female private soldier had the same gynaecologist as her. I was grateful for her tips.

Despite the attitude towards my rank and class giving birth in the same hospital as female officers, the army is a fantastic job to have whilst pregnant. I was placed on light duties for the remainder of my pregnancy. My boss was also very accommodating towards me. As my bump grew at speed, so did my appetite. I would arrive in work laden down with a big bag of food each day.

"Valerie, are you moving in? You have enough food there for a week," the guys would joke. "You're only feeding two, not the whole barracks." I was embarrassed at first but they were very supportive, showing concern for both me and the baby as I embraced pregnancy wholeheartedly.

Andy and I had decided to rent an apartment in Cork city in preparation for the impending birth. Andy was especially sensitive towards my weight gain. He would dash to the nearest shop whenever I required more sweets and chocolate Magnums, ignoring the fact that I had been gaining a bit too much weight. He was thrilled that I was no longer obsessed with my figure. I realised that he loved me no matter what I looked like, which was a good thing considering my belly was covered in stretch marks.

Whilst pregnant I continued to study, completing another level on my fitness instructor's course, exercise and fitness for kids and teenagers, with the NCEF (National Certificate in Exercise and Fitness) in Limerick University. I always had to have my head stuck in a book; I just loved learning.

The day finally came when my green army combat pants refused to fit me anymore. I certainly could not bend over to tie the laces of my boots. A single tailor in Dublin made the maternity uniforms for all pregnant women in the defence forces and there was a waiting list. In the interim I had to wear civilian clothes. There were no fancy maternity shops in those days, and certainly no online stores. I had to make do with plain loose-fitting size 22 polo shirts from Dunnes Stores as my weight ballooned.

Finally the tailor phoned. He was ready to measure me but I was seven months pregnant at that stage. He wanted me to take the train to Dublin to be fitted, but it would take a month to arrive. I told him that I expected to be on maternity leave at that stage. He was full of apologies but I was secretly thrilled. The military maternity smock consisted of a mass of green itchy fabric which resembled an army tent.

There were days when I felt so fat that I struggled to haul my body up the stairs to the office. I certainly did not have a designer bump; mine was massive. As lunchtime approached each day I could barely keep my eyelids open from the extra weight my body was carrying. During lunch I often dozed off on a couch the guys had brought into our recreational area.

At home Andy and I decided to buy our first house in anticipation of the impending birth. We were so young with little money, but we had the security of our jobs. Having a job in the defence forces enabled us to acquire our very first, albeit small, mortgage. I was horrified when I found one of the only houses we could afford. The moment Andy turned the key in the front door, a foul stench overpowered me. I looked around the house in total disgust at the layers of filth in each room. "There is no way I am moving into this house," I told him.

Then a neighbour arrived and ushered us into his own home, which was identical in structure. I realised that if we gutted the house it had potential. We signed the papers but couldn't move in for a month until our families collectively helped us to gut and furnish the entire house.

I had a loving, attentive fiancé, a new home, which was surprisingly large once cleaned, painted and gutted, and I was awaiting the birth of my first child. I couldn't have been happier. My aunt offered to take care of my baby when I returned to work after my maternity leave. I naïvely assumed that I could easily fit a child into my life and career. I knew that it may have been a little unusual to have a mother who was a soldier but I felt competent that I could cope with a newborn baby and a life in the defence forces. I still secretly harboured ambitions to return to the infantry, but decided to conceal this from Andy, fearing another argument. We had also put our wedding on hold since the break-up.

During the brief period of our break-up, Andy had arranged to travel to Kenya and Tanzania to climb Mount Kilimanjaro for charity. While he was away, I busied myself in our new home, painting and decorating. I was indeed nesting. One morning shortly after he returned home, I felt tightenings around my stomach.

"You are not due for two weeks, Valerie. You couldn't be in labour," Andy said snoozily.

"Well, according to the book, Andy, I *am* in labour," I replied.

Andy tried to convince me that I was being over-dramatic. My contractions were eleven minutes apart, but he still refused to accept that I was in labour. At six minutes apart, I phoned my sister. The tightenings and twinges had increased in frequency and intensity. "Go to the hospital immediately," she said.

Throughout our journey to the hospital Andy repeatedly pulled the car over because my contractions were so intense. Women in my family had often given birth quickly, but I assumed that because it was my first pregnancy it would take a very long time. I finally arrived at the Bon Secours, where I immediately asked for an epidural to relieve the pain.

"Why didn't you come sooner?" asked the nurse. Andy glanced away sheepishly.

A few hours later I gave birth to a healthy baby boy with a thick mop of jet black hair. Andy erupted in a flood of tears.

My newborn son mesmerised me. I was overwhelmed, tears welling up in my eyes. He was so precious, looking dark and mysterious; not in the least bit like me. I held him in my arms and stared at his tiny delicate little fingers, his soft skin resting gently against my chest. My heart melted when I held him. He was so adorably gorgeous, with sallow skin and a cute button nose. I snuggled him in closely, gently cupping his head, in awe that he was mine.

Andy stroked my hair, kissed me softly on the forehead and told me that he loved me. I had never felt so close to him, so secure. We were a family now.

Over the coming weeks, Andy showered us both with love and affection, playing the perfect father. My friends were still out clubbing and partying, but I was perfectly content to stay at home and be a mother. A steady stream of visitors filtered through our home, swooning over little Alex. We were so happy.

20

Back in the Fray

I returned to work three months after Alex was born. I had to complete my fitness test, which involved running two miles, performing push-ups and sit-ups and a route march wearing full combat battle gear.

I had anticipated this in advance and had been training since Alex was six weeks old. Unfortunately, my abdomen muscles were still not in the shape they had been prior to my pregnancy. I had also embarked on a healthy diet, following the Weight-Watchers plan in an effort to shift the four and a half stone I had gained whilst pregnant. I slowly regained my shape but was never quite the same again.

I went ahead with my fitness test. I tore my lower abdominal muscles during the sit-ups. A violent pain shot through me as I struggled to complete them. I ran the two miles around the camp field in agonising pain but refused to stop until I had passed it.

I approached my old company sergeant and asked him if I could return to the lines with the men. He instantly said that I could. I was ecstatic. Andy for now didn't seem overly concerned as he continued to play the doting father to our son.

For the next few months I was placed with a recruit platoon with many of the men whom I had trained alongside. They were by now corporals while I was still a private. I took care of the entire platoon's administration and was appointed the female liaison for the female recruits. Each day I completed the recruits' physical training with them, including all of the battle physical training.

In the back of my mind I knew that an NCOs' course was looming. I saw this as the perfect training ground for my application. The course sergeant and platoon officer both took me under their wings as I bombarded them with questions on the responsibilities of an NCO. I borrowed Andy's military notes on his own NCOs' course, which I studied daily.

During lunch periods at work I often drew different weapons from the stores. Andy taught me how to instruct on each weapon expertly. I had become almost obsessed with weapons and everything military. I had one goal in mind. I didn't just want to complete the NCOs' course; I wanted to receive the award for "Best Overall Soldier". A woman had never received it before. I was determined to prove that a woman could perform as well as a man in a tactical environment.

I had tried so hard to get past what had happened in Lebanon but it had affected me more than I was willing to admit. Sometimes at night my eyes flashed open from a dream where I was back there, reliving the hurt, pain and humiliation. I wanted to prove them wrong. I wanted to prove that I could be as good, given the same opportunity, as any of them.

Andy was initially highly supportive. We shared responsibility for our home and our newborn son equally. I loved being a mother. I would wake each morning to find little Alex snuggled between the two of us. There were days when I felt extremely guilty leaving him, but the army was also my life.

I executed my days with military precision, assuming that this was born out of my military training. Later in life I realised that this is a necessity in every working mother's life, not just army mothers. I hung lists on a large notice board in my kitchen. Bottles, nappies, spare clothes, gas bill – all received a tick before I headed out the front door laden down with bags, a buggy and often my combat equipment for an exercise that day. I was often extremely exhausted in work.

Alex had colic, sometimes staying awake crying most of the night. On one particular occasion I picked him up at nine in the morning from my aunt's house after completing a twenty-four-hour duty. At eleven o'clock that evening, I was still holding him in my arms, still wearing my green camouflage army uniform. I phoned my mother out of sheer desperation. She took Alex for the remainder of the night, allowing me finally to sleep after forty hours of sleep deprivation. Andy was away on a course at the time. He was always away completing a range of military courses – sniper courses, weapons courses, rock-climbing courses, to name but a few.

I desperately tried to juggle motherhood with my commitments to the defence forces but ultimately it took its toll on my body, and on my relationship with my son and my fiancé. I was expected to get on with things at work because I was a soldier. All of us female soldiers were. No concessions were made. If we wanted to be treated equally, we had to perform in exactly the same manner as the men. Motherhood never came into the equation.

Years later I distinctly remember an incident that took place involving another woman in the barracks. Our new contracts stipulated that we had to serve overseas regularly in order to have them renewed and to receive an army pension upon retirement. This woman was a single mother without a support network. She was told to put her child into foster care in order to travel overseas. She found even the suggestion of putting her child into foster care horrifying. Luckily she resolved the situation, but with a great deal of difficulty.

In other armies there are facilities for military mothers and fathers; the US and the UK defence forces have facilities such as crèches, schools, support networks, doctors and hospitals, knowing that behind every soldier lies a family. In the Irish army, the only facility in place is at the Curragh in County Kildare, where a doctor is available for families, but numerous unsuccessful attempts have been made to close even this facility. Therefore at times it was extremely tough for both mothers and fathers within the defence forces.

I assumed that I could have it all: motherhood, a fiancé and a career. I often left my young son at home for weeks at a time in the care of family members. A soldier's mentality is different to a civilian's mentality. As time went by I began to see it as normal, feeling less guilt. Other mothers can't even leave their children for a night without overwhelming feelings of guilt. I was becoming a hardened soldier, colder, distant, often devoid of emotion.

My relationship with Andy's mother became very strained. She watched in disbelief as my child was passed between her, my own mother and my aunt.

There are some things in my life that I can never change but if I could go back to that point I would never have put my career before my child and Andy. It wasn't worth it, but I was young and ignorant of life. I was unaware of the consequences of my actions. I was unaware that while I was chasing my dream, there was always going to be another woman only too happy to fill my shoes in my absence.

My mind and body went into autopilot. At night I made bottles and fed my baby; while during the day, I tabbed over mountains with the recruit platoon, carrying packs weighing my own body weight, a rifle and helmet. I had to keep up with the men; falling behind was not an option. I chased the dream blindly without regard for my family, not knowing that it would ultimately nearly destroy me. I was often in extreme pain as my backpack weighed me down, but I forced myself to push my body past its limits.

I was given an opportunity to take sections of men on long- and short-range patrols, acting as a 2 I/C (second-in-command) on the patrols. I also stood observing on the sidelines, being taught how to perfect contact drills with four-man teams. I was preparing wholeheartedly for the upcoming preliminaries for the potential NCOs' course. We had to complete a two-week prelim course in the 4th Infantry Battalion, which is traditionally much tougher than the actual NCOs' course in the training depot. This is why members of 4th Infantry Battalion usually top the course. There were twelve places available and over twenty-four applicants. The top twelve were going to be chosen.

I was pitted against some of the finest soldiers within the 4th Infantry Battalion. Some were what I call mountain goats – experienced climbers. I knew these men would perform outstandingly during the ground tactical testing phase. If you drop your backpack during the prelims or fall too far behind, you are dropped immediately. So I pushed myself hard every day when training.

Andy trained me in the woods and mountain ranges for the tactical period of testing. Wearing full battle gear, we ran for miles around the dense woods surrounding our home in Midleton. He barked out questions at me on field craft, judging distance, section and platoon in attacks. He roared at me, pushing me to my limits mentally and physically. My legs felt heavy, refusing to move. Obviously civilians who passed us thought we were mad but I didn't care. I would scream at Andy to stop but he refused.

"If you think this is bad, wait until you hit the ground phase. The prelims are tough; you are going to be beasted like you have never been before," he would yell. "This is what you wanted – do you want it or are you going to give up? I'm not your fiancé in the woods or mountains, Valerie. I'm training you – you either want it or you don't. The weak are weeded out – are you weak?"

There were days when I thought I'd drop, it was so incredibly tough, but in the end I was ready. I ensured that I was more prepared than anyone else. During the weekends I found my motivation from training videos. Andy had acquired a selection of videos on military units and conflicts from around the globe. As clichéd as it sounds, I watched *GI Jane* over and over again. At least she was a woman I could relate to.

The day arrived for my preliminaries and I must admit I was scared. There were two other women on the course, one of whom I had trained with. The two of us bonded instantly. Each day I was tested on a different aspect of military training. I was expected to give lessons on foot drill and different weapons. I had studied Andy's notes and with his help practised at home. I often gave "lessons" to young Alex in our kitchen or bedroom. I would pretend that he was my class, which he found quite amusing.

By now our son was almost a year old, a toddler. While in pursuit of my dream, I had missed his first steps and his first word. I didn't even know that his favourite toy was a football.

Of course, I adored him, putting him to bed, bringing him to my aunt's. But I was away from him for weeks on end, and this was not the mother he needed. It still pains me to think how much I left him behind. From time to time I watch videos of him recorded by Andy's mother. In them he plays quietly with a football. In one, he is looking out a window a few times silently, a blank expression etched on his tiny little face. Maybe he was looking for me to come home? This hurts me deeply. I can never replace the memories which I have lost and when I'm alone I cry when I watch these videos. How could I have been so stupid?

Each day on the prelims we were taken on ten-kilometre marches or runs. My pack often weighed eighty pounds, in addition to my helmet and rifle. My petite frame wasn't designed for it but I was still determined to do it. The physical pain was often unbearable so I resorted to painkillers to prop me up, crushing them in my mouth before and during marches. I kept them hidden in my combat trousers, often swallowing them midway through a march when I thought my lower back was going to snap in two from the pressure and violent pain which seared across it.

The ground phase was particularly agonising. I was meticulous about my administration in the field, remembering the rule: if you pack it, you carry it. We moved in tactical formation, crossing the Galtee Mountains, which in itself was a challenge.

It took roughly thirteen hours to reach our patrol harbour. At the steepest climb I was handed the general purpose machine gun, which is the main firepower of a section, weighing twenty-four pounds, with a 200-round belt weighing twelve pounds. We were taking it in turns to carry it. Between the pressure on my back and now on my chest, I couldn't breathe. My whole chest felt like it was caving in. We were surrounded by a dense fog with a heavy mist having saturated my rain gear. I couldn't move.

"Drop it! Drop it if you can't handle it!" roared the instructors.

This was their job; how could I be expected to be a leader of men if I couldn't even keep up? How would I lead a section of men across the mountains, if I couldn't carry my own weight?

The rest of the platoon vanished into the fog while an instructor continued to roar in my face, "Give me the weapon; give me your backpack! You have one more minute to move or you are gone, do you hear me?"

Another instructor appeared. "Leave her alone; give her back a rifle," he said.

"No fucking way! All the men carried it; she has to carry it. Do you want to be here, Sheehan, or are you going to give me the weapon and your pack?" he barked.

He was right to do what he did. All the men had carried it; I was last during this particular climb. I felt dizzy, thinking I was going to faint. For a few moments time seemed to stand still, but I kept going. Five minutes later, they ordered me to hand over the machine gun. I was a little startled. Did this mean I was being taken off the exercise?

An instructor approached me. "Well done, Private Sheehan," he said, half-smiling. "We had to do that, to see if you would break – you didn't. Well done." This boosted me for the remainder of our trek.

That evening we set up our patrol harbour in dense young forest, which proved to be very troublesome; in fact, one soldier nearly lost an eye from a whack of a branch. Over the next two days, I got little sleep, completing various patrols and attacks on the enemy, played by our instructors.

A few soldiers fell by the sidelines, but many of us hung in there. My knees were red raw from the contact drills and from falling over during the long patrols. My feet were covered in blisters and my back in boils. I had packed foot powder in a clear zip-lock bag to cool and bathe my feet whenever I could. I managed to drain the blisters using a needle, which I sterilised with a lighter. Andy had taught me many of my newfound survival skills, which made my life easier on the ground. Even though I was suffering from sleep deprivation, I pulled myself through.

At the very end of the exercise we were marched again for hours to our pick-up point. I could barely keep my eyes open but morale was high amongst those who had survived. The trucks were late arriving, so we had to perform more contact drills and rifle physical training. It had become considerably warm and every soldier's best friends, midges, were whizzing feverishly around the dense forest where we were due to be collected. We all wore face nets to protect ourselves from bites, which can be very irritating.

"Gas, gas, gas!" screamed an instructor. This was the signal to put on our gas masks in the event of a chemical attack. I scrambled for mine, but struggled to fit it correctly. As a result, my face, neck and head were covered in bites.

I arrived in Collins Barracks a few hours later, barely able to walk. I stood in the shower, covered in bruises, blisters and bites, but I had completed the prelims, being placed fourth. I was thrilled, as this meant I was selected to undergo the NCOs' course.

Over the coming days I became very weak. I had a thumping headache and my back was in agony. Each evening I lay in a haze on my couch while Alex played at my feet.

"Andy, I think something's wrong. I'm so dizzy and my head hurts so much," I said.

"Valerie, I have to do everything – wash the dishes, the clothes. We are both soldiers; get over it," he said, laughing.

"No, my head is thumping – really, I think there is something wrong."

A few days later I reported to the doctor. My blood pressure was 80/40.

"That's extremely low. Stand up and down a few times until it goes up," said the doctor.

It finally went up to 90/50. "That's better. When was your last period?" asked the doctor.

"I'm having it at the moment," I replied.

The doctor concluded that I was merely exhausted, having completed the prelims course and also because I was having my period.

I was placed on seventy-two hours of light duties. I was sent on a work detail for two days lifting lockers up and down three flights of stairs. I became so exhausted that on a few occasions I thought I was going to collapse. That Friday I finally did collapse in Andy's locker room.

When Andy realised how sick I was, he rushed me to the accident and emergency department of the Mercy Hospital where my parents were already waiting. I was admitted immediately and placed in a single room. I couldn't lift my arms or walk to the toilet. The pain in my head was blinding. A series of tests was performed, which all came back negative. I was told that I had some kind of virus, probably picked up on the exercise.

At the end of the first week I was given an EEG, recording the electrical activity of the brain. Wires were attached to my head and a light flashed into my eyes which really hurt. I had to ask for it to be stopped. Midway through the procedure, the technician stopped talking to me. I asked him for the results but he said he couldn't give them to me. However, I knew that he had told other patients that their results were clear. I was filled with fear.

Shortly afterwards a team of doctors met me in my room. The consultant spoke.

"An abnormality has shown up in your EEG. There is a slowing of the brainwaves, indicating one of three things because of where it is."

"What three things?"

"Either a tumour, epilepsy or the viral infection encephalitis, which causes swelling in the brain," he responded. "We have to keep you in for further tests."

I was left alone in shock with only my thoughts. When I told Andy, he was shocked, as were my whole family. I sank into the depths of despair when Andy visited me with Alex, who crawled all over me in bed and lay beside me watching videos. Slowly I began to feel better and my strength returned but a dull ache still remained in my head.

The next week I was given an MRI scan, which returned clear. The consultant informed me that he suspected I had viral encephalitis. He said I was extremely lucky to have escaped relatively unscathed, as many people suffer permanent disabilities. I was told I had contracted the tail-end of the virus and, because I was so fit, my body was able to fight it. My family and Andy were relieved, not having told me how serious encephalitis was.

When I returned to work, the army doctor refused to pass me medically fit for the NCOs' course. I pleaded but was refused. "The only way that I can pass you fit is if the consultant gives you the all-clear. You will have to get me a letter," said the doctor.

That is exactly what I did. I told the consultant that the NCOs' course was merely an administration course with no physical exercise whatsoever. He was a civilian, not a military doctor, so had no idea what an NCOs' course actually entailed. I certainly didn't inform him that it was going to be one of the most physically demanding courses I had yet to do. He saw no problem with me completing an administration course and passed me fit.

The doctor in the barracks was flabbergasted, but I had my letter so I had to be passed fit. The doctor couldn't override the consultant's decision. For a while afterwards, a dull ache remained in my head but I was determined to carry on. My family were horrified when I told them I was returning to work in order to complete the NCOs' course. They were genuinely worried for my health but I wouldn't listen. I still went ahead at full speed with my dream – with devastating consequences for my relationship with Andy.

21

Promotion

Before I started the NCOs' course I had to complete another exercise. We spent a month in the Glen of Imaal performing a series of gruelling exercises. Yet again we tabbed over mountains for days in hazardous conditions. At that point I was swallowing painkillers like sweets to pull me through each climb as my packs were so heavy. To prop me up I also drank the fast-release energy drink "Viper". The treks often started at dusk, lasting through the entire night, moving tactically cross-country on high ground. I remember one particular night when we marched for hours over rough rocky terrain in the torrential rain, over steep hills, deep gullies and across rivers in the shivering cold.

Back at the military barracks in the Glen of Imaal, something quite unexpected happened. The old facilities in that camp were appalling. Floorboards were missing, mattresses were damp, mould hung from the walls – and scabies broke out, spreading quickly through the ranks. On parade, the soldiers couldn't stop scratching themselves. Everyone knew it was scabies; we were all given the appropriate powder and medication but informed we were imagining it. We lined up outside the shower blocks and were ticked off as we entered and exited. We had to pack all the clothes we had worn in black refuse sacks and were only allowed to wear unused items of clothing. Some refused for a period to complete the exercise and were threatened with being charged.

Photographs of our bleak and filthy facilities in camp were leaked to the newspapers, which proved to be very embarrassing to the defence forces. Part of the camp had been renovated but most shower blocks and accommodation were below even the most basic human standards. After the photographs were leaked, we were all permitted to use the officers' shower facilities, which had warm water and weren't entrenched in rust and mounds of filth.

During the long summer evenings I ran the roads with some of my female friends. We were of the same mindset – no longer civilians but soldiers. I had forged quite a close bond with a few of them, including Amelia and another girl, Chloe. We swapped stories on love, children and all things military. On reflection, I think we all lived in a military bubble, completely desensitised from civilian life. But what was important then was that I was one of them; at least with them I felt a sense of belonging.

At home, Andy cared for our son. He sacrificed a trip to East Timor with the battalion so that I could complete the potential non-commissioned officers' course, but he really wanted to go. As a result, our relationship was becoming very strained. He was often away completing courses, as was I. We only saw each other at weekends. Alex stayed with either my parents or Andy's parents in the evenings and at my aunt's house during the day.

Soon afterwards I arrived at the Southern Brigade Training Centre to commence my NCOs' course. I had to complete another three days of testing in order to qualify for the course. I began the by-now familiar phase with a general test on military knowledge and map reading. A few applicants failed this stage of testing and were immediately returned to their unit. My friend Rebecca and I passed this stage, so we started the fourth potential NCOs' course in the Brigade Training Centre. There were forty-seven students, including twelve from the 4th Infantry Battalion, while the rest were drawn from different units in the Southern Command of the Irish defence forces.

I started my days at six o'clock, often not going to bed until two or three the following morning because of the number of military assignments I received. Therefore I temporarily moved into the barracks, as did the majority of the platoon. If I was lucky I was able to get to bed at midnight, but that was a rarity mid-week.

Every morning we stood on parade for our inspection. The instructors would eyeball us, berating us if our uniforms were not starched and ironed to perfection. Boots had to be painstakingly spit-polished for hours until they appeared almost glass-like. I had my own little secret for my boots. I bought floor polish in Dunnes

Stores and laced my boots with it. Once they were polished lightly, my black boots gleamed and sparkled, giving the impression that I had been up half the night spit-polishing them.

Each day a student was nominated as orderly sergeant. When it was my turn, I called the platoon of forty-seven soldiers on parade, lined up in three ranks. I then opened the three ranks of the platoon before dressing each of them off in a straight line. I marched them briskly from lesson to lesson. We had to learn how to instruct soldiers on foot drill and arms drill. I was often pulled aside and made to roar out orders to another section of men across the large barrack square. I found it highly embarrassing in the beginning but I found my voice in the end. For hours we stood in the freezing cold, marching around the square either in section or platoon formation. It was exhausting and my knees became inflamed from the constant pounding.

In the afternoons we usually completed battle physical training wearing thirty-pound packs, rifles and helmets. We were often taken out running on the long winding country roads, into fields, and dragged through icy cold rocky streams in preparation for the ground phase. My legs, knees and elbows were constantly scraped and bleeding, leaving me wincing in pain.

Shortly afterwards we would commence weapons training. I had studied for months in advance and by now was coasting through the course. We received a mark for each module of training, including foot drill. At the end of the course all marks would be summed up, determining

who would receive the award for "Best Overall Soldier".
I was determined to get it.

I passed my first round of testing with flying colours and
was commended on my skill. Over the coming weeks I went
through the same procedure for arms drill, method of
instruction, map reading, leadership, field craft, military law,
first aid, administration, signals, organisation of the infantry
battalions, barrack duties, military symbols and weapons.
For each test I studied for hours, often exhausted, wearing ice
packs on my knees in the confines of my room. This
combined with gruelling physical training every day left me
completely shattered. I again resorted to painkillers to numb
the pain in my back, shoulders and knees.

I scored highly in each test and was placed sixth as we
headed into the tactical phase of training. I was climbing
steadily but consistently. Sometimes the instructors would
drag me out in front of other soldiers, saying, "Look at
her! She can do it – she's had a baby and she's tiny, yet she
can do it. Why can't you?" I outran many of the men and
I performed better academically in the classroom.

A few members of my platoon therefore hatched a plan
to fix me once and for all. Each Friday afternoon we
completed either a route march or battle physical training.
Usually I was soaked to the skin, having crawled on my
hands and knees through mucky cold streams. I would be
covered in muck and camouflage cream and would head to
the showering block before Andy collected me with Alex. We
had been warned never to leave barracks without showering.

One Friday shortly before the tactical phase, we had
been dragged through freezing streams and wet, boggy

fields, crawling and running for miles wearing our customary thirty-pound packs. When I arrived in the barracks, Andy was waiting with Alex, who was crying hysterically. He had a bug and was teething. His nappy was dirty and he refused to stop crying. Andy begged me to leave before I showered, as we were headed for my mother's house, a mere five-minute drive from the barracks. Seeing Alex in such a distressed state, I left without showering and headed to my mother's house.

I was spotted leaving the barracks by a member of my platoon. A complaint was made about my personal hygiene, alleging that I permanently smelled of sweat, I rarely showered and I rarely washed my uniforms.

A week later I was pulled from the trucks as we were about to depart for Kilworth. It is the single most embarrassing thing that has ever happened to me. I was told that my personal hygiene was disgraceful. I was going to be checked for smells of sweat on a regular basis. If I smelt of sweat or my uniforms were dirty, I was going to be paraded in the hospital, showered and powdered. From there I would receive a full selection of shower gels, powders and other items.

I tried in vain to explain what had happened that day with Alex, and that upon arriving at my mother's house she had washed my clothes while I showered. I was standing to attention, trying to absorb what was happening. I had showered at least twice a day. I had a wardrobe full of uniforms that my mother and Andy washed. I never wore the same uniform two days in a row. I was so meticulous about my equipment that I even washed my gas mask in the washing machine. The instructors could never find a single trace of dirt on it, even with a cotton bud.

I returned to my room mortified, refusing to go on the exercise. I told a corporal that I was returning to unit but the NCO urged me to reconsider. Eventually I was persuaded to go back to the trucks.

Later that evening Rebecca pulled me aside. An NCO had asked her if I showered or if I smelled badly. If she wanted a single room away from me, he said, he would accommodate her. "She does shower, she does not smell and no, I do not want a room away from her," she replied.

Most people on the course were appalled at my treatment. That evening I sat in a lecture feeling embarrassed, thinking that no job was worth such treatment. During a cigarette break I wandered down to the back fields of Kilworth camp to gather my thoughts. I phoned my family and Andy on my mobile to ask for their advice. Meanwhile the instructors had been searching for me but I'd had enough. I decided to pack my bags and take a taxi ride home to Cork. On returning to camp I was advised not to take a taxi but to apply in writing to return to unit, which I did. Moments later an officer asked me to withdraw my application, ensuring that it would never happen again, which I was extremely grateful for. Thankfully that was the end of the incident and things returned to normal.

Rebecca and I had bonded well, encouraging and motivating each other daily. Over the next two weeks we performed section-in-attacks all day long, running late into the evening. We seemed to spend most of our time on our bellies or, as the army calls it, "on the belt buckle", crawling through fields, over ditches and across icy cold streams, where we constantly smacked our knees and elbows off the hard rocks. Thorns often became embedded into our hands. Our faces would turn blue but we just kept going.

Each of us had to lead a section-in-attack as part of our testing. We had practised for days and our hands and knees were raw and swollen. The testing went on for three days and some of the students failed. We had been told in our leadership classes that a leader has the ability to drive or influence others towards achieving a certain goal with their willing co-operation. Fortunately, my section all performed outstandingly for each other, giving everyone a chance at success. Each of us was combat-fit and ready.

My instructors approached me. "Are you ready, Sheehan?"

"Yeah, I think I'll be okay," I replied.

"You know what you are doing; stick to the orders, stay focused and zone out the testing board."

They slapped me on the back while I gulped down my nerves. I had my war paint on; I was ready.

While I received my orders for my own section-in-attack from the platoon commander, my 2 I/C moved the section into a good position to protect us from view and fire. I gave my orders, stipulating the situation, mission, execution, service support, command and signals. I kept a calm, level head as I gave the orders. My section crossed the green fields surrounding Kilworth camp under my command, rifles at the ready, butts embedded in our shoulders, staring through the optical lenses in search of the enemy. Moments later we came under fire.

"Contact front, contact front!" I roared, signalling for my section to take cover behind an embankment.

The most difficult aspect of a section-in-attack is locating the enemy's exact position. We immediately put down suppressive fire, firing hundreds of rounds at the enemy. I emptied my full magazine quickly and clipped on another one, continually roaring out orders to my section from behind the embankment. We had to win the fire-fight, putting down suppressive fire, pinning down and isolating the enemy. Three directing staff stood over me, examining every aspect of the attack. I zoned them out in order to perform confidently.

I searched the ground for the best position from which to launch the assault. I then issued a frago (fragmentary order) to the section before moving the manoeuvre group up the flank to the final assault line. We were closing in to destroy the enemy. Our fire support group (FSG) watched, giving covering fire using the general purpose machine gun. I dropped a soldier off into the position of flank security to cover the right-hand side and another soldier into the position of depth security, which also provided support as we moved up the flank along a ditch line. We crawled on our hands and knees, attempting to stay as low as possible to evade detection. I had my whistle ready, the signal to the FSG to lift its fire. From the final assault line (FAL) the lead scout and I had to crawl up and throw a thunder flash (pyrotechnic) into the enemy position. After the explosion we then fired a full magazine each to ensure the enemy had been destroyed. Reorganisation and consolidation followed quickly.

Adrenaline rushed through my body. It was over and I had passed a major test.

The following week my platoon was headed to the gas chamber wearing full nuclear biological chemical (NBC) gear, including the dreaded gas mask. When the instructors called "Gas, gas, gas", we had to go down on one knee, remove our helmets, cease to breathe, close our eyes, place our gas masks on and secure them properly. Each of us shouted, "Gas, gas, gas", pulling up our hoods and securing our straps. This was the drill in the event of a chemical attack. Inside, the CS tablets were lit.

Of course, a soldier still has to eat during a chemical attack so each of us was handed a hard-boiled sweet inside the gas chamber. Each soldier quickly lifted their gas mask and swallowed the sweet. Instead, I was handed a raw egg. "Come on, eat it," snapped the NCO. I was a little startled but to my relief an instructor grabbed it from me, cracking it open and swallowing it quickly. "That's how it's done, Sheehan," he said, winking at me when the other NCO turned his back. He had saved me from the raw egg and I was handed a sweet like the others.

On other occasions, that same instructor would pull me aside. "I was told to give you a bottling, so just pretend – pretend I am giving out to you," he would say. I had a very good relationship with all the instructors, so I played the game well.

We completed two phases of tactical training during the NCOs' course, each of which lasted two weeks. On one particular night I had a bad fall from a high ditch, banging my lower back on a jagged rock during a downpour. I had to be taken away in an ambulance. However, I refused to go sick off the ground and was back with the course shortly afterwards.

During the second phase of tactical training on our "dig-in", I thought I was going to collapse from exhaustion on a number of occasions. The hillside position we occupied was desolate, raging winds blowing across the fields. In our slit trench, myself and two other students lay closely beside each other in an effort to stay warm, as hypothermia was a constant threat. At one point I could no longer feel any sensation in my feet. I took my boots off a few times, convinced that my socks were soaking, but they were perfectly dry. My feet were frozen to the point where they felt like ice blocks.

"That's it, I am not going to allow you to go down," said my buddy. "Get up!" he yelled.

"I can't, I'm freezing, and I can't feel my legs anymore," I said meekly.

He pulled me up by sheer force from our trench and dragged me out onto the cold, dark field. From there he pulled me around the field, chanting "a-ring a-ring a-rosy", until my sides hurt from laughing and my body regained some heat. In nearby trenches we could hear people laughing as they watched through their night vision equipment but under the cover of darkness the instructors never spotted us. Shortly afterwards they roared "bug out", initiating our withdrawal from the trenches in our dig-in site.

Next we had to complete what later became an infamous ambush – for all the wrong reasons. We left our trenches and tabbed for hours over boggy rough terrain, where the wind howled and snapped at our faces. Rain whipped down on top of us and we were all truly exhausted. At one point, a friend of mine said, "If you ask me how long more again, I'm going to knock you out with this machine gun." We both burst out laughing. Whingeing and moaning is something every soldier succumbs to and I was no exception.

A heavy fog limited our patrol's visibility and we kept our heads bowed to protect our faces from the howling winds. Finally, under the cover of darkness at around 3.00 in the morning, we moved into an unsecured area to prepare an ambush on an enemy due in the location the following morning. We got into our ambush position and prepared for the passing of the enemy patrol. Because we were all suffering from sleep deprivation, we cut a few corners. The student commander split the platoon in two and each section was placed on opposite sides of the ambush site, in complete contradiction to all ambush procedures. He was supposed to place stop groups on the approaches and in between two sections were supposed to cover the killing area.

The stop group's mission was to give us early warning of enemy approach and also to kill all enemy that escaped from the main killing area. With the patrol split in two, on opposite sides of the killing area, we would end up killing each other in what is called a "blue-on-blue". (Luckily, blank rounds are used in these exercises!) We were placed in position on waterlogged ground but decided the enemy probably wouldn't make an appearance until dawn, so we all took out our bivy bags and kit mats. Bivy bags are used outside sleeping bags for protection, as they are waterproof and very warm. For extra warmth we covered the bivy bags with large lush green plants and long reeds, which we pulled from the soggy ground. I was exhausted but warm. As soldiers we all had the ability to fall asleep anywhere, including on the side of a hill, against strong winds in the rain. Before long the whole platoon snuggled down and drifted off into a deep sleep, sounds of heavy snoring filling the valley.

We were jolted from our cosy sleep a few hours later by the sounds of gunfire blazing in our direction, echoing across the valley from the other section opposite us. We quickly scrambled from our bivy bags. Some even had their boots off. I noticed a machine gun tumbling down the hill with a private, wearing socks but no boots, in hot pursuit. It was a good few moments before we returned fire. The enemy – our instructors – had actually walked through the killing area a number of times while the whole platoon lay in a deep sleep.

The instructors were simply flabbergasted. Never in all their years had a platoon performed the way we did on an ambush. We suffered dearly for our mistakes, finding ourselves in the squatting position of the "Cossack", stepping it out, rifles overhead, for what seemed like an eternity. Still, morale within the course was high because it was just so funny to witness.

A few days later we began another exercise known as "escape and evasion". We marched again for hours over the hilly terrain, through miles of forest, along lonely tracks to a drop-off point. We were given a limited time to escape and we had to survive without being captured for twenty-four hours, with no food or supplies.

We were split into groups of three or four. Just before we left, each group was handed a live chicken, which one of us had to place in his or her pack. We had to ensure it was still alive at the end of the exercise. We were strip-searched for contraband before we left. The women stripped to sports bras and pants and were given a full search. The males lined up in their underpants. Most of the men had no cigarettes, but my group did. I had taped a box securely between my breasts, safe from detection underneath my thick black sports bra.

We hid for hours in dense forests before finally getting captured. The instructors looked on in amazement as I whipped out my cigarettes.

"Sheehan, have you had cigarettes this whole time?"

"Of course I had," I replied.

"Fair play; well, I suppose it's not cheating if you're not caught," they laughed.

Our hands were tied behind our backs tightly with cables and balaclavas were placed over our heads as we were collectively interrogated. Suddenly my balaclava was pulled partially up. I could feel claws scratching against my skin and was told it was a rat. In fact, it was a chicken. From there we were dragged to a nearby river for further interrogation. My balaclava was pulled up until it just covered my eyes. Two instructors held my hair, and my hands were still tied securely behind my back. They forced me to my knees and pushed my head into the ice-cold water. My head was pulled in and out of the freezing water repeatedly in an effort to gain information. I gulped down mouthfuls of water, exhausted; but I didn't break. Most of us didn't break but a few did. "All right, I'll tell you everything," they laughed.

Later I was asked if I wanted to kill a chicken – all the chickens had to be killed. "There is no way that I'm going to kill a chicken," I replied.

The platoon sergeant looked on, smirking. "Well, Sheehan, if you do it, you will get fifty points. Do you really want to give away fifty points in your overall grade?"

"All right, I'll kill the chicken," I sighed.

I held the chicken in my hands and snapped its neck as it defecated down my combat trousers. The smell was overpowering. I plucked it, gutted it, and washed it out in a nearby river before cooking it in an ammunition box. Then we had to eat the chicken our group had carried all day. It was a unique experience, but I couldn't be a hypocrite and not do it, as I ate chicken all the time. A soldier needs to eat in a survival situation.

Towards the end of tactical training, we carried out FIBUA and DIBUA at Fort Davis once again. We were taken by naval ship; from there we mounted sea riders and began our assault on the fort. Hours of fighting followed in the labyrinth of tunnels and rooms but as we neared completion of the course we began to relax.

Towards the end of the day a few of us decided to take a well-deserved break. We hid in an isolated area high up in the fort for about an hour. We swapped stories, laughing and joking about our different experiences over the past few months. We had nearly all made it to the end.

The night we arrived, the weather had taken a turn for the worse. Darkness fell quickly and monsoon-like rain lashed down on the darkened fort. Once we had set up our defences, having fought through the entire day, the platoon was evacuated to the town of Midleton to escape the pounding rain, where we occupied the local Reserve Defence Forces training hall. An instructor looked at my sleeping mat, which I had cut to size. I had my equipment sized off perfectly for my tiny frame. Anything that was too big or I didn't need got the chop.

"Who the hell owns this?" roared an instructor.

"I do."

"Do you expect me to believe that you fit on that when you're sleeping on the ground?" he asked.

"Yes – I always sleep in a foetal position to stay warm."

"The best thing now that you can do, Sheehan, is get over there and make a Barbie house for yourself!" he yelled.

The whole platoon burst out laughing as I was relegated to the Barbie corner for about fifteen minutes.

Later that night I woke from my sleep to find a bunch of them staring at me. "You do fit on it," one of them said. "I swear, Sheehan, never in all my days." We all laughed.

The following week our platoon started our PT (physical training) leaders' course. It was the final hurdle. I was at an advantage having completed two fitness instructors' courses with the NCEF (National Certificate in Exercise and Fitness) previously. Apparently, most thought we would receive an easy test at the end, slacking off in their approach to study. I wasn't fooled, I knew how hard the questions would be, so I studied every night for hours. After we completed the test, the majority failed but I, along with a few others, received top marks.

We spent our final week on the course preparing for our passing-out parade. I was overjoyed and filled with excitement, but I had stiff competition from a handful of other equally dedicated soldiers, all vying for a place in the top three. We completed our final exam on general military knowledge.

I had befriended a few privates on the course, some of whom I was very close to. One in particular had often taken the pressure of the pack off my back by placing his hand beneath it when I struggled on marches. On another occasion when no one was looking, he had put me on his shoulder and run the length of the track just as I was about to drop. He had been the European kickboxing champion, so he had no problem lifting me, my pack and rifle on top of his own. He was also the one who had prevented me succumbing to hypothermia in the trenches.

In return, during our academic tests, I completed my own answers and also some of his. When the instructors' backs were turned, we often swapped papers. I would fill his answers in quickly before returning his paper almost completed. We pulled each other through. He and his best friend, who was also on our course, often sat in their car until the early hours of the morning with the lights on, studying for our exams. They were just as dedicated as me, if not more so. The three of us were good friends.

Every student was eagerly anticipating the announcement of "Best Overall Soldier". The instructors had even called out three students, whom we all assumed had received the top three places. I had done my best, given it everything that was in me; I knew I could not have done any more. I was bitterly disappointed.

The following day the platoon commander fell us in to officially announce the top three students. I felt deflated, knowing my name wasn't going to be called. My two close buddies received third and second place – but they weren't the students called out the previous day. Then the platoon commander went on:

"The student who has topped this course has performed excellently, no matter what we threw at them. They never gave up, they led by example and they helped others." He paused dramatically. "Will Private Sheehan come forward? You are the Best Overall Soldier."

Suddenly my legs turned to jelly. I could feel hot tears in my eyes but I blinked them back. It would have been too clichéd for me to cry right at the end, having spent months trying to be tough. Everyone in my platoon applauded. On that day I felt very proud to be a soldier.

Afterwards everyone congratulated me. I even heard a rumour that the company sergeant had approved my award, saying, "Well, after all that, she definitely deserves it." Everyone I bumped into in Collins Barracks shook my hand and congratulated me. I was the first woman in the Irish defence forces to achieve the award. I was overwhelmed.

My father was overjoyed. I had finally made him proud of me.

On the day of the passing-out parade, I was so excited I forgot to eat. As they called out my name, I could see stars in my eyes. I repeated a mantra over and over in my mind: *Don't faint, don't faint, stay focused, pick a spot and stay focused*. I was handed a large bronze statuette of a combat soldier by the General Officer Commanding of Collins Barracks in front of a huge crowd of family, friends, soldiers and officers. I couldn't stop beaming, later joking that the statuette was a male soldier.

"Hey, where's the ponytail?" I laughed.

"You're pushing it now, Sheehan," grinned my instructors, but they were happy for me.

On that day I was promoted to the rank of corporal, an important and overwhelming moment for me.

It was Valentine's Day. Andy held Alex in his arms, watching me and my platoon as we were marched around the square. Alex was too young to understand what was happening but I had to hold back tears when I held him later that day. He loved me unconditionally, even in my absence.

22

Betrayed

Four days later, I was at home and needed to text a friend. My mobile phone was broken, so I asked Andy if I could borrow his phone. I went upstairs to our bedroom. Suddenly a text flashed on Andy's inbox, which I opened. It was from a woman whom I knew he had been close to.

My heart stopped. I felt like a bomb had landed on my lap. I don't know what possessed me, but I texted her back for over an hour, pretending to be Andy. I was devastated and visibly shaken by the words I read. I wrestled with my emotions, struggling to keep them intact. In one text I asked her not to ring "because Valerie is walking into the room", for fear she would rumble me. She immediately rang; maybe she wanted to be uncovered.

I heard Andy's footsteps on the stairs. "Is that call for me?" he asked.

I strode across my newly varnished oak floors and hurled the phone in his direction, narrowly missing his head.

"Yes, it's for you! How could you do this to me?"

He swore faithfully that she was just a friend. However, from the intimate tone of the text messages, my female intuition told me they were more than friends. I screamed and roared at him in a full-blown tantrum but he refused to give me any answers. He was completely unrepentant, staring stony-faced at me with his arms folded.

He marched into the kitchen, slamming the door behind him. I knew he was phoning her back. I said the cruellest things to him. I wanted to cut him emotionally, the way he had cut me. If I am honest, I really wanted to punch him but I managed to restrain myself.

I slept without Andy that night, curling my body around Alex, tears tumbling down my cheeks. I was in shock.

I phoned her the next day but she flatly denied a romantic relationship existed, insisting they were merely friends. I thought back to all the times his phone had beeped through the night over the previous few weeks, and wondered why a friend would have been calling him at three in the morning. I think I chose to ignore all the warning signs, the red flags, but when I read her text messages, everything clicked into place. I had been away so much, only spending weekends at home for a few months, so I knew there had been an opportunity. I would never know the full truth, but either way I was devastated.

The next day I arrived home to find Andy had moved out, and most of his belongings were gone. My heart quickened as I realised that I had gone too far with the words that flew from my tongue. I was truly crushed. I went from room to room, crying, smoking cigarettes, barely able to function.

When he came to collect the rest of his belongings, he said to me, "Have a look at your trophy, Valerie. Genuflect in front of it every morning. Well done, you did it – but we are over."

His words pierced my heart. I had paid the ultimate price for my achievement. I had lost my family.

For the next few weeks I cried every night, curling up alone in bed, snuggling next to my mobile phone, waiting for a text message from Andy, but it never came. I begged him, I cried again and I begged him some more. I could barely eat; just the sight of food made me feel sick. Over the coming weeks I lost over fourteen pounds on a heartbreak diet.

But Andy refused to flinch. I couldn't sleep, so in the middle of the night I chain-smoked, looking out of my kitchen window with the lights off as dawn broke, unable to stem the tears flowing down my cheeks. He had believed in me, he had stood by me in Lebanon when everyone else left me, but I had left him all alone. I could hear it in his voice, see it in his face: he didn't love me any more. The passion had left our relationship, which had never been my intention. I needed him, I couldn't function without him, I felt crippled by the heartache; but he was gone and there was nothing that I could do. My world crumbled overnight. I had made a monumental mistake.

The fact that I knew her, that she had been in my home, that she was really pretty and stylish when I wanted her to be ugly, really hurt. On the other hand, I had let myself go. I hadn't paid much attention to my appearance as I was more concerned with running around the mountains covered in camouflage cream. I would arrive home each Friday evening with camouflage cream smudged behind my ears, down the sides of my face and between my fingers. It genuinely takes hours to remove, no matter how hard you scrub. I suspect she had arrived at my door wearing champagne toasted lip gloss, not a green army-issue backpack.

It wasn't the first time he had left me but this time it felt so much worse. I had lost my son too. I wouldn't see him every weekend, only alternate weekends. The three of us would never wake up in bed together again; that simple joy had been ripped from me. Alex begged for his daddy when he was gone, banging on the front door, crying and pleading with him to stay. It was heart-wrenching to watch. I blamed myself for Alex's pain and I felt so guilty.

Words can't describe the depths of love I had always felt for Andy but I didn't appreciate him or show him how much I loved him and my son. I blamed him, her and myself. In the end I began to hate him. There is a fine line between love and hate. But it is easier to admit hating a man who has left you than maybe soul-searching for the reason. Maybe the reason was me. I was so busy proving that I was as good as any man that I failed to realise the important things in life. I failed to appreciate what was standing in front of me in my own home all along, but I never expected him to leave. I had given him a beautiful son, had spent the past few years by his side. He had just cast me aside, refusing to talk to me, becoming cold and distant, even saying cruel things which cut me up inside. My heartbreak, my rejection, heavily overshadowed the immense joy I had felt only a few days previously when receiving my award for "Best Overall Soldier".

I had finally secured a promotion in the army, the one goal that had consumed me. But I deeply regret the personal price which I paid.

Andy had bought me a huge bouquet of red roses for Valentine's Day, which happened to be the day of my passing-out parade. After he left, I remembered what he had said when giving them to me. "Look at the roses, Valerie. To get to a beautiful thing, you have to pass many thorns along the way." He likened life to the rose; it has many obstacles but ends up beautiful. I tossed them in the bin, feeling physically sick. I loathed red roses for a long time afterwards.

A few weeks later an opportunity arose to travel overseas to Eritrea with the 4th Infantry Battalion. My family had seen how heartbroken I was and encouraged me to go. I felt it was the only way that I could let go of Andy – not to see him for a few months – but I was unsure. Each time I saw him, my heart ached. Even though I felt pangs of guilt, I selfishly felt I needed to escape.

The army had also desensitised me to the point where I thought there was nothing wrong with leaving my child for months. If I hadn't become desensitised, then I would not have been able to carry out my duties as a soldier. But being a soldier had also desensitised me from motherhood. On the surface I had recovered somewhat from the break-up, but I just wanted to leave Andy behind. I thought that if I put a few thousand miles between us, I would get over him.

I had done the inconsolable crying, stumbling around in nightclubs with Rebecca on my weekends without Alex, drinking vodka and generally acting . . . well, quite loopy. My turning point was waking up with a half-eaten kebab stuck to my cheek, realising I had fallen asleep sending a stream of embarrassing text messages to Andy's phone, which was incidentally turned off.

It was time to stop. I replaced vodka with yoga and positive affirmations. I was never picture-perfect beautiful but I certainly wasn't an ogre. With a bit of grooming – a good bit – I felt I could re-emerge transformed. Rebecca appointed herself I/C of my transformation from combat soldier covered in muck and camouflage cream to . . . well, pretty all right. I think I even began to have a sparkle in my eye again.

From that day forward, I chose a new mission statement: never to allow any man to hurt me like that again. Andy was welcome to his new friend with her long tousled hair, cheeky grin and designer wardrobe. I just wanted to escape from it all.

We had formed up for overseas training and again had to complete gruelling exercises in the Wicklow Mountains. I had completed so many exercises that they began to merge into one in my mind. Andy was also on this exercise but he refused to speak to me, passing me as if I didn't exist. It cut me to the quick.

On one particularly hazardous night, with extremely bad weather conditions, there were a number of accidents on the mountain that saw soldiers being evacuated by stretcher and ambulance. I found it difficult to breathe and was having chest pains. I had always wondered if my chest pains were brought on by my eating disorder. Even though I had overcome it, it had left its mark on me physically.

Finally the exercise came to a brief halt. Many of the women and men were shivering, drenched to the skin. So many soldiers had been taken off injured and suffering from hypothermia that the officers finally considered ending the exercise.

Underneath a canopy of trees I sat on the ground shaking. I threw my basha (waterproof sheet for sleeping under) over my head. Heavy rain pounded down, splashing on the leaves and bouncing on my basha. I became disorientated and didn't know where I was. It was the beginning of hypothermia. "Valerie, we are moving; come on," said a corporal. I could vaguely hear his muffled voice. I sat with my back against a large tree in isolated woodland, rain pouring down on me, unable to move or respond. Underneath my camouflaged basha, I continued to feel tightening in my chest.

I was told to wait for an ambulance to take me to the hospital. In the interim the exercise was called off. I had to wait for over an hour for the ambulance and by then the rain had stopped, with sunlight breaking through the clouds.

A sergeant approached me and asked if I had seen Andy. Andy was a sniper and for the duration of the exercise he had been placed high up on the mountainside, crawling around in the muck and dirt in an effort to locate the enemy. I paused before I considered my response. I thought that it wouldn't do him any harm to stay in the mountains a few more hours. It might allow him time to think about our relationship.

"Yeah, I think I saw him head back into camp on a truck. Hmm . . . I'm not sure," I replied.

I knew this was quite wicked and vindictive, but he had broken my heart so this alleviated some of the guilt that I had felt. Heartbreak clouded my better judgement and I was angry that he had left me.

I was brought by ambulance to hospital where I was told I was pushing myself too hard. When I rejoined the exercise Andy approached me. "I can't believe that you told the sergeant I was back in camp," he said abruptly.

"Oh, sorry about that – I thought I saw you getting on a truck," I replied innocently.

"You did that on purpose, Valerie."

"Well, all is fair in love and war, Andy. Did you have any luck finding the enemy?" I asked breezily.

Later that day the sergeant approached me. "Valerie, I know he broke your heart, but that was not very nice. He was crawling around the mountain for at least four hours after the exercise was finished."

"I thought it might allow him time to think about our family. Besides, I knew ye would go back for him," I replied.

The sergeant laughed and so did I, but poor Andy was not amused. That exercise was beyond gruelling, but at least we didn't get scabies. I'm not sure Andy has ever forgiven me for leaving him crawling around looking for an enemy that was safely back in our camp. I did feel twinges of guilt, but it was outweighed by my heartache, so I brushed it off. When Andy refused to acknowledge my existence after our years together, the guilt just drifted away.

I just wanted to leave it all behind. So I made up my mind to travel to Eritrea once and for all.

23

Journey to Eritrea

I find it difficult now to accept that I left my young son at home and volunteered to serve abroad at a time when he needed me. However, I had insulated myself well from my femininity and my own maternal instincts so as not to cast any doubt on my self-confidence. It was also a way of escaping the emotions I was experiencing following the break-up of my relationship with Andy. In time I would learn that I didn't escape; I just buried my emotions and feelings so deep that I forgot them.

So, for this reason and a multitude of others, I volunteered to take part in the United Nations mission to Eritrea, a small war-torn country in north-east Africa. Part of me wanted to escape while the other part of me wanted adventure, to rekindle a sense of freedom. The mission would allow me to achieve both of these objectives. At the time, I knew little of the country, which is bordered by Sudan to the west, Ethiopia to the south and Djibouti to the south-east. What I did know came from Solomon, the young Ethiopian boy whom I had met in my teens when I was living in Cyprus with my family. He had told me a little about Eritrean history and its cultures, but this did not prepare me for the reality of what I was about to witness. Eritrea would prove to be a life-changing experience for me, for reasons that I would only later come to understand.

I was the only mother travelling with the contingent of Irish troops to Eritrea. I had been paraded on a number of occasions and it had been emphasised to me that if I got homesick or missed my son I would not be allowed home. A senior NCO had reservations about my travelling overseas. He seemed to think that being a mother would interfere with my commitment to the job. I overheard him on one occasion talking to another female soldier. I stood outside the room, listening to what he had to say. He didn't think it was natural for a mother to leave her child. He was questioning what type of a person I was and what type of mother I was. This hurt me deeply; after all, he had children of his own and he too was travelling. It didn't seem to be as acceptable for a woman to leave her child. But, thinking back, I now believe it isn't natural for a mother to leave her child for such extended periods of time. I had just become so desensitised to many things, including motherhood.

Eventually I was paraded in front of the battalion commander and sat through the same level of questioning.

"How will you cope? You're a mother – what if you miss him? We can't send you home if you miss him," he said.

It turned out that the battalion commander, who was travelling with us, was a modern and intelligent man. He was concerned because my relationship with Andy had broken down and he was very compassionate towards me. He took on the mantle of being almost like a father to me on the trip, looking out for me as a father looks out for his daughter.

I was confused about many aspects of my questioning. There were dozens of fathers travelling to Eritrea and none of them were questioned at length in the same manner. The fact that I had just won "Best Overall Soldier" on my NCOs' course seemed irrelevant. On a number of occasions he had been told that it was fine for me to travel but he deemed my lengthy interrogation necessary. The fact that I was a mother was the main issue concerning them.

Yet again I was in a minority and I found the level of judgement I received hard to cope with. I knew that I loved my son dearly but when my mothering skills were openly discussed and I was on the receiving end of hours of questioning, I felt upset, isolated and vulnerable. I wanted to prove that I could be a soldier and a mother. I realise now that being a fully committed soldier and a fully committed mother was only ever going to be pipe-dream.

During my trip to Eritrea, Alex would be staying with Andy and his mother in their family home. Andy's mother didn't approve of my leaving and it's only now that I can fully comprehend why. It deeply saddens me that I left

Alex during a time of great upheaval in his little life. My one source of comfort was that my own aunt and mother would take care of him during the day. Andy would then collect him once he finished work, but he too spent a good deal of time away on courses during that period.

My parents reassured me that Alex would get the best of care. I felt at ease knowing how well he was loved by our families, so I buried my emotions of guilt and doubt in order to prepare myself for my impending trip.

The night before my departure for Eritrea, Andy dropped Alex to my mother's house. I had temporarily moved into my parents' home when my relationship with Andy broke down. I couldn't bear to be in my own house as it held too many painful memories for me. I didn't say goodbye to Andy, refusing to see him.

I sat with Alex in the living room, watching *Elmo*, which mesmerised him. I held his delicate fingers as he rested his head on my chest, which was comforting for us both. He was too young to understand that I wouldn't be home after a week or a month. I felt like any other mother that evening. I was sad and lonely at the thought of leaving my son. This sadness engulfed me but, as always, I buried it deep within.

As I lay with Alex in bed that night before I left, I kissed his forehead and gently stroked his soft brown hair. I held him closely in my arms, his tiny little hand in mine, until he drifted off to sleep, oblivious to my impending departure.

I awoke at seven as usual and prepared Alex's bag for my aunt. I fed him his breakfast and gathered our belongings to leave. During the short journey to my aunt's house, I felt conflicted about whether I should indeed head to Eritrea, but as a soldier, if I didn't serve overseas on a regular basis, my contract would not be renewed, irrespective of my gender. I pulled up my car, a little grey Punto, outside my aunt's house. Her front door was open in anticipation of our arrival. It was a clear summer's day with a perfect blue sky overhead.

I took little Alex out, squeezing him tightly in my arms amid a flurry of emotions. I could feel tears building up in my eyes but I managed to keep myself composed. My aunt made me something to eat and gave me a cup of strong black coffee. Her children made a big fuss over Alex but I held him in my arms, not willing to let him go yet. Finally, he toddled off into the front room and sat down on his chair next to the patio door waiting for *Elmo* to appear on the cartoon channel. My heart sank as I smiled at his innocence before returning to the kitchen for my breakfast.

My aunt knew how upset I was, though I tried to mask it. She tried to lighten the atmosphere, making sure that I was at ease with the situation. When the time drew close for me to leave, I held Alex tightly, not wanting to let him go. If I could go back to that place now, I'd never have let him go. He didn't cry as I left. He didn't understand that I was walking away from him for a few months.

I formed up with the rest of my company in Cork to make the bus trip to Dublin. When we reached Dublin, I checked in my bags. Shortly afterwards we boarded the plane that would take us to Asmara, the capital of Eritrea.

As I sat in my seat I turned off my mobile phone, feeling relieved to be leaving behind Andy and the heartache I had endured. The previous few months had been a very painful time in my life. I felt that I couldn't discuss this with anyone in the army, especially as I had been interviewed so much about how I would cope with being away from my son.

The journey to Eritrea was over nine hours long and I slept for some of it. Lost in my own thoughts, I didn't really speak to anyone on the flight. I imagined my son's face, how he would be feeling with the loss of his mother. I knew that if I was to survive the duration of the trip, I would have to detach myself emotionally from my life and family at home.

When we finally touched down in Asmara I felt both excitement and sadness. As I stepped out of the plane I was hit by a wave of intense heat. The air was hot and dry, the surrounding land dusty and barren. The military police were waiting at the airport, accompanied by an escort party to ease our arrival. We mounted the small white air-conditioned minibuses and headed to our base.

The road leading to the Irish camp was relatively quiet. The sky was pitch black, the lights of Asmara lighting up the skyline in the distance. We disembarked just past the checkpoint which marked the entrance to our camp. I climbed down from the bus and stood alongside everyone else, feeling tired and anxious. The ground was barren of all vegetation, a sea of brown dirt still swirling from the tyres of the buses. For the next six months this dirt would cause a constant irritation to my eyes.

My friend Stacy, who was also a corporal, had arrived at the camp two weeks earlier as part of the first group of soldiers. She was a colourful character, always very pleasant and willing to help. She was standing quietly by the cookhouse, waiting for us to arrive. Her long blonde hair was swept up neatly and she looked every inch the soldier, albeit a glamorous one. She had beautiful sallow skin, but her most distinguishing features were her large piercing eyes.

She led the women away, giving us a quick tour of the camp. To the left was a dining hall. I was startled by its vast size and the fact that the camp seemed so clean. The showering block was spotless, but she warned us never to drink the tap water. (If only I had listened to this little piece of wisdom . . .)

Stacy was similar to me in many ways. We would develop an unlikely bond, but our relationship was often tempestuous. We both came from families full of strong women. We shared a room and we would go through every emotion imaginable together.

There were eighteen women altogether, including myself and Stacy. The female accommodation was located on the same lines as the military police and some of the male administrative staff. The military police were directly across from my room, which often proved a nuisance to us all. The male accommodation was also located only a short distance from our rooms across the gravel square, while some male soldiers on the administration staff were also accommodated on our lines. At the top of the camp was the canteen or pub. Seated outside the canteen was a large green canvas tent which often doubled as our church and conference room. The camp was surrounded by a large fence and barbed wire. Its purpose was to protect us, but later in the trip it was of more use in preventing the soldiers from leaving the camp and sneaking back in.

Once I dropped my bags in my room I ventured around the camp to find my bearings, before making my way to the phones. I stood in the small white wooden hut that acted as a phone booth. My heart skipped a beat as I dialled. I spoke to Alex and was surprised that he was talking quite clearly to me. He asked me when I was coming home and I told him it would be in a few weeks. To hear his little voice lifted my spirit.

I also spoke to Andy but his voice was cold and distant. I had refused to say goodbye to him or even see him, which I am sure made him even colder. "We are never getting back together, ever, so just move on with your life; I have," he said. My heart throbbed when I heard his cutting words.

I found my new surroundings strange. Our room was spotless, its two beds complete with duvets and soft pillows. Stacy had acquired a CD player. It was the best army accommodation in which I have ever stayed.

Before I hit my pillow, I took the anti-malaria drug Lariam, which every soldier serving in Eritrea was prescribed. I felt a burning sensation as it travelled down my oesophagus. We had heard that it was the cheapest on the market and that's why it was prescribed to us all. It was and still is a controversial drug. It often drastically altered soldiers' moods, leading to terrifying nightmares and bouts of aggressive behaviour.

As I lay in bed, I clasped my hands in prayer. I asked Jesus to protect me and my family. I asked Him to take care of Alex and help me stay safe. I turned my problems with Andy over to God to solve because I didn't think anything else would work. I found comfort in prayer then and I still do now. I often prayed to God while I was in Africa.

I tried to sleep for a while but the incessant sounds of crickets kept me awake. I drifted in and out of sleep until the camp was woken at 6.30 the following morning. I got dressed quickly and pulled the grey sliding door open on the clear blue skies of Africa. The camp was full of activity. Soldiers wearing green uniforms and tanned suede boots were going back and forth to the showering blocks and then on to the dining hall. After my shower, I made my way to the dining hall, taking in my new surroundings. In the middle of the camp lay a huge square filled with grey gravel that crunched under my feet. This was to be the scene of our morning parades every day.

I didn't feel much like eating. The previous few days had taken their toll on me and I had lost my appetite. I took some scrambled eggs and made myself a small cup of hot tea before sitting with the rest of the NCOs to eat. The dining hall had low white ceilings and was segregated: on one side dined the officers and NCOs; on the other side dined the privates. I didn't finish my breakfast and threw most of it in the bin.

I noticed that there were a lot of Eritrean women working in the dining hall. Their black hair was woven tightly onto their heads above thick gold earrings. The older women wore traditional white Eritrean dresses while the younger ones wore more modern attire. They were very quiet, almost timid. They barely spoke any English and went about their tasks silently. I later learned that they received twenty dollars a month to work twelve-hour shifts in the camp. I don't know how they survived on this, but they did.

After breakfast I reported to my platoon where I was 2 I/C (second-in-command) of a section of men. There were a number of female privates in my platoon, all of whom I knew as I had been placed with some of them for the duration of their recruit training. They were lovely women but they were a good few years younger than me. Despite this, we were well bonded and all got along throughout the trip. We ate together, trained together and so we all established a routine early on.

Our platoon sergeant paraded us and informed us of our duties and the rotations that they would take. As a platoon we were to do a two-month stint in the camp where we were based. Our role was to act as the camp guard. After that we would complete a two-month stint in another camp called the SOC (senior officers' camp). This camp was the accommodation for all international officers serving in UNMEE. For the remaining two months we would go on to serve in the United Nations Headquarters to protect the UN HQ and its staff.

The United Nations Missions in Ethiopia and Eritrea (UNMEE) had been set up in the year 2000 to monitor a cessation of hostilities between Ethiopia and Eritrea following a two-and-a-half-year war over their 620-mile border. The Irish troops were based in Asmara as part of the mission overseeing the demarcation with Ethiopia and to protect the UN headquarters and staff in Asmara.

When we weren't on duty we had a lot of spare time on our hands. For the first two months I completed two to three duties a week. When I finished a twenty-four-hour duty I would be off for the next twenty-four hours, so I soon settled into overseas life and all that it encompassed. In the evenings when I was off duty, I would watch the Discovery Channel for hours, as there was little else to do.

I phoned Alex every day while he was at my aunt's house. I loved to hear his gentle voice. He would tell me how his day went in a few words and I would tell him that, yes, your mommy has a gun and no, I didn't shoot any bold men. Phoning home was extremely cheap. Nine dollars bought me ninety minutes on the phone to Ireland. Phoning home gave me a sense of security and stability. My mother and aunt were a comfort to me, filling me in on every aspect of Alex's development. I made the decision not to phone Andy for the remainder of the trip in order to get over him.

I didn't venture out of the camp much in the first two weeks but I had heard stories from the other women about a place called the Ber Hiba, a local hostelry which acted as a bar, restaurant – and also a brothel. Most of the troops drank there but I was almost scared to go there.

One evening I was patrolling the perimeter of the camp when I stumbled across a young blonde soldier, Collette, who was just about to go into her room. I approached her and asked her if she was all right when suddenly I saw tears trickling down her porcelain skin. She tried to compose herself. She wasn't usually a girl for public displays of emotion. I guided her into her room and asked her to sit down. She told me she had just come from the Ber Hiba. She was distressed by what she had seen and the way she had been treated. The local Eritrean women had pushed her in the toilet there. Collette was left in no doubt that they did not want her.

We spoke at length about the things we had both seen. We were both distressed at the crippling poverty all around us. During the day little children begged outside the fence by our rooms. They clung onto the fence with their hands outstretched, begging for food. We were told never to give them food or money. Despite these rules, I did both. I could never find it in my heart to walk past them. Some of them were tiny, just like my own child. I imagined the hunger in their bellies and the thought of my own son having to beg for his survival like these children overwhelmed me.

During the first two weeks, I spent my days training in the gym and running the three-mile route to the airport and back with some of the other women. The road was long with tall green palm trees lining its path. Occasionally we would see Eritrean women and men hunched over with a pickaxe, working on the road. They worked slowly but diligently under the blistering heat. We were told not to push ourselves too hard as it would take our lungs a while to adapt to the new climate, as Asmara is 6,000 feet above sea level. This often led to welcome cool breezes blowing over our camp.

Wherever I was stationed I always tried to find a running partner. I usually pushed myself harder with a partner. It also relieved the boredom I felt running alone. I noticed that one of the cooks, Luke, did a lot of running but I was too shy to ask him if I could go with him. Since I did a fair bit of running I was tempted to ask him if I could run with him, but waited a while.

I was finding the running quite difficult in Asmara. My nose sometimes bled during the runs and I would be left with thumping headaches. I had never experienced anything like that before. I had received a lot of inoculations prior to my departure. I had formed up late and so mine were given quite close together, unlike many of the other soldiers. Shortly afterwards, some of my lymph nodes started to become engorged. It alarmed me at first and the pain was often excruciating but I soon got used to it and learned how to manage it.

I felt very much out of my comfort zone in Eritrea. I was away from my son and my relationship had broken down, which left me feeling devastated and alone. This, combined with being stationed in Eritrea, once again set off my eating disorder.

An eating disorder is something that is never truly cured, just controlled. There were a few times throughout my army career when my appetite faded or I began the cycle of bingeing and purging. There have been periods of months, sometimes years, when it never surfaced, but I have learned with age to cope with it. It was a destructive method of coping but I didn't realise it back then. I knew how bad it was for my physical health and had attended the support groups, but it still took hold of me, at times almost spontaneously. When I was feeling low and unable to control my external environment I always seemed to lose my appetite. Food became my coping mechanism and often my enemy.

One afternoon I was summoned to the battalion commander's office. As I approached his door I didn't know what to expect. He was a friendly man, but it was unusual to be sent for. He stood me at ease, relieving the tension I felt. Then he spoke to me at length about my health and my eating habits. The cook, Luke, had told him that myself and some other women weren't eating much. I had noticed during the previous few days in the cookhouse that he often glanced at my plate as he passed me. I found it uncomfortable and tried to ignore it. My appetite still hadn't returned to normal and I was very thin. He asked me how I was feeling and told me that he had a daughter my age. He went on to say that only a year earlier, she had broke up with her boyfriend and stopped eating for a while. He was very understanding and seemed knowledgeable on the subject of daughters, which are, I suppose, the same the world over. He said he would keep an eye on me and that I in turn had to talk to the other women.

I promised the battalion commander that I would start to eat properly and take care of my health. As I left his office that afternoon I felt very exposed. I spoke to the other women and we all shared our stories. Some said they were eating so little because the food was awful. However, the food was delicious. I sensed their reasons were closer to my own. They assured me that they would eat more; under the scrutiny of the battalion commander, they didn't have much choice.

Afterwards I went to the cookhouse in search of Luke. He seemed caught off guard to see me. I asked why he had told the battalion commander what he did. He simply replied that it was his job. "I was concerned, Valerie. Yourself and a few other girls eat nothing, and it's not normal," he replied. "I didn't do it out of malice. I was just worried about you." I accepted his explanation and we started to chat. I was surprised that he even cared about our welfare, but he genuinely did. He asked me if I wanted to go running with him at two o'clock and I agreed.

Later that day Luke took me on the ten-kilometre route that ran on the outskirts of Asmara. The hard ground beneath us was almost a rainbow of red and brown. I had to stop and catch my breath more than once as my lungs struggled to gasp in the hot dry Asmara air.

Luke was much older than me, his face etched with fine lines, but he was a kind, attractive man. Our friendship grew and we soon found that we were running nearly every day together. He pushed me more and more and my running greatly improved. He ensured that I ate properly and made sure that my whole platoon had enough rations when they were on duty. Before long, my skin began to have a healthy peachy glow again and my weight stabilised.

24

The Ber Hiba

One of my friends called to my room one glorious Sunday morning. He and a few other soldiers were having a few drinks in the cookhouse. Sundays in camp were relatively quiet so we often sneaked into the cookhouse to meet up when we were off duty. There were no windows so we were safe from the prowling eyes of the military police. We crept around the back of the cookhouse to avoid detection. An oppressive dead heat filled the air, so I was looking forward to the air-conditioning of the cookhouse.

Sunday mornings in the cookhouse were for a select few only. Full Irish breakfasts were always laid on for us. The smell of the kitchen reminded me of the smell in my mother's kitchen on a Sunday morning. Memories would come flooding back to me of my sisters all grabbing their breakfasts – bacon, sausages, buttered toast – my mother giving out to the younger ones for coming in late the previous night while we tried not to laugh.

On this particular day the guys were drinking beer while Irish rebel music played in the background. The scene was one of camaraderie. After weeks of training and solitude within the strict confines of our camp, I was ready to relax and have some fun. I felt like I finally fitted in, that I was accepted for myself. All the cooks took care of me and watched out for my welfare. We sat around the large white tables, eating our Irish fries and drinking cheap African beer.

Two hours later and it was time to leave the camp and take a yellow taxi to our next stop. We weren't supposed to drink on Sundays, but the majority of personnel from the camp had found their own hideaways tucked away on the outskirts of the city for Sunday afternoon drinking. The first time I entered the little hotel a few miles outside the city seemed to startle some of those present. It was full of privates, corporals and sergeants. When the tables of troops saw me, suddenly all drinks were put down and an awkward frosty moment ensued. I think they were afraid that, as a corporal and a woman, I would complain about them. But a few moments later my friends strolled in behind me and ordered a few drinks for us. A loud cheer filled the room and we settled into the afternoon with ease.

It was a vast room with high white ceilings, wooden fans spinning vigorously overhead. Locals sat at the long glistening bar drinking quietly. The bar was filled with smoke billowing high in the air from the ashtrays scattered on the intricately crafted tables. I felt content and secure. This place offered me an escape from reality and the group I hung around with also gave me the security I craved. They took me under their wing and took care of me. I had felt isolated and vulnerable in the beginning but they provided me with a form of protection. They were well respected and I found that no one gave me any trouble while I hung around with them.

Every Sunday evening all Irish soldiers had to report back to our camp for a parade at 6.00. The reason for this parade was to ensure that no personnel had been drinking. A mass exodus of soldiers left the hotel around 5.30 and headed in yellow taxis to the camp. I walked cautiously down the concrete path which led to my room, passing the sergeant-major who was tending to his beloved rose bush. He looked at me suspiciously and I gave him a smile. I had escaped his scrutiny and headed straight to my room to get some toothpaste and water. I brushed my teeth for a few minutes, knowing that many other soldiers were going through the same routine. We all fell onto parade amid a flurry of giggles and nervousness.

The company sergeant called the parade to attention and walked past each of us slowly. We had to stand upright with our hands pressed firmly against our sides, waiting for him to pass us. Butterflies somersaulted in my stomach as he passed me. He would lean in close to a number of soldiers, his nostrils flaring as he tried to pick up any scent of alcohol but the only thing he could smell was fresh minty toothpaste. After a thorough inspection we would all be dismissed from parade. My heart stopped pumping in my chest as I walked off parade to find my friends waiting at my room.

I had resisted visiting the Ber Hiba with the other soldiers for a number of weeks, especially after talking with Collette. However, most of my friends went there and kept asking me to come along. I relented about four weeks into the trip, agreeing to go with them.

I was aware of the activities in the Ber Hiba, as the camp talked of little else, but this was going to be my first time experiencing it for myself. Soldiers attract women who engage in prostitution. In the poor areas of the local community, UN troops held considerable status. The 220 troops who made up our mission were seen as a ready source of income for the many local Eritrean women desperate to improve their circumstances. These women did not openly sell themselves but instead frequented the Ber Hiba, which was located little more than a hundred metres from our camp.

As I walked up the few steps into the Ber Hiba I became nervous. The restaurant was dimly lit, with brown mahogany partitions separating it from the bar. In between was the reception desk, while upstairs operated as a brothel. It was a hive of activity with traditional African music playing in the background.

I walked cautiously behind my friends to the table they sat at every night. Three local girls were sitting at the table and they gave me a look as if to say I was encroaching on their territory. My friends announced to them that I was with them and they relaxed their glare.

"Oh, you're Valerie?" asked one of the girls in impeccable English. "We've heard all about you. You're very lucky to have such nice friends to take care of you."

I gave them a bewildered look and my friends reassured me that they meant it in the nicest of ways. I was aware that some of the other women from my camp, in particular Collette, hadn't received a warm reception from these girls. The bar was filled with the most beautiful exotic Eritrean women, tall and slender with caramel skin and deep velvety chocolate-brown eyes. Their slim silhouettes floated from table to table, entertaining the patrons. There was never a mention of prostitution or exchange of money. This type of prostitution relied on discretion. The women only ever asked the male patrons to buy them a drink. Then they went upstairs where there were a number of rooms on two separate floors, each with its own number.

The only flaw from the soldiers' point of view was that each person who availed of a room had to produce their United Nations peacekeeping ID card. This system was aimed at deterring rapes, as the soldiers knew the bar owner would have their ID number if an attack were to occur. Once they produced their card, they paid the hourly fee for the room.

Prostitution is a strange phenomenon for any woman to witness but I found that I detached myself from what I saw in the beginning. I didn't question it. I didn't pass any remarks and I developed a "couldn't care less" attitude. Then, as I got to know the women involved, I came to despise it. I never thought that going into the Ber Hiba was inappropriate. I wanted to escape the monotony of camp life. I had grown bored of my new surroundings and I wanted to venture outside its barbed-wire gates.

Over the next five months I would come to understand the business that is the oldest trade in the world. The girls at my table were extremely beautiful with striking features. They boasted large egos – or so I was led to believe in the beginning. They were not, however, the loudest and most vocal girls in the bar. I was soon to learn the hierarchy that ran the order of business in the Ber Hiba. I had a privileged position amongst these women. I stood on the fence, observing them. Over time they warmed to me, letting me into their lives.

None of them went by their real names. Sasha and Isabelle were sisters, blood sisters. Isabelle was known for her vicious temper and violent outbursts while Sasha was more subdued and elegant. I had heard of their antics from the men I hung around with. I overheard them describe what happened when the sisters took them to their apartment after a night's drinking. I didn't pass judgement or give an opinion. As the weeks passed I got to know Sasha quite well. We often sneaked away from the lads and went clubbing together around Asmara. She let me into her life and unlocked the secrets in her heart.

Sasha had a five-year-old blond son, David. She had married a Danish UN worker and had moved to Denmark but hated it there. She had since divorced her husband and moved back to Eritrea. Her ex-husband had followed her, taking up a job in the UN building in Asmara. He was a decent and loyal man but I feared she had married him to escape the crippling poverty she had been born into. He bought her an apartment in Asmara, which she shared with David and Isabelle. Her ex-husband lived in the apartment next to hers. I found this set-up strange but I never pushed her too much on the topic. I believe the man was totally besotted with her so chose to overlook her lifestyle.

She often invited me to her apartment, which led me to think that she trusted me, as did many of the girls. The floors in her apartment were made from white marble and the rooms had a luxury not afforded to most Eritreans: air-conditioning. I was intrigued by the lifestyle these girls led and what drove them to live this way. Sasha held a high position in the Ber Hiba.

I had been told that Eritreans can't get a passport unless they pay US$3,000 to the government. The average monthly wage was $20; therefore passports were out of reach for the majority of the population. Sasha's marriage to a Danish man had ensured she had a passport and was able to travel freely. She didn't seem as desperate as the rest of the women.

I found Sasha to be an amazing mother. She gave David a private education and took care of him very well. He was her priority in life. She herself could speak a number of languages. She often went without to ensure that he got the education she felt he deserved.

She wanted to get a husband for her sister Isabelle. She had tried but failed with the first contingent of Irish soldiers. Isabelle initially seemed to be having more luck on our trip; she was in a steady relationship with one of my friends.

I watched the women ply their trade to the men with whom I worked. In the beginning these women had the upper hand and the power sat firmly with them. They knew how to operate. UN soldiers felt privileged in the beginning. They had beautiful women all vying for their love and attention. They were like kings in their own palace, the Ber Hiba.

The monsoon season was fast approaching and the air was filled with an awful sticky humidity. One evening in the Ber Hiba I was in the bathroom, the pungent smell of urine filling the claustrophobic room. The stench seemed much worse with the humidity. Droplets of sweat ran down my face and there was no need for any form of make-up. I couldn't wear make-up in any case, because the heat would ensure it didn't stay in place for very long.

A local girl named Sandy was looking at her reflection in the mirror and crying. She wasn't typical of the women who frequented the Ber Hiba. She was a larger, older girl whose looks were fading. She seemed quite desperate.

"What's wrong, Sandy?" I asked her.

"Valerie, I love him, I really do love him," she replied. She had been seeing one of the soldiers, who was a good twenty years her senior.

"What's happened?"

"He doesn't want to marry me and he says that I don't really love him. Please help me, Valerie," she begged. "You can talk to him, you can make him change his mind; you're his friend."

"I'll do what I can but I suggest you move on and try to find another man. He doesn't want to marry you and he has no intention of bringing you to Ireland."

"I have a small son, Valerie. I cannot live like this anymore. Please promise me that you will help me?" she asked.

I told her I would try my best, but I knew in my heart what the inevitable outcome would be.

She wiped away her tears and followed me to my seat. Our usual group sat around two tables placed close together. Sandy sat next to me and tried to compose herself. She had let her guard down. I knew I was in an awkward position. I remained loyal to the women and guarded their secrets, keeping their real intentions from my male friends.

Sandy had married young. She told me how, not long after she married, her husband had been sent to the front line to fight in the war against Ethiopia and had been killed. She was devastated. She had also been left destitute. Widowed and with no proper education, she had no way to earn money. If she was lucky enough to get a job, she would have worked for twelve hours a day for around $20 a month. So Sandy found herself, like many other girls, in the Ber Hiba. She had a family to support, her mother and young son. Her mother took care of her son while she worked in the bar late at night. They had no money and no income. The clothes she wore had been bought for her by the Irish soldier she was seeing. As time went by, she slowly realised that he had no intention of becoming her knight in shining armour. She didn't want to accept that, to him, she was simply a fleeting fancy.

She started to become visibly upset again as she saw her male patron chat up a younger, prettier girl. At that point the owner of the bar asked her to leave. She whispered in my ear, "Meet me out the back in five minutes." I reluctantly agreed. My friends had warned me not to get close to the women. They watched me now, wary of betrayal. I waited patiently and when suspicion had faded from their faces, I excused myself.

I sneaked quietly along the narrow dark corridor that led to the backyard where I found Sandy. She had been crying again, tears trickling down her cheeks. She began begging me to help her, pleading with me to persuade her patron to marry her.

I tried to make her understand that he had no intention of marrying her. She found it hard to accept this. "He used me, Valerie, he used me. He made me do the most awful things to him, things that disgust me," she screamed. "He said he loved me and he would bring me to Ireland." Sandy was a relative newcomer to the world of prostitution. I knew she did it to feed her family. She was guilty of being naïve, believing her male patron to be her escape from the cruel world she lived in.

She became more and more hysterical, drawing the attention of the bar owner again. He grabbed her by the arm, forcefully pulling her away, telling her she was barred from the Ber Hiba. He was over six feet tall with a large muscular build. He dragged her off the premises in a fit of anger. I stood by, watching silently, feeling helpless and scared.

I still didn't fully understand the business but I was learning fast. I returned to my table and the owner glanced in my direction to see my response. He needn't have worried, because I was too shocked and shaken to open my mouth. I could see relief spread across his face when I didn't mention anything.

I moved over to her man and asked him what had happened.

"Ah, she was moaning all the time about doing certain things." Sandy had refused to give him oral sex and so he cast her aside in favour of a girl who would. "I couldn't be listening to that. I'm up here to relax, not listen to some whore giving out to me. Feck her, more where she came from."

Another guy sat beside me. "Valerie, she should have known. She's not exactly Whitney Houston," he joked.

Another man interjected, "Yeah, there's plenty of Whitneys here and she isn't one of them."

I sat in the middle of them and saw the relationship between the women and men shift in my mind. The balance of power was shifting. The men bragged openly about their sexual exploits, which seemed to be becoming more aggressive as the weeks went by. The older men still retained a little respect for the girls. The younger ones – some in particular – had no respect for them at all, barely acknowledging that they were human beings.

Only the strongest of the girls survived, those who didn't show emotion, who were prepared to obtain their objective at any cost. The girls who were tough, who had few sexual inhibitions, were the ones who got by best. Sasha was there for her sister Isabelle. She too was older and more seasoned in the art of seduction.

As the trip progressed, so did our group in the Ber Hiba. Different girls drifted in and out with different men. The girls took meticulous care of their looks. They spent most of their time in the beauty and hair salons scattered across Asmara. My friend and I often accompanied them, as did other girls from our camp. Their male patrons, the Irish soldiers, paid for these expensive extravagances.

One of the most attractive girls was named Diamond while her sidekick was Angel. Of course, these weren't their real names. Diamond was around the same age as me. She stood at five feet seven inches tall, with long woven light brown hair. Her skin was very pale, a lighter shade of cinnamon. She was very shrewd but could be vicious if provoked. She took care of her turf and the women who frequented it. She ruled with an iron fist. On one occasion, she bottled a girl in the face outside the Ber Hiba. She smashed a glass bottle directly into her cheek, ensuring she destroyed the tools of her trade, her looks. The girl in question was suspected of having HIV; if she had operated in the Ber Hiba she could have passed on the disease to the other girls and men, including Diamond herself.

Most of the girls feared Diamond, but the men adored her. On more than one occasion, I walked into the bathroom to find she had some poor new girl in a headlock or pinned against a wall. I would not intervene as I knew my place amongst them. Besides, I certainly didn't want to have a bottle smashed into my face. But Diamond too eventually let her guard down with me and I often spoke at length with her. I asked her how she had become so vicious and violent. She hid this side of her personality well from the men, deep behind her exotic beauty and tall slim physique.

She also had an extremely hard life. Both Diamond and Angel were single mothers. Most of the girls lived in tiny houses with little furniture and no modern appliances. Work was very hard to come by and this was their only method of earning money. She told me there was no social welfare system in Eritrea. For most of them, it was a simple choice. They could either listen to the hunger stirring in their young children's bellies and watch the tears fall from their helpless faces, or they could work as a prostitute. I couldn't comprehend having to make such a difficult decision and I often wondered why the world we lived in was so cruel to some. In the beginning, most of the men, just like myself, did not know the dire circumstances these women lived in. It was easy to judge them.

Of course, they were the tough ones, and a little older. The girls in the Ber Hiba ranged from fifteen to thirty years of age. As the months went on I saw younger and younger girls paraded through the doors. I couldn't imagine what would lead a young girl to sell her body.

Angel often spoke to me at length about how she and many of the other girls had ended up in the Ber Hiba. As I got to know her and the rest of the women, I discovered that a lot of them had fought in the war, though some had escaped conscription by having a baby and handing it into the local orphanage. Giving birth was a form of escape for some of these girls. They would then be exempt from military service. When the Eritrean army trucks pulled up, if they had no papers to say they were exempt, they would be mounted onto the back of the trucks and often sent to the front line to fight.

In time, I learned that many of the women in the brothel, and also those working in the camp canteen and cookhouse, had completed their military service, often for a few years. Their war had been harsh; they had fought day and night in the blistering heat and were often wounded and treated in underground hospitals built into their trenches. From there, they were sent back to fight again. In my opinion, these women were a much higher calibre of soldier than some of the men I had been sent to Eritrea with. Often referred to as "the hookers" by my comrades, these women were survivors.

Eritrean soldiers would often wait outside our camp like vultures, pacing up and down with sticks and guns, waiting for their prey to appear. Their victims were the women working within. Some of the younger girls in the cookhouse had not completed their military service. Under the cover of darkness, they would have been mounted onto the back of the waiting army trucks and led to serve in military camps scattered all over Eritrea. Their families would have no way of contacting them to find out where they were. There had been incidents where mothers only found their daughters three years later.

The cooks often hid young and old women in the cookhouse at night, smuggling them out with the bread run early the following morning. The Eritrean soldiers would have given up by then and left to concentrate their search for potential conscripts elsewhere.

I had a friendly relationship with another girl who worked in the canteen. She had served in the war but had deserted. Her teeth were badly stained; she told me this was because the Ethiopians had poisoned the water in the stream where they drank. She described to me in graphic detail what the female Eritrean soldiers on the front line had to endure. She had fled successfully but many others were not so lucky. To deter soldiers from attempting to escape, the Eritreans placed mines along the perimeter of their camps and in the surrounding landscape. Only certain officers knew the safe routes in and out of each base camp.

In time I came to hate what was happening in the Ber Hiba. I came to despise the brothel and the abuse that went unseen in its four walls. How could so many men do this, to their wives, their families and their girlfriends? We had completed so many courses on the level of HIV in Eritrea. Did they not care about themselves or their partners to whom they had to go home? I began to wonder what drove men to act this way. Was it simply the need for sex? Were men just primal creatures with sexual urges that could not be controlled? As a young woman I found this very disturbing.

I wondered how I could work alongside these men in the knowledge that some of them viewed women as mere sex objects, their primary function and role in life to please a man. I heard that some of the men I knew did the most awful things to women. Some used them for sex, often not paying them. Some beat them.

On one occasion I heard about a man from my own platoon. When he was finished with one of the girls, he smugly refused to pay her. While he slept in the room above the bar, she quietly crept across the room and tried to take the money he owed her from his wallet. He woke up and gave her an unmerciful beating, punching her repeatedly in the face and breaking her hand. She ended up in hospital for a few days. Her friends told me but again I was powerless to stop it. She was terrified and wouldn't give evidence. She risked imprisonment herself if the local authorities knew she was working as a prostitute.

Towards the end, the men often just paid the girls in food. A chicken or a pizza was deemed sufficient payment for their services.

I watched another night, my insides churning, as a man bounced a very young girl on his knee in the brothel.

In the beginning, the tears spilled down my cheeks as my veil of innocence was removed. After a while, the tears simply stopped coming; I couldn't cry anymore. I thought of my own son at home when I saw starving children outside the brothel begging for food. They ran up and down the long concrete path with no shoes or undergarments. I wondered if their mothers were inside trying to get money to feed them.

I thought how unimaginable it would be if I found myself in that situation. We are all part of the human family and I felt helpless as I watched how these humans were being treated. I was saddened that there was absolutely nothing that I could do.

Sometimes I found it hard to cope with events and at times I became quite difficult to live with. My roommate Stacy and I were both very competitive and trained very hard, which left both of us exhausted. We were also both taking the anti-malaria drug Lariam, which left us feeling down and often quite aggressive. Eventually Stacy moved into another room and my good friend Sandra moved in with me. Stacy and I were both a little saddened to part. We behaved the way sisters often behave, having occasional arguments, some of which got out of hand. By the time she moved out we had made up and were the best of friends again.

I regularly witnessed bouts of aggression in the camp. This was largely blamed on the Lariam. I was having terrifying nightmares; I often tried to wake from a dream and found that I couldn't. My moods would swing high and suddenly come crashing back down. It was hard enough to be in Eritrea without having to deal with the horrific side-effects of the Lariam. I had heard that taking Lariam did not prevent you from getting malaria but rather pushed back its onset. Therefore you could still contract malaria but it would lie dormant until you stopped taking the drug, perhaps a month after you returned home. I wasn't sure if this was true, but nevertheless, after a series of sleepless nights and days that left me in a black depression, I decided that I was never going to take

Lariam again. In fact, many soldiers had stopped taking it for similar reasons.

I escaped other days from the daily life of our camp. I would take a mountain bike from the stores and cycle the few dusty miles until I reached the local orphanage. It was huge and in very good condition. I was often surprised at how pristine it was. I would knock on the big blue steel gates and a nun would come out and let me in.

I was surrounded by children, all vying for my attention, their hands outstretched, trying to grab hold of mine. I couldn't imagine how they must have felt. These children received very good care and didn't need for anything except human affection and love. I think that to be starved of either must be an awfully sad and sombre feeling. They were beautiful children and I always brought them lollipops. The little girls would hold my hands and we would skip around under the trees to shelter from the glare of the African sun.

The first day I visited the orphanage, I went with some of the other women serving with me. The babies' rooms were full to capacity, with at least ten babies per room. None of these children were wanted by society. They were all quiet, with huge chocolate-brown eyes, which stared up at me from their little cots, almost looking through my soul. I remember holding a little baby in my arms, wanting to take her home with me. My eyes welled up with heavy tears.

We sneaked away from the watch of the nuns to wander around the orphanage alone. The older girls lived on the second floor. We looked into one of the dormitories. Each bed was made up immaculately and the walls were a bright mix of colours. I had been expecting to see a dilapidated run-down building but instead it was pristine. The older girls were sitting quietly on chairs, braiding each other's hair, while the younger ones bounced around on their beds. The older girls beckoned us in – but it was too late; we had been caught. A man at the end of the corridor called us to return downstairs.

As we made our way along the corridor, I noticed another stairs leading to a third floor. At the top of the stairs were large steel gates, sealed with a thick steel chain and padlock. I asked the man what was up those stairs. He looked at me anxiously and said, "Come now, you cannot go up those stairs. Come with me immediately." I reluctantly followed him down the long dark corridors but I continued to wonder what was up those stairs. I never found out.

As we emerged downstairs a little girl came up to me and I gave her a lollipop. Her head and arms were covered in bandages. She was only about four years old and was HIV positive. The bandages were to protect her skin, as she was covered in lesions. She must have been in so much pain, but she smiled as I held her hand, which was so small and soft in mine. My heart sank as her grip tightened. I knew that at her young innocent age she would not have been aware of the seriousness of her disease. We walked across the green lawn and I said goodbye to her.

From there I ventured into the orphanage's workshop. It was quite small, dimly lit and very dusty, with wood chippings scattered across the floor. An old man worked away diligently in a dusty corner, carving the most beautiful wooden toys. They were then painted an eclectic mix of colours. I guessed that those toys would be very expensive in Ireland. He made red and blue trucks and jigsaws with African animals painted on them. African dolls were hand-sewn by a young woman. I bought many toys when I was there and later I posted them to my own son, little Alex.

That night I lay in bed, getting lost under my duvet, digesting what I had seen that day. Sometimes I found the new world in which I lived surreal. It was so far away from my own life at home. I turned over in bed and again I prayed to God, asking him to protect me and my family. I also asked him to help the little girl with HIV from the orphanage.

25

Curry and Condoms

I was among a group of soldiers who headed away for a weekend to Massawa, a beautiful seaside resort on the east coast of Eritrea, known as the "Pearl of the Red Sea". I was filled with excitement. I spent the weekend lazing on the baking hot sand with some of my close friends, including a guy called James, whose room was directly across from mine in camp. We went snorkelling, gazing at the most exotic plants, fertile coral reefs and brilliantly coloured fish before heading out for dinner in a nearby restaurant. Massawa offered a Mediterranean ambience where I felt free to relax.

When we arrived back at camp two days later I felt completely rejuvenated. However, I had the distinct feeling that James had developed a bit of a crush on me. He would lean out of his window and say things like "You complete me, you make me whole", making the shape of a heart and circle with his hands. This jovial banter continued for the remainder of our trip. If I ever felt down, James picked me up and made me laugh. He was a constant source of humour. Even though I teased him relentlessly over his little crush, he never spoke ill of me.

I trained very hard in Eritrea as I knew that the high altitude would be of added benefit to my fitness. If I could run in the airless environment of Asmara, I could easily run a marathon at home. Asmara was the perfect training ground for me. Therefore I spent my days running, cycling, swimming in the Asmara Palace, or working out in the gym. I had been consumed with ambition and I wanted to become stronger and fitter than most men. Of course, my femininity suffered as a result. I look back at photographs now and laugh at how masculine I looked in some of them.

As my fitness improved, my appetite increased. When I finished running my usual ten-mile route I would often do it all over again, but on my bike. I would be famished by the time the evenings came around. I tried to stock up on food, often walking the short distance to the local shops to buy noodles and cashew nuts. I knew that the cashew nuts would provide me with protein while the noodles would give me the carbohydrates my body needed. But I soon grew tired of the bland late-night snacks and would find it difficult to sleep if I was hungry.

One night myself and a few others returned to the camp as usual. I hadn't eaten much all day as I had been feeling a little unwell. I asked Luke, the cook, if he could make me something to eat, as he often made me midnight snacks. We made our way around the back of the accommodation and down the brown dirt track that led to the cookhouse. It was a beautiful night with a silver moon illuminating the black African sky overhead. We were cautious of getting caught so we sneaked quietly around to the back door. Suddenly we were met by the patrolling military police.

"Where are you two going?" they asked gruffly.

"I was just taking a walk," I told them.

They ushered us both back to our rooms but the hunger pangs would not let me sleep. I decided to find Luke and try once more to sneak into the cookhouse.

I ducked around buildings, emerging only when I thought it was safe to do so. I was creeping along the back of the accommodation when I heard the military police talking again. I stopped in my tracks. I knew that I wasn't allowed into the male accommodation and there would be severe penalties if I got caught. Eventually they moved on so I crept around the back of the cookhouse and along the transport lines.

As I was peering around a corner to see if the coast was clear, I saw the silhouette of two men in the distance. Curious, I took a step forward, and then realised they were locked in a passionate embrace. They froze when they saw me.

"We will keep your secret if you keep ours, Valerie," one of the men whispered.

"What do you mean my secret? I don't have a secret," I replied innocently.

"You're like a black cat in the moonlight, Valerie. Where are you going at this hour?" one of them asked jokingly.

"I'm starving, I have to get some food."

We all smiled and I continued on my journey in search of some food.

I quietly knocked on Luke's door and a few seconds later the sliding door rolled back. "Valerie, what are you doing?"

"I'm so hungry – please could you get me something to eat in the cookhouse?" I asked.

"All right, I'll meet you over there in a few minutes. Now run before you're caught," he laughed.

A few minutes later I was standing at the back of the cookhouse yet again. Was it really this hard to get some food? Eventually Luke tottered over to meet me, but just as he let me in, I heard the military police again. They were watching; they were always watching.

"Run, Val, quickly, and hide in the fridge," Luke whispered.

"What, the fridge? I'm not hiding in the fridge!"

"Well, if you don't, you're going to get charged, Valerie. We both are."

The thought of spending any amount of time in one of the large industrial-sized fridges did not appeal to me. I ducked down low along the cold floor, crawled beside the cookers and made my way into the fridge. Immediately I was struck by the cold and the hair stood up on the nape of my neck. It was eerily dark and freezing inside. I could hear raised voices outside.

"Where is she? I know she's here somewhere," said the MP.

"I don't know what you're talking about. I just came over to get something to eat for myself," replied Luke.

While their heated exchange continued, I was left shivering in the fridge. My teeth were rattling and my arms were shaking uncontrollably. I wrapped my arms around my body in an effort to stay warm. If I was going to last in the fridge without getting hypothermia, I would have to use my head. Besides, how would I explain getting hypothermia in Africa? I kicked around the floor to see if I could feel anything to sit on. My foot banged off something, so I knelt down and felt around. It was a huge metal pot used for storing and cooking sauces. I decided that I would sit on it and curl into a ball to conserve the heat in my body. As I sat down, it felt very soft and mushy. There was no lid on the pot. I quickly began to sink further and further down. Before I could stop myself I had sunk to the bottom of a huge pot of curry sauce.

Suddenly the fridge door was flung open and Luke stood gazing at me in horror. "That's tomorrow's dinner, Valerie, for the whole camp," he gasped.

"I didn't know there was no lid on it." I didn't know whether to laugh or cry.

"Oh my God, you're freezing. Are you okay?" he asked.

"Of course I'm freezing, you hid me in the fridge! I thought I was going to get hypothermia."

I finally emerged from the fridge and the cold gradually left my body. Luke handed me a sandwich but I didn't feel like eating anymore; having been shoved in the fridge and sitting in the curry sauce, the hunger just left me. I thanked him and returned to my room drenched in thick yellow curry sauce. The smell was overwhelming.

The next day I queued up to get my dinner. Everyone behind the counter was laughing. "Lasagne or curry, Valerie?" a cook asked.

"I'll pass on the curry, thanks," I replied, smirking. I noticed that half of the personnel in the cookhouse were tucking into their chicken curry. I wondered if they would have eaten it, knowing that I had sat in it the night before. I felt slightly guilty about my little secret, but I carried on as normal, not letting on that their curry had been anywhere near my bum.

Monsoon season arrived in Asmara and the children danced around the streets and lit fires to celebrate. The monsoon had been late arriving that year and the locals had been getting nervous. If it had failed to come, the crops wouldn't grow and hunger would become widespread.

One afternoon I met a nun, who was in charge of administering aid and food in a local shanty town. The shanty town was not far from our camp but we were shielded from the sights of the daily grind there. She told me how she would weigh little babies and children each day. She would fit a plastic band around their arm. If the band was too big, they received a small portion of rice. If the band fitted their tiny little arm, then they would have to remain hungry. Only those close to death were fed – the ones in most need, the little children for whom the band was too big.

I felt so inadequate. There was nothing I could do to help these poor children. I thought back to my own childhood, where there was so much food readily available. Life in

Asmara was a stark contrast to life in Ireland. I wasn't easily shocked any more but I couldn't imagine how the nun did her job, how she could listen to the piercing cries of a starving baby and keep going. I admired her devotion and selflessness. I spoke to her for a little while before saying goodbye and heading back to my room.

A few moments later, the rain came pouring down, as it did at roughly the same time every day. Huge droplets of water the size of stones bounced off my nose. I dashed into my room and quickly pulled the door shut. Sandra was sitting on her bed, listening to an Enrique Iglesias CD. The song "Hero" was playing softly in the background. I snuggled deeply into my warm duvet. My eyes filled up with tears as I thought of my life back home. I missed Alex so much that my heart ached. I should have been with him in Ireland and not in Eritrea with the army.

By this stage, I was seriously considering leaving the army when I returned home. I didn't want to do this anymore. I thought the new army contracts were very unfair. I had no wish to travel overseas every three years and leave my child at home, motherless. What would happen three years from now? Was I going to be kicked out if I didn't travel again? There were times when I was so down and lonely that I would cry inconsolably into my pillow. Of course, I refused to let anyone see my tears.

I also missed Andy, but when I thought of him, anger took over my love for him. I still hadn't phoned him. At one point he had sent me a letter on a flimsy piece of paper, which I immediately returned to sender. He had broken my heart, torn it into pieces, and I was not yet ready to forgive him. I buried my love for him, blocking all thoughts of him out of my mind.

After what seemed like an eternity, when life almost becomes still during the monsoon, the rain eased off and soldiers began to reappear outside. I was tucked up in my bed and didn't want to move. I was off duty for the remainder of the day, so I decided to stay where I was.

Moments later, a voice rang out loudly over the loud-speakers. "Attention, attention! All personnel report to the main tent in the camp."

I reluctantly left the cosy confines of my room to peer outside. All the soldiers were making their way towards the green tent. I asked one of the guys what was going on.

"Oh, it's a condom parade," he said.

"A *what*?" I gasped in astonishment.

"A condom parade; we all get issued two boxes of condoms – you know, to prevent sexually transmitted diseases."

"I don't need condoms, I'm a girl," I said.

"No, you still have to get them; everyone does."

When I reached the tent, I joined the orderly queue and started giggling along with everyone else. I thought having a condom parade was ridiculous. How much of the army budget was spent buying condoms for troops?

As I reached the table, the battalion commander greeted me. "Hello, Corporal Sheehan."

"Hello, Sir. I don't need condoms – why do I have to get condoms?" I asked.

"Don't worry, it's just a standard procedure, so you won't get an STD," he said. "The level of HIV is one in three out here in Eritrea, Corporal Sheehan."

"I still don't need condoms, though. I have no intentions of being with a local out here, or anyone else."

"I know, but you still have to get them, just in case. Everyone does; it's protocol."

"Okay, where do I sign?"

Two blue boxes of condoms were handed to me and I made my way back to my room. Condoms were readily available throughout the camp anyway. You could get them in the medical aid post and they were freely available in all of the bathrooms. I was becoming increasingly accustomed to such strange scenarios. My life in Asmara could at least never be described as dull and predictable.

We often had to attend lectures in the green tent. Sometimes the lectures were about STDs. We were taught about the different types of STDs and how you can contract them. We were shown how to use condoms and we had to fit them onto bananas.

At other times we had to attend lectures about phoning home. We were warned that if anyone mentioned anything about what was happening in Eritrea we would be charged and severely reprimanded. Fear is a good antidote to speaking out so I became afraid to tell my own parents. We were told that everybody had a right to have their own private life and we were not to talk about any personnel on the trip when phoning home. We were told that our calls were monitored by the signalmen and often listened into. If we were caught on the phone talking about other individuals, then we would be charged. When we finished those lectures we had to sign a form saying we had attended them. This was so that they could punish us if we were caught talking out of turn.

I got to know some of the young girls who worked in the cookhouse quite well. They were employed by the Irish army officers and were paid out of the canteen fund, the profits left over from the mess. One of the girls, Martha, was a beautiful girl with shiny black hair that fell to her shoulders and framed her face neatly. She had chiselled features and was softly spoken in very clear English. She always tried to dress well, despite the fact that she was so poor. She was a respectable girl who worked hard every day. Her hands were almost like leather from the endless hours of work. She would prepare vegetables and potatoes and do other menial tasks for up to twelve hours daily. She had begun a relationship with an Irish cook who worked in the cookhouse; he was many years her senior.

I had become desensitised to my African surroundings but I was becoming increasingly upset about certain events I was witnessing. I watched as the behaviour of individuals changed. I often sat down with my comrades after lunch and heard of their exploits in the Ber Hiba. I wasn't spared from the graphic details. Was this the life of a soldier that I had sought out and craved, I wondered?

They spoke of the audacity of the women asking for money. One afternoon I was sitting in the cookhouse when a man came in.

"Can I take a chicken there, lads? I have to feed the missus," he said.

"What do you mean you have to feed her?" asked one of the cooks.

"Ah, I'm sick of paying her, she has me fleeced. I'll just give her a chicken and that should shut her up."

"Work away; I think there's a spare pizza there as well if you want to take that to her," the cook laughed.

I suppose the tables had turned and the hunted became the hunter. I felt uneasy when I witnessed such things. I didn't know what to do. I couldn't complain because I'd be seen as a troublemaker. Put up and shut up is what I was told to do.

I was also very much aware of pornographic material in Eritrea – not just the watching of it, to which I was extremely desensitised, but the making of it.

I felt that the exploits of some were like a game of Russian roulette, with all of the players ducking for cover in order to protect their families and careers, but with little regard for the people who we were supposed to be helping. After Lebanon, I chose to stay silent in particular about events in Eritrea. I opted for a quiet life but I have always felt like I sold my soul because I knew some of the things that happened were so wrong.

26

On Leave

Shortly afterwards I was preparing to return home to Ireland on leave. A few days earlier, I noticed an uncomfortable swelling, about the size of a pea, on the side of my face, next to my ear. Some of my lymph nodes had been swelling throughout the trip but this was the first time that a lymph node on my face had become engorged.

I went to the camp doctor but he said it was fine. As the days passed, however, the swelling grew. A friend of mine was concerned. "That's not normal, Valerie. You need an antibiotic." I spoke to the doctor again and he reluctantly gave me some penicillin, but I told him I was allergic. "It's all I have left; the stronger antibiotics are all gone." My face had become very tender and swollen by then. I could feel another swelling under the skin of my cheek, which was very uncomfortable. I knew that I must have got some sort of infection or that my body was fighting something.

The night we were leaving for Ireland, a huge barbeque was planned for the camp. The regular Irish camp barbeques were becoming famous, or rather infamous, around Asmara. The camp cooks were very talented and their food was praised by everyone, from privates to ambassadors. Sumptuous steak and a huge array of salads were laid out in the tent. Fresh fish from Massawa was bought at the local market. No expense was spared and the music played loudly into the night.

As the night went on I saw an officer approach the green tent. He had already consumed copious amounts of alcohol and was staggering through the camp. To my shock he turned around, pulled down his pants and flashed his bare backside to the stunned troops. I wasn't very impressed by the sight.

I'd had a few drinks myself but I couldn't relax because the pain in my face was becoming unbearable. I returned to my room and grabbed my bags to head for the airport with my comrades. The next few hours were a blur as I swallowed painkillers in an effort to numb the pain of my swollen face. We had a two-hour stopover in Cairo. I sat in the shabby terminal and found myself seated next to the Eritrean athletics team. I became engrossed in conversation with a young Eritrean athlete. She told me that she planned to run away from the team and to try to seek asylum in the country to which she was travelling. She was very brave, I thought, to risk such a thing.

Finally I boarded my plane again, bound for Heathrow Airport. At that point my face was so swollen that you couldn't distinguish between my neck and my cheek. I was totally exhausted and drained. I wandered around the terminal at Heathrow in search of a pharmacy. I was so excited about seeing Alex, but this was overshadowed by the pain. My mother had told me that she was bringing Alex to Cork Airport to meet me when I landed. I wondered if he had changed, if he would recognise me immediately. Would he welcome me home or be angry that I had left him for so long?

When we reached Cork, a dense fog had descended, so the plane was unable to land and was diverted to Shannon. I was becoming agitated because Alex would have to leave the airport without me. What would he think? Would he believe that I just hadn't come home to him?

As soon as I arrived in Shannon I phoned my mother to tell her what had happened, but she already knew. I told her I was getting a bus to the airport in Cork. All I wanted to do was hold Alex in my arms. I tried to sleep on the bus journey to Cork but couldn't. My father met me off the bus. He opened his mouth in horror at the sight that stood before him.

"What happened to your face? It's so swollen – what's wrong with it?" he asked.

"I don't know – they had no antibiotics left in the camp and I was allergic to the only ones they had."

"Oh Valerie, you're going to have to go to the hospital as soon as we get you home."

When we pulled up at my parents' home, I suddenly became nervous. When the aluminium front door swung open, my mother stood there with her mouth wide open. "Is this what happens when my daughter goes to Africa – she comes home with her face the size of a football?" she gasped. "You're going straight to the hospital; I have never in all my days seen anything like the size of your face."

"Thanks, Mom, I feel bad enough," I replied.

"Valerie, Alex tried his best to stay awake for you but he has just fallen asleep," she said. It was two in the morning. "Come on, we'll try to wake him but he mightn't recognise you with the swelling."

Alex was sleeping soundly in his favourite chair. I gently nudged him and he blinked open his eyes. He jumped up from the chair and ran away from me, crawling behind the couch, refusing to come out. He didn't recognise me and my heart sank. I consoled myself that it was probably because my face looked so deformed. I gently encouraged him to come out and after a little while he did. He threw his arms wide open and flung them around my neck. It was like we had never been separated. I was filled with guilt for having left my only son.

I played with an exhausted Alex downstairs for a while. I told my parents I was too tired to go to the hospital. It could wait until the morning. I had just met my son again and I didn't want to let him go so soon.

I brought Alex to bed with me, snuggling next to him for the night. He fell asleep on my chest as I stroked his soft mousy-brown hair. I watched as he slept silently and pondered whether I should leave the army in order to become a full-time mother. It was so strange to be home.

Africa seemed so far away. I refused to think about Andy; I simply wished to move on. I took some more painkillers, then lay my head on two soft pillows and fell into a dreamy sleep.

The next morning I woke up and put my hand to my face. It felt like the swelling had gone down. My skin was smooth and I couldn't feel any trace of a lump. I raced, breathless, to my parents' room.

"Is it gone down?" I asked my mother.

"No, Valerie, it's actually worse. Your whole face and neck are swollen now and it's very bad."

She nudged my father on the shoulder and told him to take me to the hospital straight away. I'm not sure why, but he ended up taking me to the army hospital. It was the weekend so the doctor was off duty. When the medic saw my face he decided to call the doctor in. The army doctor examined me and told me I had gingivitis, an infection caused by contaminated water. On one occasion I had used the water in the camp toilets to brush my teeth. According to the doctor, some of it must have gone into my gums and infected the surrounding lymph nodes. He prescribed strong antibiotics for me and sent me home. I wasn't sure if I agreed with him. I'd had swollen lymph nodes months before I ever used the water. It didn't make sense.

I lay in a haze for the next five days in the bedroom in my parents' house. The antibiotics were so strong that I could barely stay awake for very long. Alex, who was the quietest child imaginable, often came and slept next to me, willing me to get better. I must have done something right in my life because I was blessed with the most lovable child that a mother could wish for.

After a week had passed I relented and arranged to meet Andy. The swelling in my face had gone down dramatically so it only looked a little puffy by then. I drove to Blackpool Shopping Centre and walked the cream marble floor, pushing Alex in front of me in his buggy. Time had indeed healed my heartbreak. I can never stay angry for any long period of time. I had let go of the hurt and pain and just wanted to move forward. I wanted to do the best for Alex.

When I saw Andy standing in the distance, I soon realised that I was still very much in love with him. The first few moments were very awkward. Images of his female friend kept flashing through my mind; I didn't know whether I wanted to kiss him or hit him. I knew he missed me too, because he didn't want to say goodbye. Sometimes absence really does make the heart grow fonder. At that point, though, I wasn't yet prepared to forgive him.

We went out at night together a few times and we also brought Alex away for day trips to Kerry. We all loved County Kerry. Andy and I had often gone mountain climbing there. It offered us a sense of peace and some solitude. Sometimes when life gets too much for me, I escape to the mountains. It grounds me and takes me to a happier place. I love the fresh air and the simplicity.

My feelings were very confused. I wanted my family back together but so much had happened. Andy wasn't just my ex-fiancé; he was my best friend. Of course, the "other woman" didn't know that I was home and was still relentlessly texting him. I knew that if I said nothing it would upset him more than if I questioned him. If I no longer seemed bothered on the surface, he was pulled towards me more intensely.

I opened up my heart to him again, telling him what was happening in Eritrea. He didn't want to believe some of it. I suppose it seemed so unbelievable. I had grown accustomed to it, but to someone on the outside it probably did seem a little surreal. We had been warned repeatedly during the trip not to tell anyone at home what was happening. When I look back now, I feel very naïve to have listened to these warnings. When I eventually did break my silence the floodgates opened up. I also told my parents and they talked me through how to deal with it. My father was a fountain of wisdom, giving me good advice on what to do. My mother also encouraged me to see the trip through. I gave them a brief description of what was happening in Eritrea, but I spared them the more graphic details.

The night before I was due to return to Eritrea I told my father I wasn't going back. I became hysterical. I didn't want to leave Alex again. I wanted to stay at home and sort out my own family. I didn't want to have to deal with all that being in Eritrea entailed. I cried inconsolably for hours while my father told me that I should go back. I refused but after hours of talking to him and my mother, I relented and returned to Asmara.

On Leave

While at home on leave, I had to be up at 7.30 every morning, except the first five days when I was sick. Running around after a young toddler is no easy task and I didn't see it as a holiday. Being a mother is enjoyable and I love it but I certainly would not describe it as being a holiday. However, when I returned I was placed on duty immediately the following morning. "Sure aren't you after having a long holiday!" said one officer.

27

Going Off the Rails

During the last two months of my tour of duty in Eritrea I was stationed in the staff officers' camp (SOC), which housed the international officers' accommodation. I was also working in the United Nations Headquarters building. The SOC was located a few hundred metres up the road from the main camp. Our responsibilities were to staff the entrances and carry out patrols and perimeter checks on the camp, which was quite large.

There were only two female officers in the SOC. One, from Kenya, was over five feet nine inches tall with an athletic build. The other, from South Africa, was very small, standing at just five feet. There was only one female toilet in the entire camp. The South African officer saw me using it one day and ordered me out of it.

"How dare you? That toilet is for commissioned officers only," she yelled.

"It's the only ladies' toilet in the camp," I replied.

"That's not my problem. You are not using this one; you don't hold the rank." She strutted away with a smirk.

There is a vast class difference between officers and other ranks personnel in the defence forces. Privates, corporals and sergeants are seen as third class. Senior NCOs such as company sergeants, quartermasters, barrack quartermasters and sergeant-majors are viewed as second class. Finally, all commissioned officers are viewed as first class, along with nurses.

As usual I had been relegated to the lowly level of third class and this apparently meant that I could not even use the same toilet as them. Sometimes I really wondered what century I was living in. This would not deter me and I decided to use my feminine charm to gain access to the coveted and only female toilet.

I knew a Ghanaian colonel in the camp. He was forever asking me to go out with him, so I decided to go and find him. I knocked on his door and burst into tears, recounting what had just taken place. He stormed out of the room in search of the South African captain. He stood her to attention and verbally reprimanded her. "She is an NCO and therefore she is permitted to use the only female toilet in the camp, Captain."

She tried in vain to argue the point with him but he smiled at me and I stood in victory over my opponent. I winked at her when he wasn't looking and walked off.

Eritrean civilians would arrive on a regular basis at the gates of the SOC, looking to be brought to the rooms of some of the senior international officers. They were usually beautiful looking girls or, less frequently, young men. I refused to escort them to the rooms of the officers, as did many of my comrades. Eventually a compromise was reached whereby we would inform the officers that they had guests waiting. Sometimes the guests stayed for a day and sometimes they stayed for a week. I often saw their hosts taking plastic containers of food from the dining hall over to the guests staying in their rooms. This happened on a daily basis and was largely ignored by all who witnessed it.

I came to know one of these young men quite well. He was a well-known local rent boy. He often had to wait for up to an hour for the international officer in question, who usually met him at the gate. He had regular clients in the SOC who were male international officers. The money he received from his clients was the only income he had. He described his miserable existence in detail, even repeatedly asking me to marry him to escape the cruel life he lived. We were all human, but it seemed some of us had to do anything in order to survive. At the beginning of the trip, I could never have envisaged sitting down talking to him, but fast-forward a few months and it had become quite normal.

During the long hot days in the SOC, I often spoke to the street children and listened to their stories. They would sit outside the camp and beg for food and drinks. Their begging was relentless, because their hunger was relentless. I would tell them to leave but they always came back. They had nowhere to sleep. I don't know why they were never taken in by the orphanage. Some were abandoned by their parents. Some had been orphaned during the war. What they all had in common was that they were hungry, penniless and homeless.

During the evenings we would receive rations from our own cookhouse. We always received far too much, so at the end of the night I would ask if everyone was finished. Once I was satisfied that they were, I would take the leftover food out to the street children. If I didn't give it to the kids, it would have gone into the bin. I would hide the children in a small white hut just outside the camp, laying cardboard down for them to lie on, as did other members of my platoon. In Asmara the nights were often very cold, and the cardboard at least gave them some insulation. These actions were not welcomed by some.

I became friends with Sam, a Tunisian officer in the SOC. He was very well spoken, friendly, handsome and cultured. He stood at over six feet tall with a large muscular build. Everyone in our camp had nicknamed him Jean-Claude Van Damme. He worked in a cell in the UN headquarters building. He went running most days and therefore was extremely fit. Women from our camp had been banned from running alone because of a minor incident. I told him what had happened and he offered to take me running with him.

Over the coming weeks we developed an unlikely friendship. When I was off duty, he would call for me at the Irish camp at two o'clock every day and together we would run the length and breadth of Asmara. I regularly participated in races and military challenges throughout my trip to Eritrea.

On one occasion we had to complete a charity fun-run. The route was only three kilometres, from the gates of our camp to the airport and back again. However, some of the female soldiers were injured and couldn't run it in comfort, but still were made to participate. In the days leading up to the event, some of them were getting increasingly worried. They were very fit and trained regularly but some felt vulnerable about being in competition together. I was a fitness fanatic like a few others but some were just casual runners.

I rallied our group together, ensuring that all the women completed it. We bonded together as women that day. Some of the women raced ahead and won prizes, but it wasn't about winning a medal. It was about coming together as a group of women to raise money for the local orphanage. The girl who would have come last would have tried just as hard as the girl who had come first. In the end, none of our group came last because I kept us all together and pushed us forward. Later I got a medal, which we all shared. I didn't want one of the women to feel bad about herself, even if she finished well behind everyone else. There's no pleasure or sense of achievement gained from watching someone else be humiliated. On that day, I was very proud to be a woman; in fact we all were.

The end of our trip was drawing near and all hell was beginning to break loose in our camp. Violence was becoming widespread as more and more soldiers began to argue with each other. This was largely blamed on the Lariam. One night two soldiers beat each other viciously with extendable metal batons which they had purchased locally. This incident led to a full military police inspection in which dozens of the weapons were confiscated.

Soldiers would often go missing and the MPs could spend hours, sometimes days, trying to locate them. One soldier disappeared to get married to a local girl. On another occasion, a soldier had absconded and could not be found. After hours of searching and questioning, the military police finally located him in a local bar. He made a desperate dash for freedom. There is hardly any street lighting on the far outskirts of Asmara and the roads are often dark and dreary. With only moonlight aiding their search, they gave chase across the barren brown dirt fields opposite our camp. He ran frantically over what we later learned had been a minefield during the war. Two tall muscular MPs finally caught up with him. Gasping for breath, one of the MPs lunged at the private in an attempt to apprehend him.

"Get your fucking hands off me now," the private roared, "or do you see that baton? I'll shove it up your arse and use you as a lollipop!"

The MPs grappled with him and eventually placed him under arrest. They shoved him into the back of their patrol vehicle and drove him swiftly back to our camp. However, they neglected to handcuff him, and as soon as they got him inside the gates of the Irish camp he once again made a sprint for the barbed-wired gates. There was a long grey concrete path leading to the gates, famously known as the "Chicken Run", after the film of the same name. Soldiers often tried to jump the wire after sprinting the length of the path. Some were successful while others, often intoxicated, were not. This particular private dug his feet into the criss-crossed wires and attempted to pull himself up over the fence. One of the MPs managed to grab hold of his belt and tore him back to the ground, where his body smacked painfully onto the cold concrete.

In his pursuit of freedom to enjoy all that Asmara had to offer, he had ripped open the skin on his forearm with the barbed wire and blood was gushing from the wound. He was led forcibly to the medical aid post, where he received urgent attention. The duty camp doctor sedated him and diligently stitched up his wound. He lay in the two-bedded billet under the shadow of a lamp, looking totally worn out. For about an hour it looked like he had accepted his fate. The medics relaxed their watch on him. No sooner had this happened than he made another desperate bid for freedom. As he later told me, he gave an unmerciful roar and aggressively clenched his teeth. He flexed his bulging muscles and, using only his teeth, ripped the stitches from his arm. Then he sprinted out of the medical aid post and off down the chicken run with two MPs in hot pursuit.

They followed the same routine as before and dragged him kicking and screaming back to the medical aid post. The duty doctor was called again and his arm was once more stitched up. This time after he was sedated he was locked in a cell at the end of the camp, containing only a navy mattress and a bucket, with a single light bulb dangling from the ceiling overhead. He remained in solitary confinement for three days. As his section corporal, I had to visit him daily. I would find him in very good spirits and laughing about the whole incident.

This was just one of many stories from the weeks leading up to the end of our trip. Sometimes mattresses were placed on the rooftops of billets and on the ground outside. The men would then try to jump from their roofs out onto the road in order to escape the confinements of our camp in the pursuit of alcohol or sex. The whole camp was kept constantly entertained by these events and nobody seemed to have any form of control.

Soldiers, including myself, were being charged on a regular basis and every day there was a long orderly queue outside the battalion commander's office. There were over 200 charges on our trip, ranging from the slightest to the most severe. I was found guilty four times, once for simply wearing a pair of shorts. I had failed to notice that I wasn't permitted to wear shorts while entering the UN Headquarters building. A fellow platoon corporal with whom I had played as a child wrote the charge sheet himself. On the same day I also went running fifteen minutes early. The same corporal duly noted my behaviour and I was charged, tried and found guilty.

Incidentally, the officer who found me guilty was the same officer who had flashed his naked bum during the camp barbeque. How ironic, I thought, that he could expose himself but I couldn't wear shorts down to my knees!

On another occasion I was charged for staying out fifteen minutes late and the last guilty charge was for entering the male lines. One particular officer watched me relentlessly and tried but failed to charge me on many other occasions. I heard that the battalion commander had warned him not to bring any more charges about me in front of him, but he was too stubborn to listen.

I was starting to feel unwell a lot and would often get the flu. Towards the end of the trip I nearly always had a tissue in my pocket to wipe away the constant dripping from my nose. Looking back now, I believe that the later deterioration in my health stemmed from the Eritrean trip. It makes perfect sense; it was all starting to happen back then. Maybe if I had listened to the warning signs, I wouldn't have had to suffer the way I did.

One night on duty I became really ill. The glands in my neck began to swell, my throat burned from within and became inflamed. My ears were ringing loudly and my balance was unsteady. I was totally exhausted and all I wanted to do was sleep. I was desperately hoping that my face wouldn't swell up again.

I went on duty that night but I should have gone to the medical aid post. It's extremely difficult to stay awake for twenty-four hours, but your body becomes accustomed to it. I was used to sleep deprivation. That night I went to the UN Headquarters building accompanied by two privates under my command. As the night went by I grew increasingly ill. I spent a lot of time going in and out of the toilet. My kidneys ached, my bladder burned, I had a thumping headache and the muscles at the back of my neck were becoming stiff. I had to stay in the toilet for fifteen minutes on my hands and knees until the pain passed over my body. I struggled to breathe but I had brought an inhaler from Ireland and was using it as often as I could.

We were finally relieved and I headed straight to bed at 7.30 the following morning. There was a loud banging on my door. An NCO greeted me and I was told that I was being paraded yet again. I struggled to pull my limp body up. My arms ached and my strength was vanishing. I was questioned at length.

"I heard that you fell asleep on duty last night," said the NCO, who had once been a good friend.

"I didn't fall asleep. I'm really sick at the moment and you're not allowed to drag me out of bed when I'm resting off duty," I replied.

"I'm informing the company commander and we'll inspect the CCTV footage. If you're found to have fallen asleep, you're going to be in serious trouble."

"Go ahead, because I wasn't asleep, I'm sick," I replied.

I couldn't take much more of this and I just resigned myself to accept it. I hadn't the strength to fight them. I was so frustrated.

Later that evening I was informed by another corporal, a friend of mine, that they hadn't found any evidence to support the allegations and so the charges against me never proceeded. I was so ill that I reported to the medical aid post. The doctor gave me seventy-two hours rest and I slept soundly for the next three days. I couldn't care less what they thought of me any more. I held my head high; I would never let anyone break me again.

I made a good recovery and around a week later a function was organised for the whole platoon. We all went to the dining hall for a meal and later we headed to a nightclub in Asmara. This was to be an eventful night, for all the wrong reasons.

The platoon was eagerly waiting to return home in the coming weeks. Morale was high. The nightclub was usually frequented by Asmara's upper class and was very modern, unlike other places in town. It had a proper bar, high modern stools and trendy martini glasses. The dance floor was very spacious and there were comfortable areas with silk cushions to sit on. All the privates and corporals were lining up shots on the bar and taking turns downing them. Tequilas were set alight and swigged back and the music pumped out loudly. Everyone was having an amazing time.

I was becoming increasingly homesick. I knew I was leaving the escapism of Asmara and returning to Ireland soon. As a result I usually headed back to our camp early and phoned Andy. I was phoning him every night now and over time we had grown very close again, though I still wasn't sure where our relationship would go once I arrived home. After the nightclub, I headed back to our camp to speak with him before going to bed.

I fell into a dreamy sleep, but a couple of hours later I heard someone bashing at my door. "Open this door this instant," yelled an NCO. I got up from my bed and slowly walked over to the door. As I pulled it open, I could see that it was still dark. The NCO told me that a number of male soldiers from my section had not returned from our night out and he was going from door to door in his frantic search for them. "They're not with me and I don't know where they are," I replied. The NCO looked genuinely worried and he continued his search for the missing soldiers.

Not long afterwards the three young soldiers were delivered to the gates of our camp courtesy of a local taxi driver. They had been beaten so severely that they had to be moved immediately to the Jordanian hospital in the SOC.

There were a number of nightclubs in Asmara which our troops frequented. Once they had finished drinking with the platoon, four soldiers had headed to another club, unaware that the club was reserved for locals only on that particular night. There were a lot of Eritrean soldiers returning to Asmara from the front line. These men had been almost destroyed by the effects of war. A lot of them were suffering from post traumatic stress syndrome. They came home penniless, sometimes limbless, and often to find their women in the arms of other men – sometimes wealthy foreign soldiers. This often turned the streets of Asmara into a smouldering pot of tension and violence.

The soldiers in question were smartly dressed in designer clothes, had wads full of cash and were merrily drinking champagne. The penniless war-ravaged Eritrean soldiers looked on as they continued to down bottles of champagne and flirt with their women. Enraged, they collectively attacked the three Irish soldiers. (Apparently the bar owner helped the fourth Irish soldier to escape through a hatch in the rooftop.) The music stopped playing and the nightclub was shut down. The Irish men were trapped. There was nowhere for them to hide. One of the Eritrean soldiers took off his belt and pounded one of the Irishmen repeatedly with its buckle. Blow after blow rained down on his head and body. Blood splattered everywhere, but the Eritreans were still not finished. They tied their arms behind their backs and led them out onto the streets.

At this stage a large angry mob had encircled them. The Irish soldiers were forced to walk through the streets, bloodied and beaten. They were then forced onto their knees and told to pray to God for mercy. A local taxi man intervened and negotiated their release. He then helped them into his waiting cab and drove them to our camp. He dropped them off and disappeared into the night.

The men had been battered to within an inch of their existence. They were young and had displayed poor judgement, but paid for their innocence heavily. Each of the soldiers was charged with numerous misdemeanours such as breaking curfew, unruly behaviour and more. However, they were only found guilty on a handful of the charges. I knew each of the men to be a good soldier. They were dedicated and generally well behaved. But Asmara was changing all of us forever.

I was beginning to find the atmosphere in the Ber Hiba unbearable. Many male and a lot of female soldiers frequented the bar but increasingly the Irish girls were going to the Asmara Palace. The Ber Hiba and the Asmara Palace were so close together but were worlds apart.

The Asmara Palace was like a precious jewel, like no other place in Asmara. It is an amazing city but this hotel seemed out of place when all around it lay crippling poverty. The Italians had once colonised Asmara, and it is sometimes compared to the cities of Italy. Indeed, Italian architecture is scattered everywhere. They used to call it "Mussolini's city".

Stepping inside the Asmara Palace, also known as the Inter-Continental Hotel, was like stepping into a new world. A smartly dressed porter would greet us at the main entrance to the spacious foyer, which was beautifully lined with white marble floors. Crystal chandeliers hung on the high ceilings overhead and a swimming pool glistened outside its rear entrance. It catered for some of Africa's elite upper class. I often watched as Arab Sheikhs dined for hours in its gourmet restaurant. I would sit with some of the other Irish girls at the tables opposite them and occasionally we would exchange pleasantries.

The bar was designed like an Irish bar, full of comfortable modern furniture. The staff wore crisp burgundy and emerald green uniforms. I felt like I was stepping into a bar in Ireland. Most Friday nights I would participate in the regular karaoke at the bar. Most of the other girls in the camp would come along too. The karaoke was a heady mixture of African and western music. I absolutely loved to sing but I'm not very good at it.

One evening in the Asmara Palace, I noticed Martha, the Eritrean girl who worked in the Irish kitchens. She was quite elegant and graceful and sat quietly absorbing her new surroundings. She was wearing a pair of sky-blue skin-tight leggings and a white T-shirt with huge blue polka dots on it. She glanced over and caught my eye. I walked over to her and she greeted me warmly.

"Hey, Martha, how are you?" I asked.

The lights were softly dimmed and everyone was dancing. I watched as Martha swayed gently under the fluorescent lights. She had a smile stretched the width of her face and I couldn't help but feel happy for her. Her relationship with her Irish boyfriend, Derek, seemed to be progressing. I think that he was truly beginning to care for her. While he was married with children at home in Ireland, he and his wife were separated.

In stark contrast to Martha, I was beginning to feel worse than ever. Human endurance is an amazing thing. Human beings have the ability to bounce back from anything. All the soldiers filtered out of the bar slowly and headed to the local nightclub. We usually headed into downtown Asmara but the guys said they had heard of a new nightclub. Apparently there had been a nightclub in the Ber Hiba all along, accessed through a side entrance. It was usually reserved for locals only, but was now open to the soldiers too. I decided that I may as well drown my sorrows in the club. Alcohol was becoming like a medicine at that stage; it numbed me from feeling anything.

I headed with Sam and Sandra, my roommate, to the Ber Hiba nightclub. We walked down to the entrance and were met by some burly bouncers, who looked suspiciously at me but allowed us to pass. Sam always had a smile on his face and was very upbeat. He wasn't drinking because it was during the Muslim period of Ramadan.

I think subconsciously I often seek out someone who is older than me and who displays some level of intelligence. As a friend, Sam guided and nurtured me. Sandra was a good friend too, so together we joined the Eritreans performing their traditional dance that night. Traditional Eritrean dancing consists of everyone shuffling along in a circle and moving their shoulders up and down. I found it very silly initially and couldn't help laughing, but once I let my inhibitions go, I thoroughly enjoyed myself. After a while Sam asked me if I wanted a lift home. I trusted him completely and accepted. Sandra remained behind with other Irish soldiers.

Close to the Irish camp, Sam pulled the white UN jeep to the side of the road and we sat chatting. Suddenly there was a loud bang on my window. I froze. At least half a dozen Eritrean soldiers had surrounded the jeep. They were wearing dark green uniforms and green army caps. Some had toothpicks in their mouths and they were all laughing. Some of the soldiers had guns slung across their chests while others simply had large sticks. They were either waving them around in the air or scraping at the brown dirt below their feet. I was terrified. They kept banging on the window, motioning for both Sam and me to wind down the windows. I didn't know what to do but slowly, nervously, I wound the window down.

One of the soldiers was heckling louder than the rest but his mood changed quickly. He swung up his rifle and placed its cold barrel against my temple. I couldn't breathe, my whole body filled with terror. I closed my eyes and heard Sam talking but his words simply sounded like a fuzzy blur. The soldier must have sensed my trembling terror. I suddenly felt the barrel pull away. I opened my eyes. The soldier was smiling but I was petrified. He motioned for us to leave. I sat in stunned silence as Sam drove on and pulled up outside our camp. I couldn't talk so I sat motionless in my seat. I knew that I had been extremely lucky. On a whim, they could have raped and beaten me violently.

It was times like this that I truly understood the meaning of being a soldier serving in a volatile foreign land. I lay awake in my bed that night for hours, thinking about home.

I woke up the next day feeling totally miserable and slightly traumatised. As the morning went on I heard a rumour that one officer had not returned from the previous night's escapades. At around midday he sauntered into the camp without a care in the world. He was smiling from ear to ear and pleasantly greeted all those who passed him.

That evening the company sergeant mustered a parade together in a desperate attempt to regain control of the camp. He berated us, saying careers were going to be ruined forever. He was a few months too late, though. It was like trying to get a horse back once it has bolted. Besides, how could anyone take him seriously when just that day an officer had only arrived back at midday?

Once I had finished my ten-kilometre run that day, I sauntered into the cookhouse to get some cold orange juice. The cooks usually let me help myself. I saw one of them in deep conversation with Martha.

"Hey, how are you?" I asked her.

"I'm pregnant, Valerie," she replied, smiling sweetly.

Derek gently patted her belly and she held his hand affectionately. They both looked so happy. When I looked at him, I was amazed. She had tamed him and he grew to love her dearly. They had the rest of their lives to look forward to.

"What are you going to do?" I asked him.

"I'm coming back here, Valerie. I love Martha; I'm going to take care of her." He went on to tell me that he was going to try to get a job in the Asmara Palace as a chef. He was a talented chef, as were all of the cooks on that particular trip. This largely contributed to my bulging waistline towards the end of the trip!

I stood looking at the happy couple and I could see that they were genuinely in love. Derek had had a difficult trip, as had a lot of the soldiers, but in the end he seemed totally content and happy. I admired him and some of the other cooks for all the kindnesses they showed to the local women.

As I entered my final two-week stint in Eritrea, I was saddened for a number of reasons. My good friend Sam had already returned to Tunisia on leave. I was largely stuck in camp, unable to go running. I used running to clear my mind and vent my frustration. When this was taken away from me, I found it difficult to pass the time. I returned to what I had done at the beginning of the trip – watching TV in the recreational room, mostly alone.

I had stopped going to the Ber Hiba but, one night before we left, I was invited along with some of my friends. I decided to go, to say my goodbyes. It was overflowing with Irish soldiers. There were dozens of tables and well over a hundred stools to sit on but, on that night, everyone was packed in like sardines. I had barely enough room to stand. Women were dancing on the tables, some locked in passionate kisses – they received extra money for such "girl-on-girl" displays. It was a hedonistic scene.

The soldiers left waiting downstairs would have their watches set to time those men in the rooms above. They wanted to see who would be the fastest upstairs. Cheers and loud applause were given to those who emerged after fifteen minutes.

I spoke to some of the local prostitutes and said my goodbyes. I had grown quite fond of some of them. We had shared stories and secrets on everything to do with life. I was going to miss some of them. They lived in a cruel world, relying on sex to sustain their existence. By this stage, some had climbed the social ladder and been elevated to the rank of girlfriend. Some were pregnant. I remember one girl in particular with a burgeoning bump. I stepped outside the smoke-filled bar, looking to the cloudless sky overhead. A magical silver moon shone brightly in the star-glittered sky, but I was feeling anything but magical. There had been times in Africa when I couldn't make any sense of my surroundings and the situations I found myself in. I often felt like I was going mad.

I walked down the steps of the Ber Hiba and took one last look at the place. So much had happened here. How would I ever be able to trust men again? That place would haunt me for a long time. I became unable to trust people and often unable to love people. I became almost dysfunctional within the confines of normal society afterwards.

The following evening, 3 December 2002, I sat in the airport, awaiting the arrival of the plane that was due to take us home. I didn't want to talk to people; I knew most of their dark secrets. Some soldiers were drawn to me instead. Derek, who had left Martha behind carrying his child, came over to talk to me, knowing that I would listen to him. Unlike some of my fellow soldiers, I saw Martha as a fellow human being.

We soon boarded the plane to take us to Ireland. Derek sat next to me and showed me a small nativity crib that Martha had made for him using lollipop sticks. The shops in Asmara have a very limited budget. Christmas decorations are seen as an unnecessary luxury. Martha didn't have the money to buy a real crib for her boyfriend. Instead she made one out of lollipop sticks. She gave it to him for his children at home. He was very forlorn and agitated. He reassured me that he was going to travel back to Eritrea and take care of Martha and his unborn child. Once her passport was sorted out, he would return to Ireland with his new family.

Nine hours later, the flight touched down in Dublin Airport. When I stepped out from the plane I saw the familiar grey clouds suspended overhead. I was home, but I would never be the same again. Some soldiers were greeted by their beloved families. I stood watching them – the same scenes that had been played out in my own childhood, fathers coming home to receive hugs and kisses from their children, girlfriends and wives, bouquets of flowers filled with vibrant colours jostling in their hands, tears of joy flowing. I turned my back and walked away. The majority of us were headed to Cork.

I was overwhelmed by the Christmas songs ringing out throughout the airport. Glittering Christmas decorations were in abundance everywhere. The excess of Christmas in Ireland was so far removed from Asmara.

We proceeded on the last leg of our journey. I sat freezing on the army bus. I wasn't used to the extreme cold weather of Ireland anymore. Martha's boyfriend sat next to me again on the way home. Maybe I was a comfort to him. He talked relentlessly about her. I wondered what she was doing at home. The bus stopped and he jumped out. He waved goodbye to me and that was the last time I ever saw him.

28

Coming Home

On 4 December 2002, a grey, cloudy, wintry day, I arrived at my mother's house like many times before, but so much in my world had changed. I had loved madly, or maybe badly, which is why I had overlooked the red flags with Andy. I had gone to Eritrea to escape but instead had witnessed many of the men I worked with – married, single, engaged, most at least with a girlfriend at home – visiting brothels on a regular basis. I had sat on the fence, witnessing life from a man's point of view. I had infiltrated the boys' club, but I was still a woman.

I had believed in true love and been the eternal optimist, but that trip planted seeds of doubt about every man in my mind. It began to haunt my soul. All I had left was hope but that flame of hope was fast flickering out. My illusions of true love had almost been quenched forever. I sincerely doubted that any man could remain faithful to just one woman. I wondered if all men were destined to stray, no matter how much they professed to love a woman.

I came to the conclusion that I might never be enough for any man. Would any man love me, just for me, despite my many flaws? Would I ever find my soul mate, my diamond in the sand? I had desperately tried to change, to reinvent myself, to become more glamorous and more level-headed in an attempt at winning Andy back. I had spent the last few weeks on the phone to him, trying to convince him that I was a changed woman, but a voice within told me to stop. I knew that I needed to become a much better mother and reconnect with my son. I didn't want to change my personality for any man. Sometimes I can be so level-headed while other times I can be a ball of madness, but that's me. I wasn't prepared to lock myself into a false personality just to obtain a man's love.

That day in the comfort of my mother's home, I embraced Alex, vowing never to leave him again at any cost. I was going to make him the centre of my universe, giving up my pursuit of finding true love. I threw out my self-help books on "how to win your ex-boyfriend back" and moved on.

A few days later we moved back into our home in Midleton. We were going to make new memories, replacing the overbearing heartache that lingered within its walls from six months earlier. It was almost Christmas and I had no intentions of wallowing in self-pity any longer. Now I was more confident, stronger and certainly more in touch with my femininity. Six months previously, I had been petrified that my broken heart would never mend, that I would be left alone as a single mother. But now I was ready to embrace motherhood and carve out a new life for myself.

I set about painting and decorating my home, with Alex at my side. Whilst in Eritrea I had wired money home to my father and he had installed a new heating system, re-plastered bedroom walls and cleaned the entire house. Alex and I painted a spectrum of colourful stars and planets on his sea-blue bedroom wall. We bonded like never before. One soft smile from him made my heart dance on the inside. He looked as cute as a button with his little paintbrush.

Andy continued to phone and knock on my door but I steadfastly refused his advances for a few weeks. I think he bitterly regretted his decision to leave. Finally, on Christmas Eve, against my better judgement, I let him into my home. After all, it was Christmas.

"Wow, you have done an amazing job on the house! You seem so organised," he gasped.

"Yes, I am organised, thank you very much, Andy."

Once Alex was safely tucked up under his duvet in bed waiting the arrival of Santa, Andy lingered in the living room, hovering around my over-tinselled Christmas tree.

His phone hopped and beeped but he ignored it.

"Don't you have somewhere to be?" I asked abruptly. "I'm kind of busy."

"Well, my friends want me to go out with them but I'd rather stay here with you and Alex," he said meekly.

"Go to your friend, Andy. It's Christmas Eve; don't you have a present to give her?"

"I want to spend Christmas with my family, Valerie," he whispered, before flashing me a smile.

I was about to throw a mini-tantrum at the cheek of him, but he had Christmas on his side. I simply couldn't. I had tried so hard to let him go, to get over him, but just when I was beginning to erase my feelings for him, they came flooding back. I realised that I still had a flame of love for him in the depths of my wounded heart.

"You look really well, Valerie. How was Eritrea?" he asked. He stared into my eyes and I had to wipe away the tears I felt building up in my eyelids. I opened up my heart to him about Eritrea once again but I was unaware how much it had really affected my subconscious mind.

Some months later, I was also interviewed by the military police. Our contingent of troops who had arrived home from Eritrea faced investigation over their alleged use of prostitutes and for allegedly becoming embroiled in sex scandals. The MPs centred their questions solely on what I had witnessed in the staff officers' camp and concerned the privates in my section of men. Therefore the interview was over in a relatively short space of time. I never learned the exact outcome of the investigation. It was all very much hushed up. I really did try to put Eritrea behind me, but inevitably it left long-lasting emotional scars.

Over the following months Andy tried desperately to win back my love and my trust. I suppose, like many a woman, I followed my heart and not my head. Beneath the anger, I loved him. I believed he had given up his female friend but he never told me for certain what had happened.

We began dating again, going out for meals, rediscovering our love for one another, but I refused to allow him to move into my home – the home he had dashed out of, referring to it as merely a house.

I returned to work and was placed on the lines for a period of time, but I requested to serve in the newly built gymnasium in Collins Barracks. While serving on the lines, I received a letter one day in my postal hatch in B Company. When I opened the brown envelope, I was shocked. It contained a large folded page, with black letters cut out individually; some were large while others were tiny. Newspaper articles with pictures of Myra Hindley, the moors murderer, were blown up and stuck to the page with glue. Arrows pointed to her head with my name on it and the word "whore" was scrawled across the page. I suspect it had been painstakingly put together, with considerable time and effort.

I really didn't know what had warranted it but I gave it to a senior NCO. He insisted that some people were jealous that I had received the award for "Best Overall Soldier". He was at a loss for any other reason why anybody would send me such a hateful letter. He went on to tell me that when he was promoted he received a bullet in the post with his name inscribed on it. This did little to lift my mood. I was deeply shaken and found the incident very disturbing. He assured me that he would investigate the matter and I should ignore it.

At home, I spent every available moment with my son, playing with him, taking him to feed ducks in a lake near our home and loving him like any other mother. He even began giving me spontaneous hugs, which he had never done previously.

Andy and I began training together, just like the old days. He signed me up for the Dublin City Marathon, vowing to ensure I finished it. "I will stay with you the whole way so that you complete it, Valerie." I was impressed that he was going to run a marathon for me; he really was trying. When I ran, I pushed myself further and faster with each passing day. My feet pounded the hard concrete, sending shock waves through my bones. My heart beat faster each day as I ran but I always seemed to have throbbing pains above my clavicle bones. I ran ever-increasing distances, running away from my memories, pushing myself to escape their pain, but they were slowly catching up with me. The memories of the previous few years remained in my thoughts while I ran, jumbled up loosely, all vying to be dealt with.

I had requested my appointment in the gymnasium to ensure that I would not have to spend extended periods of time away from Alex. Besides, all I felt I had yet to complete was a selection course for the Irish Army Ranger Wing, our elite special forces unit. I never intended to serve there. I just wanted to prove that a woman could do it. Upon passing the selection course a soldier is qualified to wear the *fianóglach* shoulder flash insignia. To date no woman has ever passed the course in the Irish defence forces. This in itself would have been an achievement. After that, my priority would have been Alex, which is why I ultimately did not want to serve in the Ranger Wing. It would have meant spending long periods of time away from him.

Working in the gymnasium would allow me time with my son and time to train within my working day. I had been swimming almost sixty lengths in the mornings before work, running ten to sixteen miles during my lunch break and also doing weights and core stability exercises. I was at my fitness peak for both the marathon and the upcoming selection course. Andy encouraged me and helped me every step of the way. He too wanted to complete the next selection course for the Ranger Wing.

Although my fitness had soared, something lurked within my body which I chose to ignore. I blocked out the physical pain I felt, the niggling sicknesses, to obtain my objective. I dealt with my anger from Lebanon and my memories from Eritrea by running, swimming and pushing ever-increasing amounts of weights. But soon enough all of my coping mechanisms would be ripped from me, leaving me to deal with the pain and memories from the previous few years in an exposed and very vulnerable manner. I frequently got ill – the flu, swollen glands, engorged lymph nodes, bladder and kidney infections, throbbing headaches, sore throats – but I traipsed to the doctor for antibiotics, took painkillers and soldiered on. I masked it but I never dealt with the underlying root cause.

A few weeks later I was posted to the barracks in Limerick. America had invaded Iraq and we were rotating at Shannon Airport, providing security to the American troops as their planes refuelled. I had been feeling particularly tired, nauseated and lethargic.

One evening I phoned Andy and he gave out to me. "You are not eating enough meat, Valerie. How are you supposed to run the way you do on an insufficient diet?" he said gruffly. Andy was convinced that I was anaemic, as I hadn't had a period in months.

The next morning I ate a good hearty breakfast of four sausages, a few rashers, beans and copious amounts of hot buttery toast in an effort to recharge myself. Shortly afterwards I raced to the bathroom and vomited my entire breakfast into the toilet. I was dizzy, dehydrated and weak. Later that cold cloudy day, I was running around the back field at the barracks when I felt a familiar sticky sweat pouring from my brow. I could feel my calf muscles cramping and I was still nauseated.

Oh my God, I thought, recalling the day I had discovered I was pregnant on Alex. A few days later I bought at least five pregnancy tests and watched in stunned silence as each one turned positive instantly.

That evening I lay in my local GP's surgery. "You are nearly three months gone, Valerie," she told me.

"Nearly three months? How can I be nearly three months pregnant?" I gasped.

Andy was away at the time on a standard course to be promoted to the rank of sergeant when I phoned him. I was amazed at his response. He was thrilled and instantly supportive. "I hope it's a boy," he laughed. "I think you should definitely allow me to move back in now, Valerie," he joked.

The following Monday morning I was paraded by my company sergeant and informed that my application to serve in the gymnasium had been accepted. I was filled with excitement but this was overshadowed by panic. How was I going to work as a fitness instructor when I was pregnant? I nervously approached my new sergeant in the gymnasium and told him my news. He had fought hard to get me into the gym but was very understanding, reassuring me that everything would work itself out.

I could instruct on the classes but could not demonstrate or participate, which was definitely a first in the army barracks. I would shout out orders at masses of recruits and infantry soldiers as my bump grew bigger and bigger. They were not going to escape my physical training sessions just because I had an ever-expanding bump. I often aided James, whom I had befriended in Eritrea and who was by now also working in the gym, and the other PTIs with their classes and they tended to me carefully, ensuring that I was always okay, as did the sergeant.

Eventually Andy moved back into our home. Over the coming months we lived a quiet and peaceful life for a change. He continued to spend a lot of time away on different military courses but this time I remained at home, caring for Alex and our home. I didn't fully realise how much another baby would upset the fine balance between work and home life. I truly believed that I could manage as I was working in the gymnasium and had a good support network around me. I had just managed to get it right, naïvely assuming that it couldn't possibly go wrong.

Some days in the quietness of my office I received calls from someone who would roar down the line at me before hanging up. This happened on a number of occasions. My car was also keyed. Every time I was told the same thing: just ignore it. The position in the gym was a coveted one, but I had worked hard on my own time to qualify as a fitness instructor. To some people, though, it didn't seem to matter how hard I worked.

I had been gaining an unusual amount of weight in a short period of time. I was five months pregnant, but I certainly was not over-eating. Also, I had a number of complications during my second pregnancy which I found difficult. When Andy realised how difficult my pregnancy was becoming he too put his selection course on hold. He sacrificed his professional ambitions for me. However, both our professional sacrifices would come back to haunt our relationship in later years as, bubbling underneath the surface, we were both still quite ambitious. I too had to put my dream on hold yet again, of course.

At home we began preparing for the birth of our new baby. I began nesting feverishly. We revamped our house, putting in a brand new maple Shaker kitchen with a large breakfast island. Together we transformed the almost-dilapidated house into a cosy modern home. I had also become quite good at saving and managing my money. When Andy had left me, I realised that I would have to cope alone as a single mother; therefore I took the matter of my financial future in my hands, learning once-and-for-all how to become self-sufficient.

Our Irish economic boom, the Celtic Tiger, was roaring and we found ourselves caught up in its many extravagances. Once the house was finished I asked a local estate agent about its worth. I was shocked at her response. It had well over doubled in value. Not far from our home was a magnificent housing estate, Rose Hill, nestled close to the countryside in an idyllic rural setting. I used to refer to it as Celtic Boomland. I had wandered around the show houses when the estate was in its infancy, joking that one day I would live there. When we realised that our home had ample equity, we pondered the idea of moving to Rose Hill. Sure wasn't everyone upgrading to bigger and better? We found ourselves swept away like the majority of our friends by our new-found financial situation. We viewed some houses but decided to stay put until the birth.

Towards the end of my pregnancy my weight had ballooned and I gained six stone. Everything hurt; my ankles, my hands and my face were swollen. When I walked past the office door in work the lads would joke that they would see my bump for a few seconds before they saw me. I begged my gynaecologist to induce me early, as I could barely walk, but he initially refused. I knew this was extremely selfish of me, but I couldn't sleep and could barely stand upright. My doctor finally agreed to induce me two weeks before my due date.

We arrived at the hospital and I was placed on a drip. A few moments later my doctor arrived to examine me.

"Valerie, how long have you been on the drip?" he asked, looking bewildered.

"Just a few minutes."

"You're in labour, well in labour. You're a few centimetres dilated," he gasped in surprise. "Are you not in any pain? Have you not been having contractions?"

"No, I can't feel anything."

"You should have come in during the night," he told me.

"I came in last week with tightenings and was given toast and tea and sent home. Now I can't feel anything and you're telling me I'm in labour!"

He shouted at the nurse to take me off the drip immediately, saying, "I told you about her; she gives birth really quickly."

Andy was smiling at me, holding my hand, nervously awaiting our new arrival. Fifteen minutes later, I felt a violent contraction and requested the epidural but was told it was too late.

"Give me the epidural now!" I screamed at the nurse.

The anaesthetist was called and two nurses had to push down on my shoulders as I bit through a pillow. He was just in time and was successful in administering my pain relief. Twenty minutes later a stern midwife glanced in my direction and asked, "How are you feeling now?"

"I can feel some tightenings."

"You couldn't possibly be feeling tightenings," she said adamantly.

She left, but moments later peered her head around the door.

"By any chance can you feel a burning sensation down below?"

"Actually, now that you mention it, yes, I can."

"Don't be ridiculous; there's no way you could be feeling a burning sensation."

She waltzed over to my bed and gave me a quick examination.

"Oh my God, the head is coming out!"

"What?" I screamed.

Panic quickly ensued. "Do not push, don't push," she yelled. She rang for the doctor, who came running down the hall with another midwife by his side.

A few moments later, tears filled my eyes as I heard the first piercing cries of my newborn son. I held little Christopher in my arms. "If you ever have another baby, I am admitting you two weeks before the birth," the doctor laughed.

Andy was overwhelmed, both with the quick birth and his newborn son. He was moved to tears, holding my hand tightly, lovingly stroking my hair, telling me that he had never been so in love with me. He never left my side over the coming weeks. He was the perfect partner throughout both of my pregnancies, loving, attentive and always affectionate.

This time around I took to motherhood instantly, feeding, changing and burping baby Christopher. He was adorably cute but quite different to Alex. He had mousy brown hair, silky, peachy cheeks and long skinny legs. "He'll be a good runner," I joked.

All the girls from the barracks visited. "I'm surprised your kids don't come out teaching aerobics, Valerie," they would laugh.

29

From Marriage to Special Forces

Prior to Christopher's birth, Andy had asked me to marry him again, but this time in a low-key ceremony – just the two of us. We wanted it to be a simple quiet ceremony where we would pledge our lives to one another. The day before I was discharged from hospital Andy leaned over my bed, kissing me softly on my forehead.

"I booked the registry office for next month," he whispered.

"Do you really want to marry me when I'm wearing size twenty-four underwear?" I asked.

"I don't care what size you are, Valerie. I love you and I just want us to be a proper family."

I had never loved him so much or felt so secure. At that moment I felt like he was my protector, my partner. I simply adored him and couldn't wait to spend the rest of my life with him.

A week before the wedding, my mother phoned me up.

"Is it true that you're getting married next week and you never told anyone?" she gasped.

I had opted not to tell her as she still hadn't forgiven Andy for leaving me. I didn't think she would have blessed our marriage. I had only told a few select friends. I didn't have a clue how she found out; I suppose mothers always know.

She did, however, amaze me by arranging a whole new wedding for us in seven days: the band, the photographer, the venue, the dress, the cake and the flowers. My poor father was tasked with the job of wedding planner. Every time I looked at him he was ticking something off in his black leather Filofax. While I was happily caught up in the whirlwind affair, Andy was very disgruntled about the whole situation but had no choice, as he was still seeking her approval and forgiveness.

We chose a fairly small affair with sixty guests, despite my mother's request for a larger wedding, because we still wanted to move to Rose Hill. The whole wedding cost a mere € 3,000 when weddings were averaging € 30,000 during Ireland's economic boom. We sacrificed the lavish wedding for a beautiful new home we had set our sights on. Despite the tiny budget I allocated my father, he miraculously managed to pull the whole thing off. I suspect he bribed a few people along the way.

We were married in early January 2004 in a small registry office in Cork city in front of an intimate group of family and friends. I wore a simple light golden, champagne-coloured wedding dress. The classic boned strapless bodice and princess-line gown greatly minimised my weight gain, although I had lost a considerable amount of weight in the short time since the birth. My sisters and friends carefully applied my tan and make-up. My younger sister, who happens to be a hairdresser, swept my hair up into a classic style, inserting ivory diamanté flowers all around the soft chignon she had assembled on my head, leaving a soft lock loose at the front to frame my face. Before my big moment, we sipped champagne in my parents' front room as my many aunts swished in and out. It was a scene of total chaos, which is very normal in my family of women.

After the official ceremony, we headed to Vienna Woods Hotel for our winter wedding reception. Inside the hotel waited sixty guests. I noticed that the band were soldiers. Despite the miniscule budget, everyone commented that it was indeed one of the best weddings they had ever attended. Everyone mixed easily, drinking, laughing and dancing the night away. Towards the end of the evening, most of my family and friends congregated next to a cosy open log fire where the bright red embers danced. We listened to traditional Irish music and consumed copious amounts of alcohol against a backdrop of mesmerising Christmas trees.

Shortly afterwards we sold our first home for a healthy profit. Our new home in Rose Hill was a large detached open-plan house, with a magnificent sun room with a timber-panelled ceiling. The master bedroom even had enough space for me to do my yoga. A cobble-locked driveway ran straight to our front door and young Alex was fascinated by our exotic back garden, which had a tiny pond and split timber decking. It was a quiet, tranquil area with a lovely country view, the perfect place to start our new married life together.

I thought that I had finally found and married my eternal soul mate. Everything seemed so perfect, but perhaps it was too perfect to last.

Not long afterwards Andy told me that he wanted to complete the next selection course for the Irish Army Ranger Wing, which was due to take place that September. I told him of my own desires to also complete it.

"Valerie, you have two children. In the name of God, why can't you be happy just to work in the gym?" he asked.

"It's only a few weeks and then that's it; that is the only military goal I have left," I replied. He relented.

We both set about training for the selection course. I bounced back quickly after the birth of Christopher, probably because my body was so used to exercise.

Together, Andy and I tended lovingly to our newborn son and Alex, but we were still equally driven by blind ambition. If I could go back to that place now, I think I would shake that young woman. I had it all: a husband, two beautiful children, a beautiful new home; but still I wasn't satisfied.

At night I began to have terrifying nightmares. Lebanon and Eritrea still featured in my dreams, the ghosts of the brothel still haunting my soul. The familiar swollen glands and sore throat also made another appearance, more regularly and aggressively.

A few months passed. The week before I was due to return to work from maternity leave, Christopher had been feeling very unwell. He was such a placid child who rarely cried, but that day his piercing screams refused to stop. I cradled him and rocked him in my arms but he was extremely agitated. I raced to the doctor but as soon as I arrived, Chris fell asleep. The doctor reassured me that he was okay but, still concerned, I took him to Andy at Collins Barracks, as he was on a twenty-four-hour duty. Andy reassured me that the doctor was probably right.

I held my four-month-old baby in my arms as I headed towards B Company office to check my mail. Another letter was waiting for me in the postal hatch. This time it contained an unwrapped condom.

I was so exhausted that I wasn't thinking straight. I wanted the person responsible found. I foolishly headed to the military police building and handed them the envelope containing the condom, telling them briefly about the other letter, the calls and the incidents with my car. I was only there a few minutes but little did I know that I was wasting valuable time that should have been focused on Christopher.

I travelled home to Midleton but Chris took a turn for the worse. He was screaming and sweating, and had a convulsion. My brother-in-law and other family members quickly raced to my house while I phoned an ambulance.

Driven by fear, my heart was pumping so fast that a lump formed in my throat and I could hardly breathe. Andy handed in his weapon in Collins Barracks and headed straight to the hospital.

On the way to the hospital in the ambulance, as I held little Christopher in my arms, the paramedic remarked, "Those bruises weren't there when we arrived." He immediately signalled to the driver who put on the sirens and raced quickly to Cork University Hospital. I was paralysed by fear that my baby was so sick.

In the A&E, a nurse looked over Christopher. "It's probably colic," she insisted.

"It is not colic," I said abruptly. "My eldest son had colic and this is more serious."

I demanded that he be admitted for further tests. Finally he was admitted and a series of tests performed.

At two o'clock in the morning a nurse raced into Christopher's room where I lay on a chair next to him. His white blood cells had gone through the roof. We were told that he either had meningitis or septicaemia, but more than likely it was bacterial meningitis.

"Don't worry, Valerie," said the nurse reassuringly. "Last week a baby arrived just like yours. I was sure he wouldn't make it, but the antibiotics are so strong now, he made a full recovery."

I held my baby in my arms all night, begging God not to take my beautiful son. This wasn't meant to happen; I couldn't lose my baby. I was terrified, tears tumbling down my cheeks for hours. I was so angry at the person who had sent me the condom and at myself for being so stupid, wasting precious time when I should have gone to the hospital with Chris. I was overcome with guilt.

To our relief, Christopher slowly recovered over the days that followed. I cradled his little body in my arms each day, lightly stroking his hair. Occasionally his long brown eyelashes would flutter open, revealing his sparkling blue eyes. Large teardrops stung my eyes every time he smiled at me. I remembered back to the day he had discovered his shoulders; I thought he was having some kind of fit when he kept twitching them up and down, but he was just curious. He was so funny sometimes; even at four months old, he made the whole family laugh.

Andy stayed with us, curling into a ball on a chair every night, waiting for his son to get better. He was due to travel to Nepal the following week to climb to a base camp on Mount Everest. We had sacrificed our honeymoon so he could fulfil a lifelong ambition. In the end he didn't go, opting to remain at home to tend to our baby.

Towards the end of the week the nurse's words of comfort came to fruition when Christopher's white blood cell count began to drop. We were so relieved. After he was discharged from the hospital, Andy and I remained at home to take care of him. Over the next two weeks he got fully back to normal.

I returned to work after Christopher had made a complete recovery. The military police had investigated the letters, the calls and other incidents but never found out who was responsible.

I continued with my gruelling training regime as usual each day. Over the coming months my fitness continued to soar as I ran around the woods in Midleton at the weekends with Andy. We were setting about our dream together. During the week, Andy was often away, leaving me to cope alone.

I soon found that I was struggling to balance my career with motherhood. My aunt had been an amazing support to me but I needed help at home in the evenings and mornings. I was ferrying my young children back and forth to her house, which sometimes took an hour in bad traffic. In the evenings we came home to a cold empty house. There were days when, like many other working mothers, I battled traffic in the lashing rain, unsuccessfully trying to soothe a screaming Christopher in the back seat of our car. It would often be close to eleven in the evenings when I would finally stop running around preparing for the next day, cleaning, ironing and preparing bottles. I knew my first year of marriage wouldn't be a fairytale, but I never expected to be left all alone either. However, since we were both soldiers, this is the life we had to live. Most mornings I woke up a dishevelled, tired mess, grabbing a cup of hot coffee in my thermal mug before racing out the door with only a slice of cold toast for my breakfast.

One day as Andy and I sat in our car waiting for the traffic lights to turn green, another car rear-ended us. The impact jolted me violently from my seat. I was left in agony in the area of my coccyx and lower back. Maybe God was putting obstacles in my path but as usual I ignored them. My lower abdominal and back muscles had not fully returned to their pre-pregnancy condition, leaving me more vulnerable to injury. Andy too was injured but opted for a different approach to therapy. I attended physiotherapy weekly while he received a cortisone injection in his back to relieve the pain. My dreams of attempting a selection course were shattered but Andy went full-steam ahead with his. As I had done for my NCOs' course, he fuelled his body with an ever-increasing amount of painkillers.

Andy had begun to distance himself from me in certain ways. Sometimes I felt like I was living with a complete stranger. On reflection I think he wanted a supporting wife, not one who he felt wished to compete with him professionally. When he was due to start the selection course for the Ranger Wing, I assembled all of his kit, cleaned it, sized it off, packed items in zip-lock bags and lined everything up in our hallway for him. I knew he would pass the selection course and would want to stay in the Curragh in Kildare, where the Ranger Wing is based, but there was nothing I could do to stop him. Less than nine months into our marriage, it appeared he loved his dream much more than he loved me. But it was my dream too and I didn't want to give up just yet. I knew that if he became a ranger, our family would always come second; maybe sometimes it wouldn't feature at all. I knew it would mean the start of the end for us. I refused to admit defeat until the last moment.

I finally had a moment of clarity. As I drove him to Collins Barracks, I pleaded with him to reconsider.

"I will give up everything – the army, everything. Please don't go," I begged.

"I'm going, Valerie," he said coldly.

I was a pathetic sight, begging him to choose his family over his career. "Why can't you be happy here in the 4th Infantry Battalion?" I shouted. "You're going to be promoted soon. Let's just be a normal family for once. I will give up everything for us."

He looked at me as if I was an obstacle in his path, then hopped quickly into a waiting jeep, disappearing into the misted distance.

We were as competitive as each other but ultimately I was the one left behind. As a woman the responsibility of our family fell on me. Now I knew I might never get to complete a selection course. I may have been willing to give it all up for him, yet I still found it incredibly hard to accept that my dream was now over.

Back at work, the 4th Infantry Battalion was preparing to travel to Liberia, so all personnel remaining behind had to perform excessive amounts of duties. No exceptions were made for mothers, so I was taken from the gym regularly and placed on two to three twenty-four-hour duties a week. I still continued with my training regime, taking increasing amounts of painkillers to dull the pain in my lower back and coccyx.

In the evenings I pushed Christopher in his buggy to try to get him to sleep, made bottles of formula, did the washing and cleaned the house. There were times when I rarely slept; night feeds, teething, bottles and running all merged into one, leaving me completely exhausted. This, combined with a relentless stream of twenty-four-hour duties, drove me to near-collapse. My weight plummeted. I just couldn't eat anymore. Again I had turned my focus inwards to deal with circumstances outside my control. It became my stress reliever, numbing me from any feeling, a non-verbal way of coping with the deep distress of the previous few years.

I continued struggling to combine my life as a mother with my life as a soldier. A senior female NCO in Collins Barracks commented on my gaunt appearance to my father, as did numerous others. Yet I was still rotated on an increasing amount of duties. At one point I was told I had to complete my husband's duties as well as my own. I had to carry the slack as the majority of the battalion were travelling to Liberia.

I was left to cope alone with two young children, regularly working between fifty and seventy hours a week and training each day. A soldier has to stay fit but I was training excessively and attending physiotherapy for my injuries from the car crash. Even though I realised I may never get to complete a selection course, I still harboured the dream deep down and continued to train. I clung on until the very end, hauling my body on runs, dragging my heavy legs beneath me as I pushed my body to the very brink physically.

Meanwhile, Andy passed his selection course and went on to complete the next part of his training for the Ranger Wing, his skills course, which was again based in Kildare.

Eventually I was offered a glimmer of hope, a lifebuoy, but it came too late. The only way I could escape the exhausting duties was to transfer to the Brigade Command Headquarters located in Collins Barracks, where a position was available in the operations training office. Plenty of strings were pulled as a number of people were concerned about my health. Their kindness was welcomed but I was unaware that the damage to my body had been done.

I started working in the Southern Command operations training office, under the same man whom I had met years earlier when I had first arrived in the 4th Infantry Battalion. The staff in Command Headquarters took me under their wing. I had finally escaped the gruelling regime that had become the 4th Infantry Battalion.

Midway through Andy's skills course, he had a terrible fall and tore a muscle in his ankle. He still persisted, refusing to give up, using painkillers to get him through. Luckily it was almost Christmas, so he would have time to allow his injury to heal.

When he arrived home for Christmas, the swelling was so bad that I dragged him to the hospital, where the doctor was sure his ankle was broken. It wasn't; it had just swollen grotesquely because he had refused to give in, despite the pain. At home I placed an ice pack on his ankle, rotating it with a heat pack every fifteen minutes. We spent that Christmas together but all too soon he was gone again to complete the next part of his skills course.

We got a Polish au pair, who was a blessing. However, I still didn't fully acknowledge the impact on my young children of both parents being out of the home for most of the day. Being surrounded by a Polish au pair and her friends, Christopher, unnoticed by me, began to speak Polish.

While Andy was in Kildare he was promoted to the rank of sergeant, having completed the interview just before he left for his selection course. The position was in the 4th Infantry Battalion, so I thought this might encourage him to come home, but it didn't. At a later date he actually handed back his third stripe so he could stay in the Ranger Wing. Once he passed the course, he began to warm to me again. He tried to persuade me to transfer to County Kildare, but at that point I was unprepared to leave the support network I had, my family and my friends. Who would mind my children when I was on duty up there?

Even though I was working in an office I still struggled to cope alone. Of course I tended to my children when I was home but I was missing so much of their little lives. I would race into Alex's playschool, having sped down the dual carriageway to Midleton, just snatching the last moments of my son's plays, all the other mothers staring disapprovingly in my direction.

I was overcome with guilt one day, so I decided to go to Smyth's toy store to buy the boys an abundance of new toys. Later that evening I sat with my young children in our gorgeous but lonely sun room when I suddenly realised that Christopher could speak quite good Polish, but had little English.

What was I doing this for? I didn't even know who I was anymore. I had a big house, a lovely car, au pairs, brand new toys, living in Celtic Boomland; yet I was skeletal, and had one son who couldn't even speak English, another who wished I saw his entire school plays and a husband whom I rarely saw.

I tried desperately to hold it together but I still couldn't grasp the concept that maybe I should just leave the army. I had fought for equality to men, proved myself and been the ultimate feminist. The reality now was that I had become a detached mother who craved the affection of her distant husband. He wanted a mother for his children, a homemaker, but I was so far removed once again from motherhood and my femininity that I was failing miserably at both.

The army, our ambition, was also tearing our marriage apart. I plodded along, exhausted, for the next few months. My nights in our new home were filled with loneliness. I missed Andy terribly, as did the boys. We all craved the security of a father and husband, but he was gone. I had to make a decision, as he had no intention of coming home. He asked me again if I would like to live in Kildare, where he had looked at buying a house. I was so desperate to cling on to my husband, to keep our family unit intact, that I agreed.

30

The Final Straw

A few months later we decided to buy a new house in County Kildare and to rent out Rose Hill. Andy had secured a position for me in the Physical Training Education College in the Curragh, a coveted job. He too had missed our family, but we were overlooking the finer details of how we would cope with the demands of our careers without the support network of home.

Everyone – my family, my friends, even my new boss – advised me to stay in Cork, but I refused to listen. The sergeant in the operations training office was such a kind, intelligent man, who offered me many words of wisdom, as did my own father. There are times I wish I had listened to them. Despite my many reservations, I decided to follow my heart and my husband and move my family to Kildare. I chose to leave my beautiful home, my family, my new job in operations which I loved, to high-tail it to the

Curragh, all for the love of a man who promised me a new start and for the stability of our family.

I wanted us to be a proper family, to live in the same house. But life was just about to throw me a cruel curveball. In our last weeks in Cork, my swollen glands refused to go down, no matter how many antibiotics I took. The day before we moved, I lay on the couch at Rose Hill, completely exhausted, unable to move. My body ached all over, my neck was sore and rigid, my face muscles twitched and my sense of balance was off. I could feel the whole room spinning around me. Andy was busying himself packing, but I didn't have the strength to lift my arms.

When we eventually arrived at our new home, I collapsed in a heap on a duvet on our bedroom floor. Andy seemed angry. "Valerie, what's wrong with you? Are you doing all of this just because you didn't want to move up here?" he barked.

"I don't know what's wrong with me. You could be a little more considerate, Andy," I replied.

My body had been screaming at me to stop since Eritrea but I just would not listen to it. In the end it simply shut down, but I was oblivious to the reason. I struggled each morning to open my heavy eyelids, walking groggily around my bed and banging my legs against the low wooden corners. I was permanently bruised from losing my balance. I developed vertigo. Luckily, we had a new au pair, who was a gentle kind girl and without whom I would never have coped.

I began working in the sprawling swimming pool and gymnasium in the Curragh camp but was embarrassed because I was so sick. They had expected a fit young female corporal. Instead, I arrived with barely enough strength to walk.

It was a horrific experience. I was admitted to hospital where I was told that I had a viral infection and that it would pass. I tried in vain to explain that I had been suffering like that for months, but the consultant at Naas General Hospital was very abrupt and refused to listen. I lay for days in the hospital bed, nauseous and dizzy with a thumping headache. I was given copious amounts of tablets and injections to relieve the symptoms. Tablets were becoming an ever-increasing feature of my life.

I was discharged but ended back in the same ward a few weeks later, still without a diagnosis despite being tested for everything. In the hospital I had become so weak that I could no longer walk unaided. Andy was genuinely concerned for me, telling me he would take care of me, but his new life in the Ranger Wing was sweeping him away, despite his initial tenderness. One day Andy pushed me down to the hospital café in a wheelchair, emaciated and hunched over. Fine lines ran beneath my eyes and furrowed my brow. When I tried to stand up in the café my heart began beating quickly and I collapsed onto the floor. Back in the ward later that same day, I tried to have a shower but I didn't have the strength to wash my own hair.

I was racked with guilt that I could not even take care of my own children because I was so sick. Juggling a full-time career as a soldier with being a wife and a mother was becoming impossible to sustain. I was so frustrated that I hadn't been given a diagnosis; surely something was causing me to be so sick?

I returned to work a few weeks later but was not much better. My weight stabilised, helped by the fact that I was eating regularly and not training. But at that point my vertigo was so bad that I struggled to slip the key in my front door or pop a teabag in a cup. My vision was too blurred to focus on even menial tasks.

Andy was training intensely with the Ranger Wing – fast-roping out of helicopters, parachuting, travelling up and down the country and preparing for exercises overseas. He would recount his experiences to me in detail each evening that he was home, which was rare.

At one point I blurted out, "Just shut up! You're brilliant, your dreams have come true, but I can barely walk. I need your help but all you're concerned about is your bloody career."

I felt a surge of guilt the moment the words spilled from my mouth. It wasn't his fault that I was sick. I was becoming resentful; he was living the dream that I had lost. He was able to have it all – a family, a wife and a career – while my world began to fall to pieces.

Shortly afterwards I reported to the military hospital in the Curragh camp to see the doctor. I was drained, dizzy, suffering from vertigo, and my body ached all over.

"There is nothing wrong with you, nothing," he snapped. Foreign doctors were employed by the defence forces and were often amazed at our level of sick days. He went on to say, "If you were in my country you would not even be permitted to go to the doctor. I am sick of seeing you; how many times have you been in hospital? If you come back here again complaining of being sick, I will send you to a psychiatrist. Do you hear me, Corporal?"

I slumped wearily on a plastic chair in that tiny room as he brushed me off, insisting that I was perfectly healthy.

Later that day I began heaving up blood down the toilet in my en-suite bathroom at home. I sat on the edge of my bed, weeping and feeling violently sick.

"Valerie, we have to find out what's wrong with you. You are clearly ill," Andy said gently.

That same day we drove home to Cork and visited my local GP. She booked me into the Bon Secours hospital for tests two weeks from then. "Don't worry, Valerie, they'll find out what's wrong with you there; you'll be okay," she said softly. In the interim I returned to Kildare and to work for two weeks.

There were times when Andy tried to comfort me, but because nothing had been diagnosed, he often became agitated. "Are you sure you're sick, Val? Where's the pain?" he would ask. Did my own husband think I was losing my mind?

In the gymnasium in the Curragh, my boss and all the staff were extremely supportive. They were like one big family in the gym, never pushing me for an explanation, but I felt so inadequate. My new company sergeant assured me that he would do everything possible for me, offering me a job in the administration office until I returned to full health. They were virtually strangers but were so kind to me. Initially I had been assigned to the pool, as I had previously qualified as a swimming instructor.

I had a civilian qualification as a fitness instructor but needed to complete the army equivalent. It wasn't looking likely that I would be fit enough to complete it.

Two weeks later, I was admitted to hospital in Cork for the tests. Our Polish au pair, along with Andy, took care of my children during my stay in hospital. There, they suspected I might have contracted some rare disease in Africa, although it was three years since I'd been there. I was isolated in a very large room with a little wooden hatch in the wall. I could see a church through the hatch. I questioned my faith; why would God do this to me? What was wrong with me? Looking back now, I believe God intervened in my life, to make me see sense.

A few days and numerous medical tests later, the consultant sat on my bed and ordered everyone else out. He asked me a lot of questions.

"How many hours do you work? How much money do you make? How often do you see your children?"

"Why are you asking me these questions? Am I not entitled to have a career like a man?" I asked him defensively.

"My dear, you are entitled, but you are paying the price physically," he replied. He went on to explain gently, "Mrs O'Brien, you have fibromyalgia and chronic fatigue syndrome or CFS, also known as ME," he explained gently. "Do you know how many women have lain in that same bed this year just like you, all paying the price for their careers?"

He returned the next day and I had my answers ready for him. After all my expenses, I realised that I was left with little or nothing weekly.

"You need to get better. If you do not change your lifestyle, you will not get better," he told me tactfully. When he broke it down for me like that, it seemed ridiculous what I had put my family and body through.

That night I lay in the darkened hospital room thinking about my future. I had amassed two houses, two cars and numerous loans; but I had become chronically ill, a detached mother and wife, lost all touch with my maternal instincts and femininity, all on the back of my so-called career. The ferocious roar of the Celtic Tiger and my feminist approach to life had ended up almost destroying my whole world. My relationship with my boys had suffered, I had missed so much of their little lives.

In my heart I knew that my military career was over. I wanted my children, my health and my husband, but it wasn't quite that simple. The road back to health and happiness almost broke me emotionally and psychologically, my marriage becoming a casualty along the way. I was a soldier; I didn't know how to be a good mother or a good wife. All the lights were there, the lights in my life, the most precious things in my life, which I had so selfishly neglected. I needed to switch them back on.

I pulled my blankets around my weak body, tears prickling my eyelids. I closed my eyes to sleep, but I knew the decision I had to make.

When I was discharged from hospital I was still extremely ill but Andy was so busy that he couldn't even collect me. He had been swept along with the tide of military life. I desperately wanted him to love me, to protect me, to take care of me when I was so low. But his commitments to the Ranger Wing had ripped him from my life. For him, the Ranger Wing was never about the money, as they are over-worked and under-paid. It was his passion, his commitment and his childhood dream to be in the special forces. Unfortunately, he had married a woman with similar dreams.

On a wet, cold, wintry day, Andy's father drove me back to Kildare, as he had a business meeting to attend in Dublin. I arrived home to an empty house and a dwindling marriage.

Once I returned to work the old nostalgic feelings returned. How could I leave a career I had worked so hard to build up? For a while I was deeply conflicted about my future but I knew deep down that I would have to leave the army.

Some time later, I was summoned to see a doctor in the military hospital. I was asked repeatedly about my condition. It was suggested to me that maybe I was just tired after having two children, that maybe I did not have these illnesses. Every soldier in the Irish defence forces has a red book called an LA30, filled in each time we go to the doctor. All of our inoculations are also recorded in these books. At this point my LA30 was confiscated from me. I was never allowed access to it again.

I had been ill for quite some time. On more than one occasion I was told that there was nothing wrong with me at the military hospital. But despite what was suggested to me I finally had a diagnosis which I could give to the doctor from a consultant. I phoned the Bon Secours hospital and spoke to the secretary of the consultant who had seen me. She later sent a letter to the head doctor in the military hospital stating that, yes, indeed I did have fibromyalgia.

Despite my failing health I later completed a lifesaving course over four weeks. I swam in the army swimming pool for hours every day, mostly in combat gear. I fuelled my body with painkillers, antibiotics and the quick-release energy drink Maxi-Muscle Viper. The moment I returned home each evening I collapsed into bed, sleeping until the following morning while Andy took care of our kids. At that point he was unsure whether I should leave the army, as we had two mortgages. He was worried about the financial implications. I tried to explain that most of my money went on childcare, but he was still concerned.

I finished that course but it finished me. It was the final straw for me physically. I was so used to the physical pain, it was part of my life. Afterwards my muscles ached so badly that I couldn't even climb out of bed in the mornings. I had used my mind to overcome the physical pain over the previous few months, but I couldn't do it anymore.

When I finished the lifesaving course, Andy and I spoke at length about our future.

"Is there anything else you'd like to do, Valerie? You can't go on like this."

"Well, I always wanted to become a beautician, actually," I replied.

"A beautician? Really?" he laughed.

"Yes! I'm good at biology; how hard could it be?"

I simply couldn't perform as a soldier any longer. I don't fully blame my inoculations; I think it was a combination of a multitude of factors: my lifestyle, my training, pushing my body to the extreme as well as the inoculations, of which I had received a large number in a short period of time before my departure for Eritrea.

I was sent for by an officer in the Curragh camp. He told me I had been pushing myself too hard, and that I should not have any more children. He asked me to speak to my husband about getting a vasectomy, handing me the number of a doctor who could perform the procedure in Clane Hospital. I was genuinely shocked. I thought it was my decision whether or not to have more children in the future, not the defence forces'.

My odyssey through the army was filled with personal and professional tragedy, but I do have many happy and some hilarious memories. I met some genuinely kind soldiers whom I was proud to serve with. But after that incident, I just wanted to leave.

31

Moving On

I remained in the army for one more year but I spent a lot of my time on sick leave. I attempted to return on a number of occasions, but my body could no longer cope with the physical demands of military life. Being a soldier was in my blood; I found it a heartbreaking decision to make, but I had to think of my family and my health.

During that year I tried desperately to get well. I never gave in to the pain or the illnesses. I refused to live the rest of my life sick. I continued with physiotherapy twice weekly and saw a specialist for my teeth-grinding, which was becoming a major problem when I slept. Each specialist I met told me the same thing: "You have to change your lifestyle, slow down."

Andy and I also attended marriage counselling but it was becoming increasingly difficult to plaster over the wounds we had inflicted on our relationship. In the end I attended our counsellor alone. I had to break the soldier

down and bring back a civilian, a wife and a mother, as I no longer knew how to function within the confines of normal society. She gave me the tools to readjust to life outside the defence forces, but my marriage was still under so much strain. I think Andy found it difficult to cope with my illness while I remained riddled with guilt for not listening to my body, not putting my family before my career.

Andy was away so much and I found it hard to forgive him for leaving me alone when I was at the lowest ebb in my life. He struggled to forgive me for the past nine years.

I found it extremely difficult to leave the army and wasn't sure how I would carve out a new identity for myself. While on sick leave, with Alex at school and Chris at playschool, I spent my time watching daytime television. The novelty quickly wore off and I started to become frustrated and bored. I decided that I needed a focus, a goal, something to keep me going. I knew that if I intended to return to work someday, I would need some sort of qualification. Being an army corporal was of no use to me in the real world.

So, while I was still officially in the army, I returned to college part-time on Saturdays to study as a beauty therapist. It kept me going as the rest of my world fell apart. I was terrified to tell the principal of my illnesses, afraid she would not allow me on the course.

Once I began training at Portlaoise College of Beauty and Complementary Therapies, it had numerous effects on my life. Not only was I going to qualify as a beautician, but also, because I was studying anatomy and physiology,

I began to understand the way in which my body worked. It also helped me to reconnect with my femininity. Before this, the only make-up I laid claim to was a brown eyeshadow from Tesco, which I applied with my finger.

While studying for my beauty course I finally realised that my frequent use of antibiotics was lowering my immune system. Therefore I reassessed my medication and my diet. I started a fully organic diet, using manuka honey to reduce my swollen glands instead of antibiotics. There were still many days when I couldn't get out of bed because my body ached so much, but I wouldn't give up. Often at night I would wake up drenched in sweat. I constantly had the flu; it never seemed to leave me. I got bladder and kidney infections but, instead of antibiotics, I drank cartons of cranberry juice in the mornings to flush them out of my system. Sometimes it worked, sometimes it didn't.

They say that depression is sometimes frozen anger. Of course at that point I was angry but I had suppressed that feeling. In its place I felt overwhelming sadness and disappointment. Struggling with chronic pain, struggling to get better, I began to battle depression. My self-esteem also hit a new low. At that stage I was back up to a healthy weight but my confidence had dropped considerably.

I had spent years building up a career that I had to walk away from. I had a condition that many didn't understand and which at times I didn't understand myself. I wished that I hadn't been diagnosed with such a misunderstood condition. I learned to live with my sickness and fought every day to get better. Slowly, over a period of a few months while at college, I began to recover. I still had dark days but they were fewer.

I managed to pass all of my exams by studying each night while my children were safely tucked up in bed. In the mornings I practised waxing, manicures, make-up and facials on my neighbours. I rediscovered all things girly. It was so different to the world in which I had previously immersed myself. I loved the creativity it allowed me. It certainly was not as easy as I had initially assumed.

I would arrive home to Andy on Saturdays, saying, "I had such a great day."

"Valerie, I don't think you ever came home saying you had a great day in the army," he would laugh.

I don't know how my tutor transformed me from combat soldier into beautician when I didn't even know what a cuticle was, but she did. Finally, in November 2006, I qualified as a beauty therapist, learning to embrace my femininity, rather than concealing it under camouflage cream.

Andy had decided to travel to Liberia with the army for financial reasons and also because our military contract stipulated that we had to serve overseas every three years. This was another reason that I had come to the decision to leave the army. I didn't want our children to be without a parent for twelve months in every three-year period.

However, because he was travelling to Africa, I instantly became suspicious. I had seen what had taken place when I was in Africa with the army. All of my memories from Eritrea came flooding back, only this time

I was the wife of a soldier heading to Africa. I had seen how acceptable it was for our soldiers to frequent brothels nightly. I didn't have the peace of mind of not knowing what was actually going on.

I was convinced that Andy would cheat on me out there. Sure, hadn't I seen it all before? I refused to trust him. I began checking his phone, questioning his whereabouts, checking his emails, driving him further and further away from me. Wouldn't that drive any man away?

As I scrutinised his every move, we began arguing daily. Our marriage had been on the brink of collapse for months. We blamed each other equally. He blamed me for inflicting my illness on myself, for pushing myself too hard, for not putting our family first. I blamed him for leaving me all alone to cope. I am not sure under the circumstances that we could have prevented the outcome.

I was still suffering physically, so Andy and I decided it would be best for me and the children to move back home to Cork after I finished my beauty course, just before he went to Liberia. We packed up our belongings in County Kildare and returned to Rose Hill, where I had the support of my family and friends.

During the moonlit drive home, we had to cross a toll bridge on the motorway. I dug in my pocket for some money and threw it into the automatic basket. I was so tired that I didn't notice I was also throwing away my engagement ring, which I had placed deep in my pocket when packing. It flew into the basket, my marriage slipping through my fingers. I never got it back.

A few days later, standing in the soft light of our bedroom, Andy told me that our marriage was over. We were still arguing daily, each filled with anger towards the other. I almost froze in that moment, realising that I still loved him, despite everything that had happened. Andy was still very handsome, but time and pain were etched across his face, his once-smooth complexion looking rugged, flecks of silver glinting through his soft silky black hair. His light green eyes looked saddened, hollow, pained in his sunken cheeks.

I was heartbroken and devastated, but I was too weak to hate him. I tried to block out the overwhelming emotional pain by focusing on our children. If I am completely honest, I am not sure my heart had ever been fully open to him after I returned from Eritrea. I think a part of it had remained frozen, tucked away under lock and key.

When Andy left our home to travel to Liberia, I sat on the window ledge of the bay window in our bedroom, knees tucked closely into my chest, tears filling my eyes. As I gazed at the lingering moon behind our antique white floral curtains, I knew that I couldn't let him go like this. I dashed downstairs, hopped in my car and flew after him. To my relief, I spotted him at the crowded train station. I just wanted him to know how much I loved him. I tried to pull him in closely, to hug him, but he brushed me off coldly, darting me a fierce look which ravaged my heart. Then he boarded the train and vanished out of my sight.

I turned to walk away down the cold platform, extending my stride to quicken my pace, sobbing quietly, desperately trying to hold it together. Long gone was "Miss Best

Overall Soldier" with her glacial ice-maiden façade. Now she had well and truly melted. But it was too late.

Later that evening I slipped out of my clothes and climbed into my empty queen-sized sleigh bed, wrapping my soft white lace duvet around my body, remembering the first weeks we had spent in that very bedroom. Lazy hazy Saturdays, we had called them. Now they were a distant memory. At that moment under my duvet, I was sure Andy had squeezed out the very last drop of love I had ever felt for him from my heart. Our hearts had collided when we were young but so much had happened that we didn't seem to fit together anymore.

I locked myself away in Rose Hill for the next few months, cocooning myself from life, striving to get better and bond with my children, but I was still battling depression. On Christmas Day my whole family were to come to my house for dinner. I stayed up until four in the morning, decorating my sun room like Santa's grotto for my children. I indulged in Christmas wholeheartedly, hanging sparkling fairy lights everywhere, even putting up two over-tinselled Christmas trees. I wanted to make it extra special for my boys because Andy was overseas.

On Christmas morning I woke my boys and we sat underneath our large glittering Christmas tree, unwrapping the many gifts Santa had left. I gazed out our frosted kitchen window at our little pond, frozen solid. A blanket of brilliant white snow covered our garden. Our cherry blossom trees stood still, ice clinging to their wispy branches. I always play Christmas songs for the entire

348

month of December; that year was no exception. My little boys' laughter bounced around the living room as we sang along to the classic tunes, the aroma of my cooking wafting through the house. It should have been a perfect Christmas.

Just as we were leaving for church, the phone rang. It was Andy. Alex and Chris were bursting with joy as they spoke to their father. When they were finished, I spoke to him. I pleaded with him to give our marriage another chance, but he refused. "I don't love you any more. Just move on, Valerie," he said abruptly down the crackling phone line. The ghosts of my past had driven him away from me; this time it looked likely forever.

I managed to get through Christmas Day with the help of some rescue remedy, which I had been frequently using. That beautiful but sad Christmas Day, seventeen members of my family and friends arrived at my front door for dinner. I put a broad smile on my face for my children and my family, but the depths of my heart were torn apart.

I didn't know then that Andy too was falling to pieces that day. He sat on a beach in Liberia and drank a full bottle of whiskey after we had spoken. I thought he loved me deep down. I certainly knew that he adored his children and missed them desperately over the holidays, but so much damage had been done. Our careers in the defence forces, our lifestyles, had shredded our love, helping to collapse our marriage.

A few months later, in March 2007, I handed in my green army backpack and equipment, signed the official documents and was discharged from the Irish defence forces.

I felt like such a weight had been lifted from my shoulders. I drove through the vast Curragh Camp, lined with high green trees, for the first time as a civilian in over ten years.

A few days later I was sitting at our long mahogany kitchen table in Cork, golden spring sunlight creeping through my kitchen blinds, when the phone rang. It was Andy. My heart thumped so fast when I heard his voice.

"So, you're finally a civilian, Val," he whispered.

"I am indeed," I replied.

We spoke for hours over the coming weeks, resulting in a huge phone bill, but it was worth it, as we decided to give our marriage one final chance. When Andy returned from Liberia that summer, we moved back to Kildare and sold Rose Hill. We cleared every single loan we had, downsizing our entire lives.

I was learning to balance my life and becoming an all-encompassing, fully committed mother. The joy I receive from my two little angels is amazing. We live a very simple, post-Celtic Tiger life.

My health returned slowly as I changed my lifestyle. The casualty was my marriage. Ironically, the wife and mother Andy had craved had finally arrived. I just couldn't forgive him for leaving me when I was sick, weak and vulnerable. I felt he had deserted me, maybe because he blamed me for inflicting it upon myself. He couldn't forgive my ambition and I couldn't forgive his absence. I also had deep-seated issues with trust and was unprepared to trust him, no matter how many times I tried. That was my demon, not his, born out of the brothel in Asmara.

A short few months after we returned to Kildare, we finally separated.

When I was twenty-one years old, I never could have imagined that the very things that had brought us together – our common interests, our ambition and our military careers – would finally tear us apart.

I grieved over the loss of my marriage. I shed tears for months, thinking how we never got to do all the things we had planned. We had never even taken a family holiday. The day came when we simply had to move on, to let go. I had to stop feeling sorry for myself; it was too late to correct the last ten years.

When we stopped blaming each other we both took responsibility equally. We had been through so much together that, once the hurt and pain subsided, we salvaged a very good friendship. Today we remain close friends, committed to raising our children together.

I have learned to cope alone without love and to rediscover who I really am. There is life after the army and a marriage breakdown. I have spent the last two years reconnecting with my children and civilian life. It hasn't been an easy road back. At times I felt very lost and almost gave up. The punishing regime of army life for a woman left little time for family or femininity.

I wrote this book to revisit my past and to heal. I have relived both the pain and the happiness, but this time around I have cried proper heartfelt tears from the depths of my soul, allowing me finally to deal with my demons. I realise that Eritrea was an extraordinary scenario and I have finally learned to trust men again, having dealt with the lingering memories of the brothel in Asmara. I never truly grasped how much that place had scarred me emotionally.

Martha, my friend from the cookhouse, remains in Eritrea with her six-year-old Irish daughter Martina. They live in a slum, having been outcast by society and family, but an Irish charity, Vita, is trying to help them. Martina's father, an Irish soldier, died soon after we returned from Eritrea. The Irish Department of Foreign Affairs is still denying the young child a passport. I pray that she isn't forced into a life of prostitution out of sheer desperation when she is older, as they are extremely poor. There are also more Irish children who remain behind.

I have honestly had enough of the whole feminist charade. After spending ten years as a woman in the Irish army under very challenging circumstances, I have finally managed to redirect my life for myself and my children. I have dealt with and overcome my past and am ready to move forward with a positive and hopeful mindset with the help of counselling, family and friends. I have finally become comfortable in my own skin.

When I think back to the extreme poverty I witnessed in Africa, the children with HIV in the orphanage of Asmara, I am embarrassed at how caught up I became in our Celtic boom and in my career and how detached I became from my own children. I go to Lidl for my shopping and my favourite clothing line is now "Haute d'Atmosphere", more commonly known as Penney's. I am unashamedly embracing motherhood, my femininity and life. I spend quality time with my children, sharing the simplest pleasures in life such as swimming, painting, going on picnics and bringing them to the latest *Harry Potter* films.

Maybe in time I will be lucky enough to find love again, my diamond in the sand. For now, I feel I have finally moved out of the shadow of men, basking in the sunshine of my God-given destiny, that of being a woman.

My new journey has brought me back to motherhood, health, a simple lifestyle and happiness. For me, having it all was merely a pipe dream. I find motherhood far more fulfilling than I ever did my military career. I have learned from my many mistakes in the past. I have finally closed that chapter in my life and a new chapter has begun.

My two young boys share similar dreams to their father. They both speak endlessly of a life in the military, which I would support. If I ever have a daughter, though, I'm not sure I would encourage her to follow the same path.